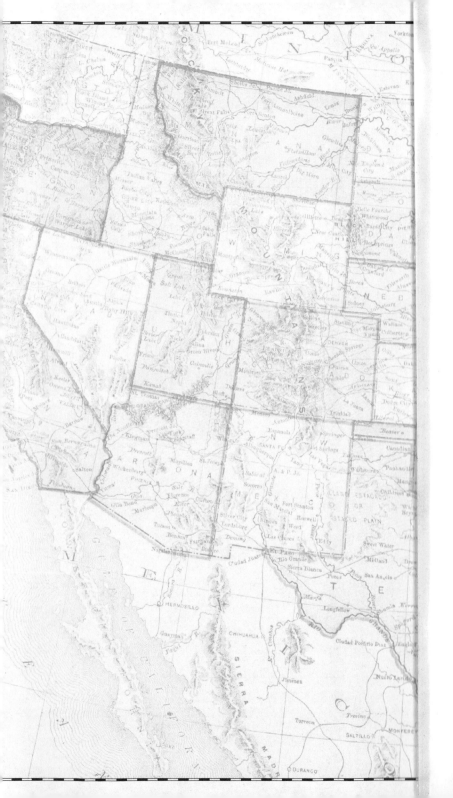

THE LAST GREAT WALK

THE LAST GREAT WALK

THE TRUE STORY *of a* **1909 WALK** *from* **NEW YORK** *to* **SAN FRANCISCO,** *and* **WHY IT MATTERS TODAY**

WAYNE CURTIS

RODALE

Rodale books may be purchased for business or promotional use or for special sales. For information, please write to: Special Markets Department, Rodale Inc., 733 Third Avenue, New York, NY 10017.

Printed in the United States of America

Rodale Inc. makes every effort to use acid-free ∞, recycled paper ♻.

Book design by Christina Gaugler

Library of Congress Cataloging-in-Publication Data is on file with the publisher.
ISBN-13: 978-1-60961-372-3

Distributed to the trade by Macmillan

2 4 6 8 10 9 7 5 3 1 hardcover

RODALE.

We inspire and enable people to improve their lives and the world around them.
rodalebooks.com

For Louise

CONTENTS

INTRODUCTION

Early on a warm spring day a couple of years ago, I set off on foot from downtown Manhattan for Tarrytown, a leafy suburb about thirty miles to the north. My plan was to follow along the same route and along the same streets that a man named Edward Payson Weston walked on March 15, 1909, the day he left New York en route to San Francisco. I knew precisely where to go because reporters dogged Weston for much of that first day and wrote up his route in considerable detail.

Weston was a famous walker, a term that may create some confusion. But through much of the latter half of the nineteenth century, the fleetest of foot could actually make a living as a walker, just as one could command a salary as a poet. Professional walkers tended to come from the lower classes. They walked and walked, sometimes absurdly long distances (Weston once walked five thousand miles in one hundred days), and people often wagered on whether solo walkers would achieve their targets, or if they would beat another when competing head-on, like mares in a sweepstakes.

Had you been around when Weston was walking, he likely would have caught your attention as he passed by. He was born in 1839 to a middle-class family that had long disapproved of his chosen career. So he often exhibited a sort of sartorial overcompensation, wearing clothing that he believed would convey a certain stature and be memorable in the bargain.

His fondness for extravagant dress was often noted in reports about his travels. On a long 1867 walk to Chicago, he emerged from his hotel room, a reporter wrote, in "an elegant suit of broadcloth, patent leather boots, and green kids to match." Two years later, on a walk from Bangor, Maine, he was "conspicuously dressed in a showy uniform with a lofty white plume stuck in a military cap." A year later, he walked in New York "attired in purple velvet pants, white stockings, ordinary laced gaiters, and a spotted linen shirt." At other times he favored a naval suit similar to that worn by Marine Corps officers, "with shoulder knots, and a forage cap of beaver richly ornamented with bullion and surmounted by a white cockade." Further accounts of Weston read like an inventory of lapsed fashion: He'd wear a "volunteer's tunic," cricket or yachting cap, knickerbockers or leggings. A California correspondent noted his "white hat, short roundabout, knee pants and red woolen stockings." And this: "When walking in the summertime, Weston wears a white blouse waist similar to a Lord Fauntleroy waist, knee trousers and leggings," reported one newspaper in 1909. "He wears this sort of clothing so that he can be easily detected, and so that he will not be mistaken for some person riding on a train." He was also given to capes.

His fashion choices probably didn't help, but by 1909 Weston was already on his way to becoming a relic. Long-distance walking competitions were falling out of favor—as a point of context, note that 1909 was the year of the first race at the new Indianapolis Motor Speedway. But pedestrian competitions hadn't completely faded. Two days before Weston left New York in March 1909, a walking match had started up at Madison Square Garden—a six-day go-as-you-please race, with the winners dividing a pot of $5,000. Contestants included walkers from France, Italy, Belgium, Holland, Ireland, Greece, Germany, Switzerland, Scotland, and England, and representatives of the Igorot tribe from the Philippine Islands. A military team and a group of letter carriers represented the United States, as well as Indians from the Mohawk and Sioux tribes, against a field that included Guido Pallanti, an Italian walker and the recognized world champion since 1904. Large crowds came out to watch, but even then it was seen as a sort of retro spectacle, a glimpse not so much at the modern, but at a feral endeavor that had crept out of a burrow and that many, no doubt, believed would soon creep back in.

Also contributing to the notion that Weston was a vestige of a bygone era: The day he left New York City, he turned seventy years old.

———

Following in Weston's footsteps, I started at City Hall Park, which today is a peaceful Edwardian oasis of trees, shrubs, and marble set amid gleaming white, gray, and brownish towers that appear to squeeze upward owing to Manhattan's narrowing toward its southernmost tip. The park is anchored by an elegant urnlike fountain designed by the same sculptor who had a hand in creating Central Park's Bethesda Fountain. To the north is New York's City Hall, a Beaux Arts structure that somehow manages to be both frivolous and stern at once. City Hall faces south, built on what was at the time the northernmost edge of the city; few anticipated that New York would continue to grow the way it did, leaving City Hall to turn its back on most of the city. Six years before Weston set off, the park's gaslights had been replaced by modern electric lights.

I arrived shortly after dawn and spent a moment watching a maintenance worker wading up to his knees in the fountain, trying to unclog a drain. Nodding sympathetically, I turned north and began my walk, leaving the worker in a pale, champagne light and heading up Park Row. Passing the elegant pedestrian entrance to the Brooklyn Bridge, I soon entered an urban canyon flanked by the neoclassical US Courthouse and the US Court of International Trade, a pair of monumental buildings with intricately articulated stone brackets and pediments and columns, the sort of details rendered invisible when passed in a speeding cab but forming a visual symphony when viewed on foot. (This area around Foley Square hadn't yet developed its heroic character when Weston walked through, but a plan for grandeur was under way.) The urban drama of the intersection had attracted a trio of twentysomething Italian tourists, who took turns snapping pictures of one another lying down in the roadway during gaps in taxi traffic. I slowed my pace, waiting to see if any of them would be run over as sacrifices on the altar of some Instagram photo album (they weren't), so I pushed on through the lower foothills of commerce before winding my way to Broadway. I then turned up Fifth Avenue, striding into one of the most impressive urban chasms in the world—the sun brighter and shimmery now, and the vistas long and attenuating—and continued on toward Central Park.

"There is a turning point in walking," Weston said in 1908. "A person will walk a short distance without tiring. After about a mile of it the tired feeling is noticeable. After two miles the walker wants to rest. If he sticks it out until he has walked three miles the tired feeling begins to disappear. When he has walked five miles he is prepared to walk a dozen more."

At Eighty-First and Broadway—about five and a half miles into my walk—I was inclined to agree with Weston. I was actually feeling stronger than when I began, and the constant, steady movement was bracing. Still, when I passed what might have been the sixtieth Starbucks along the route, my will broke and I went in, finally succumbing to the persistent promise of a coffee and a slice of lemon pound cake. Also, I really needed to charge my iPhone.

I first came across a mention of Edward Payson Weston about twenty years ago. I had been researching an early-twentieth-century mayor in the basement of a public library, a fluorescent ghetto of noisy microfilm readers amid the aroma of decaying acetate. I happened upon a brief wire service story about a man's cross-country journey on foot in 1909. I skimmed enough to get the gist—a seventy-year-old man was walking about forty miles a day for a hundred days en route from New York to San Francisco. *Good for him,* I thought, and then I scrolled ahead in search of the page I needed.

A few minutes later, I had another thought: *Wait . . . what?* Forty miles a day? A hundred days in a row? At seventy years old? I scrolled back and read the story more carefully. I jotted down a few notes. A couple of weeks later I went back to the library to track down more about this man and his adventure. Weston, I learned, was walking's Hank Aaron—someone who stood far above all the rest. I started gathering stray facts: He had almost singlehandedly triggered a boom in long-distance walking in the years following the Civil War. He favored tea over water and also liked lemonade and would sometimes drink stout or ale. On warm days he would line his hat with cabbage leaves and ice for its beneficial cooling effect.

Over the next two decades, a time during which access to historic newspapers mercifully shifted from microfilm to online databases, I continued to gather information on Weston and his 1909 walk. There was much to read, it turned out. Weston and his journey attracted press coverage by the mile— the *New York Times* ran his dispatches from the road several times each week, and he was often the subject of front-page stories in towns through which he walked. Massive, cheering crowds thronged to witness Weston's feat; in Chicago, New York, Denver, and elsewhere, lines of spectators often ran for miles and several people deep, as if a famous movie star escorted by British royalty were passing by in a parade. Even in the smallest of towns, hundreds of people would turn out in the rain or dead of night to cheer him on, and many would then follow in his wake for a mile or two, as if he were an elderly Pied Piper.

This struck me as all rather quirky and fit with my notion of the dullness of life for the average Edwardian-era American. But as I read more about all the clamor and attention he drew on his walk, I realized I wasn't learning solely about a singular man taking a remarkable walk. Something more was at play. And I came to believe that Weston's walk marked a critical turning point in our nation's history.

By the early twentieth century, I concluded, America had more or less decided to stop walking. The *New York Times* claimed that Weston's 1909 walk was the first "bona fide" walk across the country, but I came to see it as the last great cross-country walk, the farewell tour for a form of mobility that had for millennia defined us as humans. Some of the reports had the formulaic trappings of last-hurrah stories—a sort of misty-eyed coverage about the final trip of a beloved steamship, or the last carrier pigeon, or the last train ascending a mountain on a cog railway about to be sold for scrap. With Weston's walk, the era of the long walk was drawing to a close.

From 1909 forward, distance walking would be relegated to a sideshow activity—quite literally, as walkers were shunted from streets to sidewalks. The automobile would dominate travelways with its steely power and its flash and brute sexiness. Edward Payson Weston was a heroic emissary from the past engaged in a fruitless battle against the future. (Also making the news the year of Weston's walk: The British aviator Henri Farman completed the first flight of one hundred miles; Robert E. Peary arrived at the North Pole, conquering one of the two last unmapped polar frontiers; and a company started producing a material called Bakelite, heralding the age of plastic.) Weston's walk was a battle fraught with symbolic meaning, and so the figurative bleachers were filled with throngs of cheering fans who knew the ultimate result but longed for a good fight anyway. No wonder the crowds showed up and were enraptured.

My iPhone needed recharging at the Starbucks because I was tracking my walk using a GPS app, which turns out to have a large appetite for battery power. Sitting there sipping coffee as the phone drank its voltage from the wall outlet, I gave some thought to living on the cusp between two ages—that of machine and that of information. The machine is leaden and anchored to place; it smells of grease and mechanical effort. Information is ethereal, unmoored, and invisible; it's odorless, save for the moment a new gadget comes out of a box imbued with a thin, plasticky smell of expectation and novelty that wears off in a matter of minutes.

The man in whose footsteps I was following that day was also walking a cusp between two ages. He was walking out of the age of romance and heroism and into that of pragmatism. Even the early industrial age had had something of the heroic about it, but that had faded and industry was now settling down into something more routine. Two years after Weston walked across the country, Frederick Taylor published his groundbreaking book *Principles of Scientific Management,* and he was instrumental in reshaping factories and offices with his prescriptions to turn every human action into a set of numbers that could be parsed and tweaked to coax every bit of efficiency from every worker; Henry Ford was starting to make automobiles on assembly lines; and efficacious business-minded city managers were increasingly replacing politics-tainted mayors. The heroics of individuals and their sheer determination was fading; that approach was redolent of the nineteenth century and wouldn't do for the modern age, which was all about the machine. Nor would walking do when personal machines could handle the job more efficiently.

Weston was at once extraordinary and very ordinary. He was extraordinary in that he could walk forty miles a day, day in and day out, for months at a time. Few could muster that sort of stamina. But he was ordinary in that he grew up at a time when virtually all Americans walked long distances without thinking much about it. Indeed, some of his contemporaries obstinately refused to be swept up in the fuss about his great walk and instead issued dismissive harrumphs. When Weston undertook a long and well-publicized walk from Maine to Illinois in 1907, a writer editorialized in the *American Gymnasia and Athletic Record* that "perhaps the most remarkable thing about the walk . . . is the fact that it is generally considered such a feat." The writer was dismayed by the all the fawning attention and lamented the passing of an age. "What was once long ago a not uncommon occurrence becomes a matter for front page newspaper prominence and calls for the attendance of mayors of cities, yards of editorial comment and is the subject for talk by hundreds of thousands of men, women and children."

Weston was a long-distance walker professionally from his early twenties through his forties. That is, he made a living walking in competitions in which the public would bet on the outcome and often pay an admission fee to watch the race. He continued walking later in life, possibly through ingrained habit but also because he had a bit of the crusader in him. Even in his fifties and sixties he routinely walked ten or twelve miles each and every day, in part because he was convinced something disagreeable would occur if he didn't. (In this he echoed the Russian composer Pyotr Ilyich Tchaikovsky, who was a year younger than Weston and took long walks after lunch every day. "Somewhere at sometime he had discovered that a man needs a two-hour walk for his health," Tchaikovsky's brother recounted, "and his observance of this rule was pedantic and superstitious, as though if he returned five minutes early he would fall ill, and unbelievable misfortunes of some sort would ensue.") Early on, Weston competed in matches on circular tracks, both indoors and out, but he was more at home on long walks of several hundred to several thousand miles, from one city to the next, across open countryside. He was no Thoreau, an idler who viewed walking as a route to a more profound understanding of the world and himself. He viewed walking mostly as a way to get from here to there and would arrive feeling happier and fitter than when he left. "I feel as young as I ever did," he told one reporter as he marched west. "I have always said that walking would keep a man young." On another occasion he proclaimed that "walking is the road to health. If Ponce de León had realized its value he would not have sought for the fountain of perpetual youth in Florida."

Weston maintained a detailed timetable on his long walks, outlining where he would head and how far he would cover each day. He grew agitated if he fell behind. When walking, he was more interested in maintaining a brisk pace and staying on top of his blisters than he was in what he observed along the way. I'm pretty sure Weston never stopped to whistle at a warbler he spied on the limb of a spring maple. Yet he was prescient in viewing walking as the surest route to good health—"as good an exercise as a man can take," he said. And he was ahead of the time with his opinions about cigarettes (he was fervently anti-tobacco), and he often spoke about the danger of cars and the laziness they engendered.

Weston's message found an audience in his own time—magazine and newspaper editors more often hailed his vigor and determination than expressed puzzlement at the attention he was receiving. But his efforts were quickly obscured as the automobile age advanced. The real enthusiasm of editors and the public was reserved for the prospect of moving faster and more independently and with less physical effort by means of a machine. "The excitement it gives to life!" one writer enthused about cars in 1905. "No man, still less woman, can be dull and possess a motor-car." This was the glimmering future, and the future invariably trumps the musty past in matters of public attention.

The question I was asked most frequently when working on this book was "Are you going to retrace Weston's walk from New York to San Francisco?"

Let me answer that at the outset: No.

For starters, I'm no Weston. He was a remarkable specimen of a mobile human. I'm not. I couldn't walk forty-mile days for weeks at a time as he did, and I'd be hard-pressed to achieve a week of twenty-mile days. But the chief reason for my not attempting his feat is that, except for some of the downtowns of larger cities, the routes he followed have changed drastically, as have the behaviors of the people who use them. Following his route would be more or less a suicide mission. The roads Weston walked—across New York State and on to Chicago, then down to Denver and through the Rockies and the Sierras—simply don't accommodate walkers today. Many of the unpaved roads he followed are now interstates or multilane state highways, and long stretches don't possess sidewalks or much in the way of walkable shoulders. And Weston spent a lot of time walking on railroad tracks, which today is also impractical and full of potential hazards, legal and otherwise.

Anyway, drivers are so distracted now by texting, talking on the phone, and fiddling with their GPSs that I'd be just another number in the distraction lottery, and eventually my number would come up. The truth is that I'd undoubtedly be distracted while walking, as well. I'd probably be reviewing e-mail as I walked, or checking my stats on the GPS app or pedometer, or tweeting about how I was checking my pedometer. (Perhaps the most emblematic way to die these days would be to have a driver veer off the road while texting and run me down as I walked in the opposite direction, also texting.)

Our land is now the empire of steel and petroleum; to trespass here on foot is to do so at considerable risk. It's as if we've returned to the African savanna, where we likely first walked upright, and are again at the mercies of big game. If I were hit by a car, people would naturally wonder: What was I doing walking along that road? Was I mad? Was I drunk? People would shake their heads and think it was a shame, but it was really no one's fault but my own.

———————

Around noon, I left New York City and walked into Westchester County. The density of the city was now unspooling and unraveling; the green spaces between homes and buildings, rather than the buildings themselves, started to define the landscape. In making this transition, I crossed an unseen divide between a walking culture and a driving culture. Sidewalks became more ancillary and exposed; a utility pole with a hulking gray transformer box sat in the middle of one sidewalk, all but blocking it. I had to dart across an entrance ramp to the Henry Hudson Parkway while hoping that cars whose turn signals weren't activated indeed were not turning. Attempting the crossing during the afternoon rush hour would have been even more problematic.

The landscape I walked through gradually evolved into something less intricate visually and composed of coarser elements. The detailed Italianate architectural elements on upper floors of tall buildings fell away, replaced by backlit plastic signs and expansive parking lots. My interest in my surroundings started to flag. I'll also admit I was growing weary physically. My feet were feeling raw, and I was striding with less vigor and more tentativeness with every step. There was also chafing, the details of which I shall spare you. I began thinking how nice it would be to sit down in an upholstered, smooth-running train making its way back into the city. In Yonkers, I saw a sign for a rail station at Ludlow Street and descended a hill toward the Hudson River. I waited twenty minutes for the next train; a hard wooden bench had never been quite so comfortable. According to my GPS app, in the nearly seven hours since I'd left that morning, I'd covered 18.7 miles and—when actually moving—had averaged 3.4 miles per hour, less than Weston's typical pace of 3.5 to 4 miles per hour. At this point, Weston was just getting under way; I was happy to be finishing up.

Part of my goal in this book is to explore, revive, and expand on the message that Weston was intent on publicizing—advocacy for the long walk, once common and now rare. As such, this book is only in part about a single man and his obsession, and just as much about mobility, about how we choose to get around and how that impacts the health of our bodies and our minds. Above all, it's about what we lost when humans, starting roughly a century ago, opted to stop using their legs to get from here to there and instead chose to regularly climb into a metal box harnessed to a series of small explosions. Some of what has happened in the intervening century you might easily guess, but much of it you might not. Walking is more complexly knitted into our bodies and minds than you might think. How we move can determine our relationship to the land and people around us and even, to some degree, how we understand ourselves.

Not walking, I believe, is one of the most radical things we've ever decided to do. Here's why.

PROLOGUE

In 1909, a Wellesley College student named Louise Rand Bascom wrote a paper in which she discussed a couplet she'd overheard in her home state of North Carolina:

Johnie Henry was a hard-workin' man
He died with a hammer in his hand.

These were lines from a simple folk song, and as far as anyone knows, it was the first time they were discussed in the academy. This occasioned the launch of a cottage industry of John Henry studies, with folklorists and other academics chasing a legend that dates to at least the 1870s. The song told of an African American laborer who competed against a steam-powered excavator to see who could tunnel deeper into the dense rock of a mountain in the same amount of time. John Henry managed fourteen feet, compared with the engine's nine, and was declared the winner. Upon completing his task, he asked for a drink of cold water, then keeled over stone dead.

Both John Henry and his legend grew over time. He eventually was described as being ten feet tall and working with a twenty-pound hammer in each hand.

Still, the essential parameters of the legend rarely varied: Man beats machine. Then dies.

PART I

Body

CHAPTER 1

LEAVING NEW YORK

*If Edward Payson Weston succeeds in reaching California on
foot he will have demonstrated one thing at least, and that is
that some old gentlemen have stranger notions than others.*

—***CHICAGO DAILY TRIBUNE,*** April 28, 1909

March 15, 1909. At twenty-five minutes past four on a clear, chilly late
winter afternoon in 1909, an elderly man walked out of the main New York
post office, opposite City Hall in lower Manhattan, and paused for a
moment on the uppermost step. He was wiry and taut and stood about five
foot eight and weighed around 125 pounds. He wasn't remarkable physically, but he wasn't the sort to blend in, either. On this March day, he wore
a blue frock coat and a large white hat ("a sombrero in all but color," as an
observer described it) and what one reporter referred to as "mouse-colored
leggings." In one hand he held a small cane, and with the other he fidgeted
with his trademark mustache, a large and silvery thing that draped his upper
lip, resting a few inches below twinkling eyes, which seemed to find private
amusement in public commotion.

Edward Payson Weston was planning to take a long walk. He was off to
a late start—inside the post office, a crowd of well-wishers had mobbed
him, delaying his departure. Edward Morgan, the city's postmaster, had
emerged from his office to greet him personally. With a wry smile, Morgan
handed Weston an envelope containing a letter, asking that he deliver it to

his counterpart in San Francisco. Morgan reminded Weston that he could collect eighty-five cents upon delivery. Everybody laughed.

Morgan also wished Weston well on his seventieth birthday. A few hurrahs were offered. And once the small talk and good wishes tapered off, Weston said his farewells and exited the post office through tall doors. Ahead of him was City Hall, with its Corinthian and Ionic pilasters, a neoclassical pile with French trimmings; above him, the mansard-roofed post office stood with the whimsical sternness of a bulldog wearing a derby hat. But people, more than his Beaux Arts surroundings, defined the scene: A minor mob had followed Weston out of the building, and a far larger and more raucous crowd had amassed out front to witness the first steps of his walk. One reporter sent to cover the scene estimated that ten thousand spectators clogged the streets and sidewalks around the post office, cheering and clamoring for a glimpse of the elderly walker. When he emerged, they let loose with a roar and pressed in to get a better look. "For a moment it seemed that the police guard would be swept away," the *New York Times* reported. Weston later admitted that the commotion "frightened [him] to death," his anxiety no doubt compounded by his fear that an eager, oafish spectator might step on one of his feet and hobble him before he even began. This had happened on a long walk he had undertaken two years earlier, and the experience left him skittish and wary.

Weston at last doffed his hat to the crowd, then plunged down the steps and into the mob. He slowly made his way forward, thanks chiefly to the brawn of two strapping policemen, longtime friends Ben and Dan Rinn. The Rinns were minor celebrities in their own right—a few years earlier, they had been first on the scene when President Teddy Roosevelt's horse-drawn carriage was broadsided by a streetcar in Pittsfield, Massachusetts. The brothers happened to be nearby on vacation; one ran for medical help, and the other held the streetcar motorman captive until local authorities arrived. (The accident earned a small footnote in history: A Secret Service agent died in the crash, becoming the first agent killed in the line of duty.)

A posse of New York mounted police officers aided the Rinns in crowd control, riding into the rabble and parting a way for the walker. Veterans of Company B of the Army's Seventh Regiment, led by one Captain James E. Schuyler, also did their best to keep the crowd at bay. Weston had aided the company in a small espionage matter years ago, and some of the regiment had reunited to escort him on the start of his journey. The regiment had also hired the Metropolitan Band to follow him during the first part of his walk, and it was noisily striking up a brassy tune, which attracted even more gawkers and followers.

As a path opened in the crowd, Weston started to gather speed and gradually hit a stride of about three and a half to four miles per hour. "He is a marvel of endurance and determination," wrote an admiring reporter in the *Times-Leader* of Wilkes-Barre, Pennsylvania. "He is more like a tireless machine than a human being."

At minimum, Weston would need to be a marvel. His plan was to walk that afternoon and evening to Tarrytown, about thirty miles up the Hudson River. He would follow the Hudson the next day toward Albany, then turn west and go on to Chicago and then on and on, across the windswept plains and over and around the formidable Rockies and High Sierras, eventually arriving in San Francisco after some four thousand miles on foot. He told everyone who would listen that he was confident he would make the trip within a hundred days. This pace would preclude much dawdling, and essentially meant he'd have to walk forty miles every day, not counting Sundays, which he always took as a day of rest.

Even if he succeeded, this trek would not be his longest walk—years before, in England, he had once covered five thousand miles in a hundred days—but this would surely be his most challenging. And by any measure, it would require a lot of steps: approximately 8.2 million, or more than eighty thousand each and every day of his walk. A typical American today walks an average of roughly five thousand steps daily, or somewhat less than two and a half miles, doing errands, foraging around in the kitchen, chasing after a football in the backyard, crossing the shopping mall parking lot, walking down a row of cubicles to discuss with a colleague a recent memo. Weston would do that sixteenfold every day. What's more, Weston embarked on his cross-country trek in an era when the nation was not well suited for transcontinental crossings unless you were traveling by rail, in which case you could argue that the cross-country transportation network was at its apogee. While sleeping in a plush, well-tended Pullman car, you could make it from New York to Chicago in sixteen hours. (Today, it takes about twenty hours on Amtrak.) Three years earlier a train had made it from San Francisco to New York in seventy-one and a half hours, and the Harriman Special regularly made the trip in five days. But walking anywhere outside cities could be slow and sloggy. Roadways were primitive at best—

outside the cities, hardly any long-distance routes were paved with mac-adam or brick or cobblestones. Most were composed of loosely compressed dirt liable to turn rutty when wet and dusty when dry. Hotels and inns could be found in the small towns Weston passed through in the East and Upper Midwest, but, like the towns themselves, these became more fugitive and widely scattered as he pushed westward, and he would have to count more on the kindness of strangers.

Weston faced another danger: Noisy, belching horseless carriages were taking to the roadways in ever-greater numbers. In 1909, some 126,593 cars had been manufactured—more than half of them touring cars, acquired for recreation rather than commerce. Inexperienced drivers, who had to be wealthy enough to splurge on what was still a novelty, would weave pell-mell down rough, potholed streets. Walkers, once kings of the road, now found that they had to scuttle to the margins to avoid being hit, and almost every day some metropolitan newspaper ran an account or two of a pedestrian run over by an automobile. A 1905 book titled *Automobilia* was filled with poems, anecdotes, and jokes involving these new conveyances. Among them: "Have you made a record with your automobile yet?" someone asks a driver. "Oh, yes" is the cheerful reply. "Two dogs, a chicken, three small boys, and a street cleaner, all run over in less than an hour."

The day Weston left New York, a man named Arthur Subers was cross-ing a street in downtown Chicago on foot. He was run over by not one, not two, but by three automobiles in succession. Subers miraculously escaped without serious injury. It was, perhaps, the first triple pedestrian–automobile accident in history. Subers had gotten in the way of progress, and progress would not be stopped.

━━━━━━━

Three weeks before Weston set off from the front steps of the New York post office, an essay appeared on the front page of the influential Parisian newspaper *Le Figaro*. It was titled "The Founding and Manifesto of Futur-ism." The essay was by and large an obituary for anything that moved at a pedestrian's pace, and a celebration of anything that zipped along speedily. It was written by a lavishly mustachioed Italian writer and theorist named Filippo Tommaso Marinetti, who recounted a recent episode in which he was driving an automobile and encountered two oncoming cyclists—"their stupid swaying got in my way," as he put it. He avoided them, but his car ended up in a muddy gully. He emerged from the "maternal ditch" as if being born anew into a world where speed was now sacred—it ennobled man, and those who did not embrace swiftness (like those on their stupid bikes) would be left behind and one day awaken to find themselves on the refuse heap of civilization. The decaying past was slow moving, embraced only by nostalgists who longed for a static landscape and lowing cows.

"We declare that the splendor of the world has been enriched by a new beauty: the beauty of speed," Marinetti wrote. "A racing automobile with its bonnet adorned with great tubes like serpents with explosive breath . . . a roaring motor car which seems to run on machine-gun fire, is more beautiful than the Victory of Samothrace."

Marinetti and his followers saw in speed not just dispatch and expediency and inevitability, but also an aesthetic and moral good, and something that would improve the lot of all mankind. Unknowingly, he was laying the theoretical foundations for streamlined designs in cars and trains and for ever-widening road networks. In his other writings he noted that "slowness is naturally foul," and he heralded "a new good: speed, and a new evil: slowness." Marinetti and his followers called for a great public works project in Venice to fill in "the small, stinking canals with the rubble from the old, collapsing and leprous palaces." To the north, he wanted to straighten the Danube, allowing it to flow unhindered and expeditiously. The future was sleek, the future was fast. For a time, Marinetti was influential among the emerging fascist movement, and he pushed (unsuccessfully) for futurism to be made the official state art of Italy.

It was into this world that Weston, the walker, walked.

━━━━━━━━━━

"Walking with elasticity of step and freedom of action that was the absolute contradiction of age," Weston pushed on through lower Manhattan with "a springy step and a generally jaunty air," according to the *New York Times*. Another correspondent wrote that he looked "as blithe and as vigorous as most men half his age." The *Atlanta Constitution* marveled at the huge crowd that had turned out to "cheer the plucky old trudger." The *Boston*

Globe's headline: "Weston Off on His Long Walk; . . . Elderly Athlete Cheered by Thousands at Start."

Behind the public tumult and outward pep, Weston's nerves were undoubtedly running high. While publicly confident, he was privately worried about whether he'd actually make even the first thirty miles to Tarrytown. He'd started preparing for this walk months earlier by walking twenty-five or thirty miles daily. At the outset of his walk he was on his home turf, having lived in New York for many years. But his warm-up walks hadn't gone terrifically well. One of his feet came up sore, and his doctor advised him to ease up on his training regimen. So Weston walked just five miles daily immediately prior to his departure, and five miles was barely a warm-up for a walker of his stamina and habits. The afternoon he departed, he later said, he was still "suffering from great pain," although he was confident he could work through it; he always did, he said, insisting that a good walk was the best tonic known to mankind and could cure just about any malady, including that of the foot.

Surrounded by the jostling crowd, Weston turned north up Lafayette Street past City Hall and continued onward to Fourth Avenue. Those on the fringe would surge ahead and jockey for the best viewing positions along the curb to watch as Weston passed by. He soldiered on through the teeming assemblage, glancing upward at the buildings from time to time to ensure he was still headed in the right direction.

All the commotion no doubt provoked some nostalgia. Decades earlier, from the 1860s through the 1880s, a much-younger Weston had drawn crowds even larger than these—along with similarly fawning newspaper coverage—for his astounding feats of pedestrianism.

The Walking Man, as Weston was known, possibly the most indefatigable long-distance walker ever to stride across our planet's surface, was born on March 15, 1839, in Providence, Rhode Island. His father, Silas Weston, was a descendent of *Mayflower* passengers and worked mostly as a school principal and teacher, but sometimes as a shopkeeper. He stood six foot four and liked to play the bass viol. Edward's mother, Maria, wrote children's books. They had two girls and two boys, with Edward being the older of their sons. He weighed four and a half pounds at birth and was so frail he wasn't expected to survive.

As a child, Weston was considered a sweet and obedient boy, though weak of constitution and often somewhat sickly. Still, he was perpetually restless. ("There was no keeping him still," his Sunday school teacher once recalled, adding that he "was the most uneasy bright boy I ever saw.") His father left New England in pursuit of adventure and California gold in 1849 and remained in the West for three years. When he returned (largely gold-less), Weston was captivated by his father's tales and wrote up several of his accounts. He had these printed in pamphlet form, which he then sold along with the newspapers he was hawking as a newsboy on the passenger rail lines to New York and Boston. When Weston was fifteen, his mother recruited a friend who was also a coach in an effort to improve her son's health. The coach first instructed Edward to abandon coffee, then put him on a regimen of milk and vegetables. He also instructed him to undertake short, vigorous walks every day.

Weston complied, on both diet and exercise. His walks grew longer and soon progressed from being a prescribed chore to a favored pastime, one that he maintained through life. "I like to walk," Weston said matter-of-factly when interviewed at age sixty-nine. "In fact, I'd rather walk than eat, and . . . I am fond of my meals."

In his late teens, Weston took on a variety of jobs, including working as a clerk in a merchant's office in Providence and apprenticing himself to a jeweler for several months. He didn't care for either position and soon abandoned both. He continued to write, however, and apparently penned a few stories as a correspondent for local newspapers. He left a faint footprint when it came to his writings, and his brief career as a writer evidently failed to instill in him the ability to frame tight, coherent thoughts. He both wrote and spoke with a sort of flowery formal Victorian diction that matched his role as a character striding from the past. "As a writer Weston was not a success," noted the *New York Sun* when Weston was in his early thirties. "His sentences, like his speeches, were long and intricate, and also like his speeches, contained comparatively little that the mind of others could take hold of. They sounded well, but said little."

He also worked for a traveling circus, but gave that up after he was nearly killed by a bolt of lightning while riding a wagon in Massachusetts. He then headed north and worked as a drummer for a Canadian circus, undaunted by his lack of drumming experience. He eventually returned home. His father had passed away ("a man restless in his brain, and finally died insane," wrote Weston's childhood minister), and to make ends meet his mother stepped up her book writing. Her son became her chief salesman, selling them door-to-door and continuing to walk great distances while selling. (This would turn out to be good training not only for walking; Weston self-published a few small books and pamphlets about his later adventures and sold them along his walking routes.)

When Weston started his walking career, around the time of the Civil War, information was still largely tethered to foot travel. Postal carriers brought the news from family as well as from foreign countries, and that news traveled at a walker's pace. The telegraph had surfaced in the 1840s, allowing essential information to move from town to town and city to city with unimaginable speed, although it often then traveled to its final destination by foot. In 1876, Alexander Graham Bell was awarded a patent for the "acoustic telegraph," upending communications forever. By the time of Weston's 1909 walk, word of his travels moved quickly ahead of him—by telephone from friend to friend and by telegraph to newspapers, which would print updates about his walk and alert readers to his impending arrival.

The hundreds of people who lined the streets to applaud Weston as he walked by included not only the idle and merely curious, but also older Americans who remembered hearing of Weston's earlier walks or had grown up with tales of his extraordinary stamina. His fame was widespread. He'd been called "the walkingest man in America," the "country's greatest walker," the "father of the long walk," "undoubtedly the greatest pedestrian that ever walked," and the "purest walker of all time." He'd been dubbed Weston the Walker, Weston the Walkist, and Weston the Pedestrian. The last of these monikers proved the most enduring. Often he'd just be referred to as the Pedestrian. A trail of "first" and "best" accolades spooled out behind him. In 1868, he was the first in America to walk 100 miles in under 24 hours (he did it in 22 hours and 20 minutes, then topped that record by 50 minutes three years later). He was the first to achieve 550 miles in six days of walking. In 1875, Weston walked 115 miles in 23 hours and 40 minutes, and did so without taking a single rest. "Any horse which could be guaranteed to get over the same amount of ground in the same time would bring an almost fabulous price," the *New York Times* noted, perhaps as a compliment.

And now, at age seventy, Weston was about to start up his rambling again.

Weston began his journey to San Francisco by walking north. This seems unusual, but Weston often traveled against expectation. His plan was to walk through the Bronx and Westchester County, then to follow the east bank of the Hudson River to Troy before crossing the river by foot and heading west. Taking ferries was tantamount to cheating, he would sometimes tell people. He'd stride north until he reached the first pedestrian bridge, then cross it.

Weston walked through a New York City that was in the grip of vast and sweeping changes. All around him, he was witnessing artifacts of yesterday mingling with harbingers of tomorrow. Not only were horses giving way to cars, but also sputtering gas streetlights were yielding to the steady glow of electric bulbs. Moving about had never been so technologically complicated, yet so easy and effortless at the same time. New York in 1909 was in part a large and complex clock that ran on an almost frictionless movement.

In front of the post office where Weston began his trek, clanging streetcars with passengers hanging off the sides converged. These already had an air of the antiquated about them. More modern New Yorkers were heading underground. Five years earlier, in October 1904, New York's first subway had opened with a rumble beneath City Hall, where the Interborough Rapid Transit Company had thrown open the doors of its elaborate station filled with arches that made it look like the catacombs of a Romanesque church. (It later proved too small for modern trains and was abandoned in 1945.) Passengers could hop on board and be whisked at speeds up to forty miles per hour northbound to 145th Street in Harlem. The day the subway opened, a million New Yorkers came out to ride the future; lines at some stations stretched two blocks. This was the first in what would be an extensive underground network lacing the island and outer boroughs. (In truth, this wasn't actually the *first* subway. In 1869, directly below City Hall, an entrepreneur had secretly built the Beach Pneumatic Transit, which was essentially a human-size pneumatic tube powered by fans creating both propulsion and suction, much like systems for moving deposit tickets at drive-through bank stations today. The single car ran slightly more than one hundred yards through a tunnel eight feet in diameter; efforts to extend it the length of Manhattan were doomed, though not because of technology, but rather cutthroat local politics. While it lasted, the pneumatic tube served as a minor diversion for New Yorkers who would descend into the earth, be sealed in a capsule, and be whisked the length of a football field. The pneumatic tube tunnel was later destroyed during the construction of the BMT line.)

New York was, in fact, rapidly becoming a city of moles. Between 1908 and 1910, three major tunnels were completed under the Hudson and East Rivers, edging the ferry system toward irrelevance. After thirty-three years of failed attempts, the first successful underground link between New Jersey and New York opened in 1908, with train tracks connecting Hoboken and Nineteenth Street. As Weston walked through a city dusty and clamorous with construction, workers were just finishing up on the downtown Hudson tubes (today serving as Port Authority Trans-Hudson Corporation train tunnels), which would open in the summer of 1909. And in 1910, railroad service would begin through the North River tunnel, the world's longest and most impressive underwater tunnel, which linked Pennsylvania Station with Weehawken, New Jersey.

The extraordinary and elaborate Pennsylvania Station, modeled on Rome's Baths of Caracalla, was nearing completion as Weston headed north a few blocks to the west, and it would open a year later. Ten blocks north and several blocks east, the even more opulent Grand Central Terminal on Forty-Second Street, which had been under construction for six years, still had another four left to completion. The result would be a massive Beaux Arts celebration of rail transport and city life. Penn and Grand Central stations, two of the world's great temples to pre-automotive transport, established high-water marks in rail travel. Between 1900 and 1920, the number of passengers carried by rail doubled nationwide, and the number of rail miles they traveled tripled.

As an army of engineers made it easier to venture into the city and traverse its grid laterally, others were busy colonizing the sky. This upward rise was enabled not so much by the invention of the elevator—rudimentary versions of which had been around for centuries—but by pairing it with electric-powered motors and at last conquering the public fear that cables would snap and their scissor-gated boxes would become plummeting tombs. Elevators were essentially vertical railways, whisking people up and down with remarkable efficiency. The first modern elevator appeared in 1853, after Elisha Otis invented the safety brake. At the New York World's Fair that year, Otis stood on a platform that had been raised by a rope, and then had an axe-wielding confederate sever the rope. The platform dropped for a fleeting moment, then abruptly stopped. That short drop helped convince the public that elevators were safe. New steel-framed buildings could also be built much higher than masonry structures, and architects took notice of the impressive fifty-story Metropolitan Life Tower, completed in Midtown Manhattan in 1909. Towers began soaring into the clouds (though the term "skyscraper" still appeared in quotation marks in the 1911 *Encyclopedia Britannica*). In 1909, New York, like many other American cities, was crouched and prepared to leap.

New York had long been a city of brisk commerce, but it was now increasingly taut and lean—a city that brooked little waste or excess, and where movement was economical and efficient. Manhattan was a beehive, always in motion, with creatures moving seemingly at random, but each actually infused with high purpose and direction.

When Weston walked through New York headed to San Francisco, the country was balanced precariously, as if at a tipping point between a misty, romantic past and an uncertain, if hard-edged future full of pragmatic new technologies. In 1902, the novelist Henry Adams captured this moment when he noted in a letter: "My idea of paradise is a perfect automobile going thirty miles an hour on a smooth road to a twelfth-century cathedral."

Just two months before Weston strode out of New York, Theodore Roosevelt departed the White House, and his fellow Republican William Howard Taft stepped in. Roosevelt was fit and hale and would proselytize about personal fitness and manliness. ("I wish to preach, not the doctrine of ignoble ease, but the doctrine of the strenuous life," he once said.) In his post-presidential years, Roosevelt nearly died while exploring unmapped parts of the Amazon. His replacement, in contrast, fought a persistent battle against obesity. In college Taft's nickname was "Big Lub." He is perhaps best remembered for once getting wedged in a White House bathtub and having to summon servants to free him; they used butter as a lubricant.

Weston was walking from one era into another, and those cheering him along the route seemed to sense this shift. "This long walk is an effective protest against the present-day craving for speed in locomotion," a writer for the *Nation* noted about Weston. "Pedestrianism is rather a fine art than a means of locomotion." Weston was an emissary from the past, and he was striding defiantly into a future governed not by poets, but by mechanics.

At Twenty-Sixth Street, Weston turned and headed westward for a bit, then sheered north on Fifth Avenue, making his way up toward Central Park. Those accompanying him—his police escort, former army comrades, the marching band—began to huff and flag and fall behind. At Fifty-Ninth Street, he turned west, passing the opulent Plaza Hotel, which had opened just eighteen months earlier. He then walked along the southern edge of Central Park to Columbus Circle, where he paused for a ceremonial tribute: the brass band and Company B ("many of whom looked as if they had walked themselves out," wrote one reporter) formed a line and blared out "Auld Lang Syne."

Weston walked up Broadway through what is now the Upper West Side and then into Harlem. The great immigration of African Americans from the South had not yet begun, and the sidewalks would have been teeming with European immigrants; in 1907, more than a million immigrants passed through Ellis Island. He stopped for refreshment at 125th Street. "He looked fatigued at this point, the excitement having drawn heavily on his vitality," the *Times* reported. His trainer, Charles E. Hagen, fixed him a cup of tea into which he cracked a raw egg. "There is nothing so good as fresh eggs as a stimulant," Weston once told an interviewer. "On the road I have a couple beaten up in hot tea every few hours."

Revitalized, Weston walked on, crossing the treacherous Spuyten Duyvil Creek dividing Manhattan and the Bronx. Here the city became less densely urban and more open and village-like. He skirted the meadows of Van Cortlandt Park, which had the feel of a savanna edged by forest. Darkness descended as he departed New York City, and he was guided onward by the headlights of his support car and lantern light. He walked into Westchester County, where the mounted police of New York, who had accompanied him in relays from the downtown post office, handed him off to Yonkers policemen on horseback. The Yonkers police "were very kind, and their interest was very noticeable," Weston said.

About quarter past nine, Weston walked into the heart of Yonkers, where two thousand cheering fans turned out to welcome him. He signed the guest book at the city hall, then headed over to a packed YMCA auditorium. Ten policemen had to clear a path through the crowd so he could mount the stage. He delivered a short lecture on the benefits of walking.

The audience may or may not have been attentive to what he had to say; many likely came out for the sheer spectacle, and to take stock of the slight, loose-limbed aged man who was walking to San Francisco. Afterward, Weston dined on a light meal accompanied by a few others, and around 11:00 p.m., he stepped outside into the March night.

———————————

Although Weston would undoubtedly recognize much of contemporary Manhattan, with its street grid and shadowy urban canyons, it's unlikely he'd find familiar reference points in Westchester County, or any of the outlying towns and counties he walked through a century ago. The friction-less freedom of movement emerging in the country's urban areas was impressive, but that shift was nothing compared with the revolution about to sweep rural precincts. This, of course, was thanks to the internal combustion engine, the horseless carriage, the automobile, the personal vehicle. A machine that allowed anyone with a measure of daring and sufficient funds to become, literally, superhuman.

Inventors had been tinkering with self-propelled vehicles since the eighteenth century. Throughout the nineteenth century, rough forebears of the modern car had appeared, noisily and rambunctiously, on the nation's dirt roads. Some were powered by steam engines, a few by batteries, and most had big wheels and were tall, spindly, and delicate-looking, like the horse-drawn carriages they were designed to replace. Almost all were unreliable for anything but short jaunts.

Automobiles and their drivers were amid their own transition. Cars were evolving from curious contraptions made in garage-like factories to the products of a thriving, large-scale industry. The first American automobile manufacturing company was established in 1896 as the Duryea Motor Wagon Company; in 1897, Ransom E. Olds founded what would become Oldsmobile. The Studebaker brothers, known for their well-crafted horse-drawn carriages, started producing gasoline-powered carriages in 1904. Other entrepreneurs scrambled to get into the automobile game, arriving from the worlds of bike makers, manufacturers of electrical components, and wagon builders. By the time of Weston's walk, some seventy-five manufacturers produced a variety of high-wheeled, self-propelled motor buggies. Rural roads that had long been marked with three ruts—worn in the center by horses' hoofs and then by the flanking carriage wheels—gradually were replaced by something novel: a simple pair of ruts.

Makers and owners of the new motorcars sought to prove that these weren't merely playthings for the wealthy. Impressive displays of automotive derring-do became staples of news accounts in the first decade of the twentieth century. In 1903 a Vermont doctor named Horatio Nelson Jackson made the first transcontinental drive at the wheel of a used two-cylinder, twenty-horsepower Winton, piloting it from San Francisco to New York in sixty-three days. In 1905, the first motorcycle made the trip from New York to San Francisco. By 1907, this sort of thing was old hat: "So many automobiles have gone across the continent that the trip by motorcar is no longer a novelty," the *New York Times* yawned. The record transcontinental crossing was by then fifteen days.

But cars kept driving from here to there and beyond, and new records continued to be set. In February 1908, the first race from New York to Paris took place (with drivers routed by way of Alaska and Siberia), demonstrating that the automobile could conquer the globe (two cars made it to Paris, and the American was declared the victor after the German was disqualified for skipping the Alaska leg and for shipping the car partway by rail). Also that year: the first drive across the United States by a family, setting the stage for a century-long tradition. In November 1908, the headlines in American papers read, "The First Automobile to Cross the Syrian Desert." And on June 9, 1909, a twenty-two-year-old Vassar graduate (and young mother) named Alice Huyler Ramsey set off from Broadway in New York with three girlfriends, headed for San Francisco in a 1909 Maxwell DA. (They arrived safely forty-one days later.) She became the first female driver to cross the whole of North America.

Automobiles were proving themselves mechanically day by day. But they had yet to find their place in a shifting society, as evidenced by a rise in pushback against "arrogant" automobilists. In 1906, the president of Princeton and future president of the United States, Woodrow Wilson, noted that "nothing has spread socialistic feeling in this country more than the automobile." The automobile was "a picture of the arrogance of wealth," he said; pushy car owners were quickly alienating the public with their newfound ability to bully others off the road. The *New York Times* was one of many public voices calling out obnoxious drivers hogging the lanes. The "man on wheels, arrogant, self satisfied, imbrued with gore and sanguinary strains, fights for undisputed possession of the earth which he is coming to look upon as his," the editors wrote in 1909. "How fretting it is to the automobilist to be delayed in his whizzing journey athwart the fresh greensward by driving into some unaesthetic foot-passenger of earth and clogging his gear with anatomical fragments."

By 1909, the year of Weston's walk, automobiles had just arrived at a critical point, about to transition between a novelty for few to a necessity for all. In October 1908, five months before Weston set off, Henry Ford introduced the Model T. Between 1909 and 1910 Ford manufactured nearly twenty thousand automobiles, which sold for $950 apiece. Then Ford more or less perfected the assembly line, ratcheting up production and dropping the price. A decade later, he was manufacturing more than a million cars a year; by 1924, a basic model Ford could be had for as little as $290. General Motors, which would quickly rival Ford as a manufacturer of cars, was founded in 1908.

The democratization of the automobile was under way. As cars became more affordable, pressure was applied to improve the national infrastructure to accommodate their growing numbers: better, more reliable roads and a network of gas stations and auto mechanics were needed to keep these contraptions moving.

A small war erupted between drivers of cars and those who insisted on walking. The first speed bump, for instance, was constructed in Chatham, New Jersey, in 1906. "Goggles, hats, a monkey wrench, sidecombs, hairpins and other articles flew in all directions," reported a newspaperman who was sent out to report from the scene. "The crowd gave a cheer and decided the borough's plan was effective." This was a variation of an old struggle, of one species moving in to dominate a niche formerly occupied by another. Careless drivers of horse-drawn carriages had long caused the deaths of pedestrians. But putting humans up against automobiles was a far less equitable match. A car isn't as nimble as a horse (it can't rear up to come to a full stop) and has more weight and thus more mass, and basic physics decrees that an object with more mass encountering an object with less mass at speed will have unsurprising results. Drivers and walkers were beginning a long process of working out rules of engagement, and coming up with terms of cohabitation.

"Several alleged walks across the continent have been heralded from time to time," the *New York Times* wrote a month before Weston set off, "but their accuracy has been so vague as to be valueless for records of bona fide achievements." Weston's walk, the paper later proclaimed, was the "first bona fide walk . . . across the American continent."

The first bona fide walk across the country? Nearly a century and a half after the nation's founding, nobody had walked clear across it? This strains credulity. After all, the first Native Americans, horseless until the Europeans, at some point crossed the continent on foot to arrive at the Atlantic Ocean after making their way across the Bering land bridge millennia ago. Granted, this may have required multiple generations to accomplish. And unheralded British and French trappers no doubt walked from eastern ports westward two centuries prior in pursuit of beavers and other valuable rodents, and some must have marveled at the setting sun on the Pacific Ocean. A little more than a century before Weston's big walk, Lewis and Clark documented a route overland to the Pacific coast—although horses and boats were involved.

Others had since made their way across the continent (or the bulk of it) on foot. This included a former Civil War reporter named Stephen Powers, who in 1868 walked 3,556 miles from Raleigh, North Carolina, to San Francisco, following dirt lanes and relatively new railroad tracks. In 1884 Charles Lummis, a twenty-six-year-old journalist, walked from Cincinnati to Los Angeles to start a new job at the *Los Angeles Daily Times,* covering some 3,507 miles in 143 days. Lummis published a book about his trek eight years later. "It is the simple story of joy on legs," he wrote in his preface.

To the north, three young Canadians left northeastern Nova Scotia on foot in early 1906, also destined for San Francisco, at the prodding of "six well known sporting men of North Sydney" who put up a wager. The challenge for the trio was to leave on foot without a dime in their pockets, then return within a year (walking all the way back). If they managed to earn their way and save $200 in the process, they'd be rewarded with an additional $600 from the sporting men (about $15,000 in today's dollars). Their plan? Sell "pedestrian cards"—ten-cent postcard-like mementos—along the way to underwrite their walk.

Curiously, they set off on the last day of January. Less curiously, they ran into harsh winter weather in New Brunswick, then Maine. What happened next is subject to some conjecture—tattling reports surfaced of train hopping, and then the trio appeared in Montreal, where a newspaper noted "Social Life in Montreal Proved Too Tempting, and Some of Them Yielded to Seductiveness." Two of the original walkers pushed on; another man joined them. One of the walkers circled back on foot to Nova Scotia soon after, claiming that he'd made it to San Francisco and back. (*Toronto Daily Star:* "Pedestrians Faking.") Two of the walkers eventually arrived by some means, possibly foot, in Vancouver, British Columbia, where they put down roots, one as a warehouseman and the other as a police officer. They did not return east to claim their $600. This, admittedly, falls short of "bona fide" in the matter of coast-to-coast walks.

So, perhaps Weston's trek was indeed the first "bona fide" walk across the continent from sea to sea, if by that you mean a well-documented trek complete with witnesses all along the route.

Weston himself was, in fact, less definitive about his cross-country trek than the *New York Times:* "This is probably the first and only attempt ever made to cross America under surveillance during the entire trip," he said before departing, displaying, for him, an unusual lack of hyperbole. His "surveillance" was to consist of a valet, an agent, and a trainer, all of whom planned to follow along by automobile as best they could. The car would carry changes of clothing for Weston, along with eggs, tea, a bit of meat, and a large supply of ginger ale. "A special contrivance" had been rigged up to provide him with ice along the way. This was at least the second long walk on which Weston had been accompanied by a car. On the first, three years earlier, he said, the automobile was "very helpful, as I wore out several teams of horses."

March 15, 1909. It was near midnight as Weston and his dwindling posse pushed on north of Yonkers, then walked through quiet Dobbs Ferry and Irvington. At twenty minutes past one, he at last arrived in the riverside enclave of Tarrytown. He walked to the hotel where he had arranged for an overnight, stepping into his room nine hours after setting off from lower Manhattan.

Undressing as he prepared for bed, he made a small but unsettling discovery: a blister had formed on the ball of his right foot—something that rarely developed unless he was walking fifty or seventy-five miles in a day. He was "astonished," he later said, and set about lancing it with a needle. He then soaked both feet in a saltwater bath, dried them, and applied a lotion before finally lying down, his first day drawing to a close.

All things considered, it had been a good day—a surge of adulation and commotion at the outset, which Weston always seemed to welcome and from which he appeared to draw energy. Yet the crowd hadn't been so rambunctious as to get out of hand. What's more, his injured foot seemed to be faring well. And no overeager fan had jostled and hurt him.

But this had been only one day, and a fairly short one at that: he had tallied up a modest distance—just thirty miles. He faced at least ninety-nine days ahead of him. He would have to step up his pace if he was to make it to San Francisco on time, something that his spry physique was surprisingly well crafted to do.

Weston was examined earlier in his career by a prominent phrenologist, J. A. Fowler, one of a cadre who deduced personality traits from the shape and size of the skull. "His forehead is unusually high for one who is so fully developed in the base or across the brow," Fowler noted, with more than a hint of admiration. This indicated that "he is a man of reflection as well as one capable of storing his mind with useful information."

And much of what Weston stored behind his unusually high forehead was how to walk, and do so fast and efficiently.

CHAPTER 2

UPRIGHT BEARING

Know that length of stride is an indication of loyalty, good counsel, extensive ability, strong-mindedness, and anger.

—POLEMON OF LAODICEA (c. AD 88–144)

March 16, 1909. Edward Payson Weston slept six hours in Tarrytown, then arose and began the second day of his walk. If he felt sore or creaky or was bothered by the small blister he'd discovered the previous evening, he didn't show it. He offered gracious but harried farewells to the staff at the hotel and then set out into the bright chill of an early March morning, resuming his trek at about quarter after eight. His outfit was again dandified and attention grabbing, but now he sported a straw hat instead of his felt "sombrero." He hoofed the first six miles to Ossining in an hour and forty minutes, averaging a little over three and a half miles per hour. This was an accomplishment given road conditions that required he constantly watch where he stepped. By early afternoon, he arrived at the Hotel Raleigh in Peekskill, a four-story establishment that advertised "rooms with bath" and catered to "the comforts of autoists." A small crowd had gathered in advance of his arrival and heartily cheered him when he appeared. He stepped inside to warm himself and tend his blister, then lay down and closed his eyes for a customary midday rest.

An observer in Peekskill noted that Weston had arrived "at a sharp gait." Indeed, commentators often mentioned Weston's walking style, at times referring to his "peculiar" form. (One of his nicknames was the Wily Wobbler.) But conflicting accounts suggest that the peculiarities of his gait were inconsistent.

"At each step the body receives a slight jerk, which at times of fatigue becomes almost a swagger," one onlooker reported. Other times, he'd take two normal steps, and on the third hop forward slightly, adding an inch or two to his stride.

Generally, Weston preferred the French army method when walking: keeping his knees bent at a slight angle and landing on both the heel and ball of the foot simultaneously. "The foot is planted firmly and rather flat, and there is very little spring in his walk," wrote one sportswriter after watching Weston walk in 1876. He went on: "But his progression is constant; there is none of the pause which may be observed between each step in ordinary walkers."

The *New York Times* reported that Weston displayed "an elastic, swinging stride." A reporter for another metropolitan newspaper wrote that "his head, his waist, his forearms, moved in harmony with the backward-forward throw of the shoulders and the forward-backward push of the legs," a description that is as detailed as it is hard to envision. Another noted that "the action . . . was principally from the knees" and that his upper body moved little. The *British Medical Journal* noted in 1876 that "his walking is almost entirely from the hip."

In fact, Weston employed a variety of gaits to match his goal of the moment, and at times would switch them up to rest different muscle groups during long marches. In walking demonstrations, he liked to show off three different gaits he employed for different speeds: a four-mile-, a five-mile-, and a six-mile-per-hour pace, with each gait varying slightly. During a talk at Steinway Hall in New York in 1870, where he was introduced to the audience by the prominent newspaper editor Horace Greeley, he demonstrated his walking prowess by undertaking a mile around the auditorium, doing seventeen laps up and down auditorium steps and through the aisles, wearing a black velvet suit and striped hat. "He went around the room like a high-pressure steam man," reported the *New York Sun*. Unfortunately, Weston's demonstrations weren't captured in motion pictures or Eadweard Muybridge stop-action photographs or even in print by observers, so we're left to imagine how a high-pressure steam man would walk.

═══════════

Weston was conscious of his gait in ways that most of us aren't. We walk how we walk, without giving much thought to how it reflects our athleticism or individuality. One leg, then the next. Repeat. However, our gaits are as unique as our thumbprints—and increasingly, thanks to new technology, used as identifying traits.

Consider this story: A man enters a convenience store waving a gun. He departs a few moments later with a pocket full of cash and, quite possibly, a case of beer under his arm. He knew he would be seen by video surveillance cameras, so he took steps to ensure he couldn't be identified, such as tying a loose T-shirt over his lower face and wearing nondescript sunglasses and one of those baggy sweatshirts from the approved Convenience Store Robber ensemble. He'd watched enough crime dramas to know to wear gloves so his thumbprint wouldn't betray him. Harder to disguise is his height, which a preternaturally unrattled store clerk determines thanks to the measuring tape affixed to the doorframe for just such an occurrence.

But there's another biometric that will almost certainly aid in identifying him. Watch how he walks and moves on the grainy black-and-white video that local law enforcement posts on YouTube: maybe a bit of a lurch, perhaps a slight sidewise drift, maybe long, limber strides as he flees out into the night across the parking lot. That distinguishes him from last week's robber, who moved in short, jerky steps. If you happened to know the perp, you might have a flicker of recognition—"*Oh, he moves a bit like Eric.*" And you might be right. It might be Eric. Among biometric researchers, the thinking is that, with the algorithms to analyze video and a sufficient database to tap into, software may one day identify individuals based in large part on how they walk, the same way software links the whorls and loops on your finger to a vast database and can report with a high degree of confidence a simple fact: We know who you are.

This sort of research has been under way since the late 1990s and gained urgency after the 2001 attacks on New York and Washington, DC, and the 2005 train bombing in London. The US government's Defense Advanced Research Projects Agency (DARPA) and Department of Homeland Security, among others, are interested in analyzing the way we walk—our unique gaits—and DARPA has been sponsoring "human identification at a distance" studies since 2000, which combines gait cues with facial and gesture analysis. It's a hot field right now, and has been heralded as a less invasive approach than retina scans or blood tests or fingerprinting. One academic thesis on the algorithms of walking put it this way: "Advantages include the fact that it does not require subject cooperation or body contact, and the sensor may be located remotely."

The University of Southampton in England is among those at the forefront of this research and is home to the School of Electronics and Computer Science biometrics tunnel. Subjects walk through the short tunnel and their movements are captured from various angles by eight cameras. Software reduces this information to a handful of data points—the angle of the knee when advancing, the length of the step, the cadence of the walk—from which it determines a signature for each individual. Once it's got a person's number, it won't be thrown off if he changes clothes or dons disguises. (It works best when it augments facial recognition technology, as gait alone is hard to sort out from background noise.) Still, the university has reported identification with about 90 percent accuracy, and is working to improve that.

At least one security contractor is looking to introduce gait recognition at London's airports. Passengers would be captured by several cameras as they walked up to and through traditional security checkpoints—say, approaching the millimeter wave scanner—and the data obtained would then be checked against an international gait database for no-fly suspects or other flags. It's essentially fingerprinting from a distance.

Identifying people by how they walk is nothing new. We all do it, consciously or not. Many of us recognize spouses, siblings, and close friends by their walk signatures; some of us lope, some bob up and down, some stride with an alarming single-mindedness of purpose. We can identify people even without cues like a telltale hat or a mane of hair. "'Tis Cinna," says Cassius in Shakespeare's *Julius Caesar*. "I do know him by his gait. He is a friend."

In 1977, a series of experiments were done at Wesleyan University on six students (three male, three female) who lived in the same dorm and were roughly the same height. All were asked to wear dark, nondescript clothing, and glass-bead reflective tape was wrapped around their joints (ankles, knees, elbows, wrists), with additional tape affixed to their hips and shoulders. Each was videotaped walking across a dim room and the exposure adjusted so that only the glare of the reflective tape was visible on the monitors. In stills, you see just a tall, tapering collection of dots, like an assortment of blurry, decorated Christmas trees.

Two months after filming, the six test subjects were brought back into the lab and shown the videos, then asked to identify who was who based solely on the movement of the reflective tape. Identifications after watching the moving dots on the screen were twice as accurate as random guesswork.

Other studies using similar conditions (light tape, restricted vision) show that people are often able to recognize themselves by their own gait, even though they rarely view themselves walking. This discovery was made in the search for a better understanding of proprioception—that is, how we sense the position, location, and movement of our body and its various parts. When people use the expression "sixth sense," they are usually referring to paranormal or superhuman powers. But we are all born with a natural sixth sense: Our muscles allow us to define and understand space simply by moving though it.

The field of biometrics can be cleaved into two divisions. Static biometrics strives to identify individuals based on fixed characteristics, like fingerprints, ear shapes, or facial features. Dynamic biometrics analyzes traits such as voice and speech modulation, keystroke patterns, or gait.

Human movement and locomotion first arose as a subject of serious study during the Renaissance. Sir Isaac Newton, Leonardo da Vinci, mathematician Giovanni Borelli, and many others were fascinated by body dynamics. In the nineteenth century, Ernst Heinrich Weber and Eduard Friedrich Wilhelm Weber used a stopwatch and measuring tape to gauge the efficiency of gaits. Their book, *The Mechanics of Human Walking Apparatus* (1894), correctly described the pendulum-like motion of the leg, but attributed to gravity an undeservedly large role. Still, the best-known studies of human motion—then and now—were undertaken by Eadweard Muybridge. The photographs he shot during his research in the 1880s have migrated from science to popular culture (they're everywhere—in magazines and posters in dorm rooms, on greeting cards), in large part because of the surreal, serene beauty of the sequential photographs depicting people playing with children or striding, unself-consciously unclothed, before a series of height markings. (He also studied animals such as horses and achieved fame as the first person to conclusively prove that a galloping horse was, in fact, fully airborne in midstride.)

The 2012 Ig Nobel Prize for fluid dynamics—awarded at Harvard by the science humor magazine *Annals of Improbable Research*—went to a pair of California researchers who published a study in the American Physical Society journal *Physical Review E*. It was titled "Walking with Coffee: Why Does It Spill?" ("While often we spill the drink, this familiar phenomenon has never been explored systematically.") It's the sort of study that lends itself to parody, but underlying it you'll find a fascinating truth about the biomechanics of walking: With each step, we almost imperceptibly speed up and slow down. We're essentially a pendulum when we walk, slowing at the apex of each step and then speeding up as we swing through. This pattern leads the coffee to oscillate in the cup, and our imperfect, uneven steps amplify those oscillations, leading to minor catastrophes and laundry bills. (Among the study's suggested solutions: Start walking slowly, and leave a gap of at least one-eighth of the cup's diameter between the coffee's surface and the mug's lip.)

The cadence of walking has been studied by numerous other researchers, who have added further insight into why it's so difficult to carry a cup of coffee. "As the body passes over the weight-bearing limb, three different deviations occur from uniform progression in a straight line," note Verne T. Inman and colleagues in *Human Walking*. "With each step the body speeds up and slows down slightly, it rises and falls a few centimeters, and it weaves slightly from side to side."

Walking is a skill that's partially instinctual and partially learned. In the nineteenth century, talk of gaits would not infrequently devolve into a disagreement over the most efficient style one might adopt: either the straight-leg manner of walking or the bent-knee approach. Weston's preferred gait—the French army style—generated significant debate.

Armies have always depended in large part on the speed of their infantries, and infantries often walked very long distances. The Roman army was famed for its exploits in marching, and for its superb road system, which nearly circumnavigated the Mediterranean and extended through France into Great Britain. These smooth, wide roads were essentially an early form of troop transport. Even laden with sixty pounds of weaponry and gear, Roman soldiers could move at about three miles per hour. When rail became widespread in the nineteenth century and permitted the more efficient wholesale movement of troops to the battlefront, the infantry still traveled on foot after disembarking, or as historian John Keegan wrote, nineteenth-century generals were "no better able to move or transport their supplies than Roman legions had been." Getting about by foot remained the linchpin of military strategy until 1916, when the armored tracked tank appeared at the Battle of the Somme and proved that something with an engine could maneuver reasonably well over uneven terrain.

How should armies march? Armies experimented with different gaits. The Prussian army famously popularized the goose step—an exaggerated swinging of the leg up to nearly hip height (some armies, lacking the vigor of the Prussians, raised the leg to only calf or knee height). This was thought to keep soldiers in order by ensuring they would be a fixed distance from the ranks immediately ahead, but it was used chiefly for ceremonial occasions. It didn't make much sense for long marches across open terrain.

The French army, in contrast, was the leading proponent of the bent-knee method of long marching. The gait was modeled after infants learning to walk, with the knees angled and the body canting slightly forward. The idea was that by pitching forward, gravity would help pull one along and make it easier to cover vast distances. In some ways, the French army's bent-knee walk looked almost as silly and unnatural as the goose step.

A 1908 article in the *New York Times* pondered, "Is our method of walking correct or incorrect?" The story rehashed the debate over the straight-leg versus bent-knee approach to walking. It noted the justification for the bent-leg walk—that it's the natural tendency of babies—and posited that walking straight legged was simply behavior learned from elders. Not all went along with this idea. Some scientists countered that babies simply didn't have the musculature to straighten their legs, and the crouched posture that better prepared them for falling is something they would naturally grow out of. The reporter wrote that a "famous wrestler" tried walking the bent-leg way across the lobby of a hotel and "was quite disgusted at the result." A physician also dismissed bent-leg walking, claiming that "it's just a fad. . . . Soon somebody will be getting up and saying that if we blew our noses differently it would improve the race. It's all nonsense."

Walking defines us, sometimes as a culture, sometimes as an individual. Few studies have compared individual gaits across cultures (crowd behavior in different cultures has been more widely studied), but some research suggests that, for instance, some African women practice a more economical, energy-conserving stride because they've trained themselves to carry heavier loads more efficiently. And in Japan during the Edo period (1603–1868), long-distance messengers were trained to swing their left arms in tandem with their left legs and their right arms with their right legs rather than counterbalancing with the opposite-side swing, as is natural. One can with practice break from cultural walking norms and don a gait like a frock, as in the case of the French army's bent-knee walk or the goose step. Or one can move naturally, not thinking about it, just trying to get from one place to the other while finding that sweet spot between speed and reduced effort. When we find what works best for us, our gait becomes our fingerprint.

How to walk properly and efficiently has been the subject of long study, although this is mostly aimed at answering specific questions for specific audiences. A modern racewalker, for instance, must abide by narrow restrictions, and so has a different definition of an efficient gait than someone out for a casual stroll. Is the walker walking a long distance? How long? Is the goal to walk fast and far, or just far at any speed? Is the walker recovering from injuries?

As previously noted, Weston's favored walk was what he called his "flat-foot shuffle." He swung his forward leg out with knee bent slightly, slapping the whole of his foot down at once, avoiding a heel strike. (Observers said this caused him to wobble a bit from side to side.) His toes were usually turned slightly outward. "Heel and toe," he said, referring to the most popular style of walking, "will do for a time but it ruins the heel." Of note: Weston would be disqualified from modern racewalking, which codified rules in 1996 that require that one's knee be straight when the leading foot hits the ground and remains so until it swings past the vertical.

Studies using high-tech pressure plates have shown that modern race-walking is actually less energy efficient than normal walking with a slightly bent knee—the racewalker wastes energy with the up-and-down movement that's forced by the unnaturally straight leg. So a modern racewalking stride is essentially a fabricated step designed to accommodate the sport's judges, not the walkers themselves. Some racewalking advocates have noted the foolishness of this and recently agitated to eliminate the straight-leg rule. Some point out that modern technology in the form of small computer chips embedded in shoes could easily determine if a competitor is failing to keep one foot on the ground at all times and could be programmed to assess penalties accordingly for those who fail.

Likewise, research suggests that walkers who stretch out the very longest stride possible at each step are doing themselves few favors. It seems self-evident that taking longer steps would mean moving farther with less effort, but it's not true. "Over striding results in higher horizontal deceleration forces," notes one study, and puts unneeded stress on the shins. As it turns out, people are most efficient when walking their "normal stride length." And that, according to research involving a three-axis force plate, is 88 percent of the distance from your hipbone to your anklebone.

And how should you place your foot? Should you advance flat-footedly like Weston, or perhaps land lightly on the balls of your feet, like a runner? Neither. The natural and most efficient step involves the heel striking first, and then essentially rolling to the balls of one's feet as the leg pendulum swings from fore to aft. "We lose less energy as our heels collide with the ground than we do when we walk toes first," the authors of one study found. "Landing heel first also allows us to transfer more energy from one step to the next to improve our efficiency, while placing the foot flat on the ground reduces the forces around the ankle (generated by the ground pushing against us), which our muscles have to counteract, resulting in another energy saving."

So what it comes down to is this: For efficiency, walk using your natural gait, at a pace that feels comfortable to you. While doing so, be aware of any unneeded motion up and down or side to side, and strive to reduce that. But how you walk naturally is just as much a product of evolution as your opposable thumb and ability to process symbols. It's what we've got going for us. It's hard to improve upon what feels natural. Use it or lose it.

———————

Among the more concise descriptions of Weston's walking style was one related in *Physical Culture* magazine by H. C. Long, who awaited Weston's arrival during a long tramp. He asked a nearby railwayman, who had seen Weston before, how he should identify the walker. The railwayman answered: "You'll see a little man with white whiskers, carrying a short stick, and walking all over his body. He'll be moving sort of slow. Yet take your eye off him and he'll be out of sight before you know it."

"Walking all over his body." Like scales on a fish or feathers on a bird, Weston was perfectly evolved to move long distances by foot.

"He has the mechanism of walking to perfection—the ability to use just the minimum of energy in covering a given space," said George L. Meylan, physical instructor at Columbia University. "Of course, he has the 'bent-knee' method—that's the French army way—the body forward, and the leg muscles used only in the middle of their range. It's just the natural way to walk; our stiff-legged method, product of high hats, stiff clothes, and canes is purely artificial. But Weston has perfect mastery, perfect balance."

Picture one of those pop culture diagrams depicting human evolution, starting with a hunched ape who gradually rises to the erect *Homo sapiens,* a creature that strides purposefully and with elegance and ease. That man at the far right of the graphic, moving with confidence, stamina, and efficiency? That's Edward Payson Weston. The Walking Man.

Weston's path to becoming the Walking Man started with a wager in 1860 when he was twenty years old and living in Hartford. Weston bet George Eddy, an acquaintance from Worcester, that Stephen Douglas would defeat Abraham Lincoln in the upcoming presidential election.

The wager involved no money. But both agreed that whoever lost would walk from Boston to Washington to attend the presidential inauguration, completing the walk within ten days. Had Douglas won the election, Weston might well have remained an obscure jobber or forgotten scribbler of ephemeral accounts. (Also, if Douglas had won, it's unlikely Eddy would have seen him sworn in; he later admitted that he would have skipped out on the bet.)

Of course, Lincoln won. Weston waffled a bit and didn't actually commit to the walk until about Christmas. But when he decided he was in, he was all in. He announced he would leave Boston on February 22 and arrive in time to see the president's inauguration on March 4, 1861, covering the distance in ten days.

The young Weston wasn't sure how feasible this was. So he set off on a trial jaunt January 1. He walked thirty-six miles from Hartford to New Haven, doing so in ten hours and forty minutes. A born salesman, Weston also dropped off 150 advertising circulars for an unknown "literary work" he was hawking at houses along the way. "I did not feel the effects of the walk at all," he reported in New Haven, and he stayed awake and alert until eleven that night. The next day, he turned around and walked back to Hartford, selling "several" copies of the book he'd touted the day prior. "Some idea may be formed of the condition of the roads," he wrote, "from the fact that when I reached New Haven there were no soles to my boots." ("It did not affect me in the least," he was quick to add.)

His plan to walk to Washington did not sit well with his mother. Fretful as ever about her twenty-two-year-old son's health, she pleaded with him not to go. When he insisted, she wrote the governor of Massachusetts, John A. Andrew, asking him to intercede. "Please pardon the intrusion of a stranger," she wrote. "I am a mother and I appeal to you in behalf of a child." She went on to tell the governor of her son's reckless wager and his foolish determination to carry it out. "Were my son a robust young man, the act I deprecate would be less rash. Such is not the fact."

It could well be a matter of life or death, she continued. "My family physician, who has known him from a child well, gives his opinion that his life will be forfeited if he attempts to do as he intends. He is impulsive. On nervous excitement he may keep up some days, but his muscular strength is inadequate to the task imposed."

There's no record of the governor having responded. It seems slightly odd that a mother would write a governor and ask him to intervene with a bullheaded son. Perhaps this was part of a publicity campaign for the walk. If so, Weston may not have been hale and hardy, but he was already shrewd and clever.

Weston already knew about the power of the press. On a second trial walk in late January, again between New Haven and Hartford, he managed to walk seventy-six miles ("four miles farther than the direct road") in less than twenty-four hours. (This time he distributed 350 advertising circulars for books.) Perhaps prodded by Weston, the *New York Times* took notice of his long winter walk, noting that he accomplished his task on roads "covered with ice and slush." The paper of record went on to observe that "he starts from Boston on the 22nd of February to walk to Washington in ten days." People along the route had been alerted.

Planning for his trip to Washington was complete, save for one detail. He desired a companion along the way, who could also verify his feat. It was unlikely that anyone would voluntarily walk the full distance with him, so Weston persuaded an acquaintance in New Haven to supply a horse, carriage, and driver for the sum of eighty dollars. Weston was not a man of means, so to pay for the vehicle and driver plus expenses for a friend, he expanded on the scheme he employed during his pilot walks in Connecticut and turned to advertising. He convinced five businesses to underwrite his journey—a sewing-machine manufacturer, a druggist, a photographer, the Rubber Clothing Company of New York, and a man from Boston whose business he refused to mention because the man failed to pay up and Weston wasn't fool enough to give him free publicity, despite his frequent post-walk grousing.

The Grover and Baker Sewing-Machine Company was the lead sponsor. It agreed to pay him one hundred dollars to distribute five thousand copies of a booklet touting its sewing machine along the route. Other sponsors also provided circulars, which were collated and wrapped in packets for distribution to homes and businesses. (The Rubber Clothing Company even provided him with an "entire rubber suit of the best quality.") Weston also relied on supporters along the route in other ways; hotels would provide him with a room and restaurants with a meal for free in exchange for the publicity he brought them.

For the inauguration walk, Weston's plan was to leave from the state house at noon on February 22. He arrived punctually, and the weather was agreeable, given that it was late February. The circumstances that greeted him, however, were not. At ten minutes before noon, Constable A. G. Dawes walked up and notified him he was under arrest. The matter? A claim of $10 that Weston owed the Boston firm of Bean and Clayton for an unresolved debt. While he was trying to sort this out, a man named D. F. Draper appeared on the scene and slapped him with another affidavit, claiming that Weston owed him $25, a debt evidently stemming from an earlier visit to the city. Weston's deft touch at generating publicity about his walk already had proved a double-edged sword: It served as a beacon to those who'd been trying to track down the Walking Man and serve him papers.

All this was inconvenient in the extreme—Weston had no money to clear his debts. They talked and haggled. Draper eventually accepted a note that guaranteed payment against expected income from the sewing-machine company; the lawyer for Bean and Clayton accepted a promise in writing that he would pay them upon his return to Boston. His creditors allowed the deputy to free him, and he made his way before the crowd for some hurried public remarks. At 1:48 p.m., nearly two hours behind schedule, he aimed his feet toward Washington, DC, and set off, with a couple hundred excited Bostonians tagging along and cheering. A cadre of his more indefatigable friends kept him company for several miles, until the pack reached the village of Newton, where he continued on, followed by his two friends in the carriage.

He started out of Boston at more or less a gallop. He covered the first five miles in forty-seven minutes, topping six miles per hour. He blew through Newton and reached the outskirts of Framingham around 6:00 p.m., where a troupe of drummers met him and escorted him to a local hotel. Here he paused briefly for supper and some socializing with Framingham's grandees. At 7 o'clock he was back outside and hoofing it again, now through deteriorating conditions, with snow and rain starting to spit from the sky.

He neared Worcester that evening and was met at the city limits by another welcoming committee. This one did not involve drummers. It was, in fact, the local constabulary, who warned him that if he entered Worcester, he'd be arrested, again for an unpaid debt—he owed a local hotel about $50 for a stay he'd skipped out on two years prior. He pushed on, and pleaded and importuned, and was detained for about two hours. Weston didn't deny the charge ("I managed my affairs very injudiciously, and it may be extravagantly," he admitted). In the end, two of his fans and supporters, people who scarcely knew him, stepped forward and signed papers to guarantee payment, with Weston's repayment due to them two months' time. Weston was then free to continue on his southward journey.

For the rest of his walk, he fell into a routine, one blessedly free of creditors. He'd walk twelve to eighteen hours a day, often retiring early and briefly, and periodically napping along the way at hotels or private homes. (When he visited his sponsors at the Grover and Baker Sewing-Machine Company on Broadway in New York, he "mounted himself upon a table and took a nap.")

He often began his day's walk in the dark, at times leaving shortly after midnight and other times at two or three in the morning. His early-morning jaunts were not without complications—he faced delays at toll gates along some roads, since the walker and his carriage-bound companions were required each time to wake the gatekeepers, then wait long minutes for them to dress before they emerged with a lantern, collected the toll, and unlocked the gates so the party could continue on its way.

The winter weather was mostly seasonable and cooperative, with a few lapses. Weston had to wrestle his way through a two-foot snowfall in Massachusetts. A day later, he faced a rain deluge, although this allowed him to don his new rubber suit and offer a glowing testimonial to his sponsor.

The rain resulted in deep mud, which, his companions reported, sent him several times into fits of great irritability.

The grueling schedule notwithstanding, his limber body fared well, although not perfectly. A dog chased him outside one city and he sprained his left ankle getting away; near another he twisted his big toe. One day he mysteriously couldn't keep his eyes open, and repeatedly said he wanted to lie down in the snow and sleep. This caused some alarm, and he talked of abandoning his walk, but then was afflicted with a sudden and copious nosebleed, which, strangely, invigorated him. (The nosebleed "seemed to relieve him greatly, and waken him up," wrote one of his fellow travelers.) In New Jersey, both his ankles starting feeling tender and giving him trouble, and his companions ("for an experiment," one noted wryly) suggested to him that he climb into the carriage and ride with them to the next town. "He will not listen to us," they reported, "and [he] becomes exceedingly irritable, which makes him push forward more briskly." Chest pains caused him some concern on his sixth day out, but he concluded that this was the result of too much mustard on a sandwich he'd had.

Foraging for food along the route was not hard. This often involved little more than extending his arm and returning it to his mouth with something delectable to eat. Hotel and tavern keepers plied him with nourishment wherever he stopped, and generally refused payment. He received doughnuts right out of the fry pan at one hotel, and spectators who appeared along his route handed him refreshments that included milk, bread, and a mix of molasses and water, the latter a sort of early precursor to the energy drink. He made it clear to potential benefactors he didn't care for cider.

On rural lanes he walked alone, his carriage following behind. When he passed through villages and towns, residents invariably gathered to see him. In New Haven, a contingent waited for him for six hours; in Milford, great bonfires were lit to greet him. The Bristol Brass Band waited for him for two hours outside Bristol, Pennsylvania, then merrily escorted him into town. The Stars and Stripes was fluttering everywhere along his route, although whether these were to hail the walker or mark the impending presidential inauguration is unclear. It's said that Weston preferred to believe they were for him.

He continued blithely on Sunday, and this caused some delays when he had longer waits at river crossings for ferries, which maintained limited hours on the Sabbath. In Philadelphia, he refused a ride to his hotel room on a new steam elevator, claiming that "he would not alter his mode of travel until he arrived at Washington."

North of Baltimore, his companions directed him down the wrong road, an error that wasn't discovered for twelve miles. (This "caused the pedestrian to be very irritable.") Then, thirty miles outside Washington, DC, the horse refused to continue on, and the trio wasted precious time and a few miles of unneeded walking trying to scare up a replacement. Weston finally told his companions they should abandon the horse and carriage and take a train to meet him in the capital. He then hurried off down the road by himself.

Weston walked into Washington—his lips "very much parched"—and made his way to the Capitol Building, touching its granite wall the moment the clock struck five on the afternoon of March 4. He had completed his journey in ten days (plus some change). And he arrived, as promised, on inauguration day. Yet he'd missed the president's inaugural ceremony by four hours. (His failure to witness the swearing-in was the source of the friction with the sponsor who wouldn't pay for Weston's distribution of the advertising flyers, insisting that the agreement had called for him to arrive in Washington before the swearing-in in order to collect his fee.)

Weston stopped by the inauguration ball that evening but didn't stay. He was fatigued and retired to a hotel, where he slept for thirteen straight hours. He remained in Washington another six weeks, mostly because he was out of funds. (All he had earned in fees for distributing advertising had been promised to creditors.) But his residency had benefits: During his stay he was introduced by a Rhode Island congressman to Stephen Douglas, the losing candidate, who extended an invitation to stop by his house. And he was invited to a gala, where Douglas introduced him to the newly inaugurated president, Abraham Lincoln, who expressed admiration for his pluck and "great powers of endurance." The president offered to buy him a ticket for a train back to Boston. Weston refused, insisting he would walk back to show that he could do it in less than ten days. ("Good spunk, but unprofitable business," a newspaper commented about his proposed return on foot.)

In the end, Weston ended up taking the train anyway, using money loaned by a sympathetic hotelier. The Civil War had just broken out, with the Southern troops firing on Fort Sumter on April 12, less than two weeks prior to Weston's planned departure. Riots then flared in Baltimore on April 19, and he thought it best to avoid the dangers along the road.

In certain essential ways, Weston's first great walk was emblematic of the rest of his career: an instance of failing upward. He didn't make it to Washington, DC, on time, but he was close. His walk did get attention in newspapers. One noted that in arriving several hours late he "failed to come up to scratch," but conceded that "he has acquired a reputation, however, and considering the unfavorable weather, he tramped smartly."

Perhaps more important, the attention his walk drew agreed with him. During his ten days on the road, he no doubt thought about ways he might make a living at walking from one place to another. Later in life, his daughter said she knew the family bank account was in dire straits when her father uttered a phrase with which she became too familiar: "I feel very much encouraged."

The Washington walk certainly left him "much encouraged." It would not only set him on an unlikely career path as a professional walker, but also help trigger a mania for walking that captivated the nation—and then much of Europe—for more than a decade. It was also, one speculates, wistfulness for these accolades that coaxed Weston out to attempt one last feat—his most daring of all.

In 1859, exactly one-half century before Weston set off on his great walk, Charles Darwin published his influential work, *On the Origin of Species*. This settled little in the debate over whence man arose, but set off a cascading series of arguments that has yet to draw to a conclusion. The animal kingdom had been divided and subdivided into taxa since the seventeenth century, with much argument over where each animal should be shelved. But Darwin put forth the controversial proposal that this arrangement wasn't actually fixed. Species change constantly, like flowing rivers, many evolving into something else over time. His startling conclusion: Man did not come from Adam's rib. He started out as an ape.

In the half century after *Origin's* publication, an army of serious and self-taught anthropologists, part-time adventurers, and wily hucksters had poked and scraped at the earth with trowels and shovels and brushes in search of evidence to confirm or refute Darwin's ideas. Bone hunting flourished in the late nineteenth and early twentieth centuries. Just a year before

Weston walked west, the Piltdown man skull turned up in a gravel pit in East Sussex, England. (The skull wasn't publicly presented to the Geological Society of London until 1912.) The worker who found it at first believed it to be a fossilized coconut, but then the importance of the find became clear. The discovery was one of a trove of skulls and femurs and other calciferous remains being extracted from the earth, including Java man in Southeast Asia (in 1891 and 1892), the Taung child in South Africa (1924), and the Peking man in China (1923 to 1927). Before the jury of the world, the exhibits were trotted out one by one as paleontologists and other experts in evolution made their cases as to when and where apes first started down the long, elusive path of becoming human.

The Piltdown man, which many archeologists insisted was the conclusive "missing link" between ape and man (it had a large braincase and a primitive, apelike jaw), eventually proved to be a colossal hoax—certainly among the top five hoaxes of history. It was in fact a clumsy pastiche of human skull and orangutan jaw, both stained with an iron solution to simulate aging. In the end, Piltdown man served chiefly as proof that if people fervently want to believe in something, they will. What Piltdown proponents wanted to believe was that the first humans were distinguished by their powerful brains, and that only after developing intelligence did they learn to walk upright. What's more, it was hard for many people at the time to accept that human evolution occurred in such a dark and primitive continent as Africa, since that meant they themselves descended from Africans. The idea that Edwardian gentlemen and the modern-day bushmen were brothers, both having evolved from the same upright primates with small brains, was hard to accept. It took many decades before those of a scientific mien agreed to agree.

Walking upright—with the head held high above the torso and legs and forward movement driven by swinging one leg and then the other like a pendulum—is what first defined us as humans and in large part separated us from the remainder of the animal kingdom. While chimps and apes can move short distances on two legs, humans are the sole example among the two hundred or so primate species that elected to throw our lot into walking upright exclusively.

Virtually all evolutionary biologists now accept that becoming fully bipedal was the first fork in the road of human evolution, and the most significant change sending man down an evolutionary track separate from that of the apes. Yes, the size of our brain, our ability to use tools, our penchant for reflecting on our own lives ad infinitum, and our deft skills in manipulating symbols (like letters of the alphabet) also make us human. (The opposable thumb? Not so much. This evolved in primates some sixty million years ago to aid in catching insects and grasping.) Our large brains and our ability to invent and use primitive tools all came along much later—millions of years later, it turns out—long after we had adopted our upright posture. By standing upright and moving about on two rather than four legs, we defined ourselves as humans.

Walking on two feet wasn't an inevitable development. In fact, hominids—the taxonomic family that includes humans—weren't the first animals who evolved to get around this way. A number of dinosaurs actually walked upright on two legs, and they employed various degrees of uprightness—some stood fully erect, while others inclined toward the horizontal and had a distinct lean.

Walking upright, essentially, comes down to filling an ecological niche.

Long after the dinosaurs went extinct, a great many species of apes and apelike creatures occupied central Africa, competing for resources where overlaps in their niches occurred. Most could scramble efficiently through trees in the dense equatorial forest, moving along limbs to harvest bananas and other fruits. The forest canopy in large part allowed them to scamper from tree to tree without touching the ground, and they could grasp limbs with both hands and feet. Where gaps in the tree canopy proved too large to span, they'd move to the ground and scramble with relative ease on all fours.

And then something remarkable happened around six or seven million years ago. Sediments extracted from deep on the seafloor suggest that, globally, Earth's climate steadily became cooler and more arid. This may have led to a gradual drying out of parts of Africa's equatorial forest, changing its composition and resulting in more open grasslands. Or perhaps unstable geology was at play. Around the two branches of the East African Rift, which passes through latter-day Ethiopia, Kenya, Uganda, and Tanzania, the land was sinking in parts and simultaneously upthrusting in others, forming a mountain range along one edge. These hills would have pushed clouds farther aloft, wringing out the rain, with a similar result: The dense forest to the west of the hills grew patchy, with stands of trees interrupted by open savanna.

Faced with an altered environment, primates living in the area had to adopt new strategies for foraging. Over millennia, as the forest canopy thinned and grasslands between trees grew more expansive, ancestral apes with mutations in their genetic makeups that made them better able to traverse their new environment were aided by a subtle evolutionary advantage.

What advantages did moving about on two limbs confer over four? What precisely happened in a biomechanical and evolutionary sense to favor primates who began to walk upright?

At least two dozen reasonably sound theories have surfaced since Darwin's time. Some notions are simple and straightforward. Perhaps we started walking upright to reduce the exposure of our bodies to the harsh equatorial sun, while also reaching the cooling breezes higher off the ground. Or maybe standing tall on two feet allowed early hominids to see approaching predators more readily—the survival of the tallest. Or standing upright made us appear bigger and more fearsome, and thus allowed us to dominate other species.

These notions persist—not as single-bullet theories about bipedalism, but as part of a complex web of reasoning. Other theories surface and thrive for a time, but then evidence tips them into disfavor. Like many species on the tree of evolution itself, these ideas flourish, then die off at the end of a frail and attenuating limb.

Among other explanations for bipedalism is that of the "aquatic ape." This is a hard one to fully grasp, because it's difficult to contemplate without imagining something animated by Pixar, with a soundtrack by Randy Newman. The theory was promoted by Welsh writer Elaine Morgan (1920–2013) starting in the 1970s and posits that early apes waded into the water in search of food and soon adapted to buoyancy, keeping their heads above the water and learning to swim. Their upright state, developed through natural selection, conferred certain advantages that continued to benefit them when back on land. This theory might explain certain human oddities: for instance, our relative hairlessness except for the tops of our heads (the thinking being that hair was needed to protect us against the sun's rays while swimming) and our breathing's independence from our stride, unlike with other mammals. But the theory has the disadvantage of having virtually no fossil record to support any of the hypotheses it puts forward. Also, if water was the natural environment in which a large part of our evolution took place, why do so many people panic in the water and drown? It seems that natural selection would have disposed of this strain of human long ago. Few scientists take the idea very seriously today, although it persists in some circles.

Another intriguing theory, equally simple: We started walking upright because males wanted more sex. This has the advantage of confirming what everyone already knows. And in some particulars, the theory is compelling. The notion's chief proponent is C. Owen Lovejoy, a biological anthropologist at Ohio's Kent State University. His theory, often called "male provisioning," doesn't require the African savanna; the transition could have occurred in the forest. The idea is that after giving birth, a female protohuman had to spend much of her time caring for the infant. This restricted the amount of time she could spend foraging for insects and fruits, and the resulting poor nutrition for her and her offspring led to a longer nursing time. And while nursing, she was unavailable for sex.

Enter the male protohuman. He would bring food to the nursing female to speed the feeding cycle, thereby freeing her up for copulation. The gesture would also create what would today be called bonding between the pair, giving him priority status for future sex. The male who could carry more by moving upright to free his upper limbs would thereby be advantaged. As Lovejoy notes, "The males of such pairs were most successful if competently bipedal and capable of proficient provisioning." That is, the man more able to haul more food got more sex, making his genes more often passed on.

Not all embrace the theory. As Ian Tattersall, an evolutionary biologist with the American Museum of Natural History in New York, pointed out in an interview, "It makes a nice story. But I don't think many people are convinced."

And as anthropologist Craig Stanford notes, all theories are essentially stories. And the best stories often rule the roost for a time since we're hardwired to find a good tale compelling. But eventually the evidence fails to support these stories. Evolution, it turns out, is likely more random and less scripted than a good yarn.

Regardless of how we came to walk upright—whether by swimming or sex or some other trigger or combination thereof—those who have studied the rise of bipedalism tend to agree that the main advantage conferred is far more prosaic: simple economics. By walking upright, we acquire more rewards while expending less. As Stanford tautly puts it, "Bipedalism is a strategy for foraging that works in the right environment."

Widespread environmental changes may have accelerated the evolution of upright walkers, but current thinking holds that the first hominids may have learned upright walking while still in the forest. Here's a Pixar version of how this might have unfolded: Imagine two creatures somewhere in Africa. One is an early hominid, walking mostly upright, perhaps a bit awkwardly. The other is a forest ape, a knuckle walker who gets around on both his feet and the thick pads on the backs of his hands. Both ceaselessly canvass the land around them in search of food. They may move at roughly same speed, but the hominid has a subtle but indisputable advantage: He requires fewer calories to move about than his ape cousin does. Which means he can travel farther and cover more terrain in a search for food. It's a very slight but critical advantage.

Being bipedal is not inherently better than being quadrupedal. Modern humans don't actually have a distinct advantage in the calories-burned-per-mile contest when compared with modern four-legged animals, like deer or horses. In certain circumstances, we may be fractionally more efficient than modern quadrupeds, but in other circumstances, we're not.

The thing is, we weren't competing for resources with the forerunners of deer or horses. We were competing with other primates— say, the chimpanzee. And walking upright on two feet is much more efficient than scrambling on four, at least when moving at relatively slow speeds and over long distances. According to a 1992 study, a hominid walking on two legs can travel eleven kilometers on the same expenditure of calories as a chimpanzee traveling four kilometers. Other studies have shown that this efficiency also generates less internal heat as a by-product of muscle use, and by standing upright a hominid is less afflicted by the harsh rays of the sun than an animal that's hunched over and exposing a broad back. This presumably allowed the early hominids to forage longer in the direct sunlight. The quadrupedal apes and chimps retained their advantages in the forest, burning fewer calories when harvesting from trees. But in open spaces, especially the plains and grasslands that had started overspreading central Africa, bipedal foragers gradually outcompeted the quadrupedal primates.

And this selection process didn't just separate hominids from apes in the trees; it also gave early *Homo* species, ancestors of modern humans, an advantage over other hominids competing for scarce resources. Evolutionary biologists in the past half century have concluded that predecessors of modern humans weren't the only ones to walk upright; many branches of our family tree did likewise, although they eventually died out, because bipedalism alone wasn't sufficient for their survival.

This included the australopithecines, hominid cousins of early *Homo* species. The fossil record shows that this branch of humanlike primates had shorter legs, and so their forays were likely shorter range than those of *Homo*. "Put simply, *Homo* could have moved faster at an energetically advantageous walking speed than would have been possible for the australopithecines," wrote Leslie C. Aiello and Jonathan C. K. Wells in the *Annual Review of Anthropology*.

By being able to walk farther while burning fewer calories, modern man's predecessors could expand their territories and forage from a broader area. And that brought other benefits, some accidental, which accrued from generation to generation.

For instance, walking man found new uses for hands and arms, which at first served little purpose but to aid in balancing. These vestigial limbs were recruited into undertaking new tasks, such as carrying fruits and grains and offspring. Starting around 3.4 million years ago, they were used to craft and employ tools and weapons.

Another happy by-product of walking: It released early humans from tying their breathing to their gait. Most mammals have a breathing pattern synchronized to their gait. But by walking upright, we broke that bond, allowing the fine control of respiration necessary for speech and other evolutionary advantages.

But the most enduring—if indirect—advantage was the size of the human brain. The idea that first the brain expanded and then man started walking upright persisted into the early twentieth century, until a series of discoveries, notably the 1924 discovery of the Taung *Australopithecus africanus,* eliminated that idea. It was later posited that the human brain grew in tandem with our walking upright, the idea being that we suddenly had these hands available, and we needed to figure out what to do with them. Again, evidence renders this chronology impossible. The larger brains in our human ancestors likely didn't appear until about two million years ago, three million years or so after we'd started down the path of bipedalism.

Anyway, the long and short of it: Walking began as an advantage for finding food in the forest, then expanded when an ecological niche opened with the rise of the African plains. Over the next few million years, give or take a million, bipedal primates (including the forerunners of humans) started the process of dominating a far larger niche: the entire globe. And about two million years ago, the first members of *Homo erectus*—the hominid that shared many traits with modern humans—first began to roam out of Africa, walking into Europe, the Levant, Asia. Again, it was the ability to walk long distances that allowed them to expand into a wide geographical area, albeit over multiple generations. It was walking that allowed us to eventually inhabit every habitable landmass around the globe, from the Arctic to Tierra del Fuego.

We got where we are today, both literally and figuratively, because of walking. Standing upright and moving forward one step at a time is more than simple locomotion. Walking makes us human.

———————————

March 17, 1909. Weston awoke at the Hotel Raleigh in Peekskill after a brief nap, then willed himself to rise. Walking still invigorated him, but he was now seventy, not the twenty-two-year-old who first demonstrated a knack for it on his long stroll to Washington. He gathered up his entourage, headed out the door, and soon picked up his pace, continuing north along the east side of the Hudson River. Road conditions continued to be dreadful, with each step putting his ankles at risk on the rough, rutted, and frozen roadway. He avoided sprains, though, and finally arrived at Fishkill at about ten that night, stopping for a rest and a meal at the Union Hotel. Then off again: another five miles in the dark to Wappingers Falls, where he walked to the hotel and slept briefly. The next morning, more of the same: up and out early again, this time headed for the town of Hudson. Again, the roads seemed to be engaged in a conspiracy to thwart him. "With the exception of seventeen miles of macadamized road between Poughkeepsie and Rhinebeck," Weston wrote, "it has been one long continuation of frozen, narrow, deep mud ruts" where he had to constantly watch his footing. And then came a blanket of fresh snow, making the footing even more treacherous.

He slogged on, through the towns of Stuyvesant and Castleton. The roads failed to improve—"worse than any I encountered," Weston said— and he slowed his pace further. He trudged into Rensselaer, eighteen miles north of Stuyvesant, a pleasant, prosperous town just across the Hudson River from Albany, well after dark. Some two thousand well-wishers awaited him. After a fifteen-minute rest and a bit of glad-handing, he resumed walking, finally arriving in Troy, about eight miles farther along, after midnight on March 18, more than two hours late. It was nearly 1:00 a.m., but his spirits were bolstered by a crowd of some six hundred who greeted him at the city line and escorted him en masse to his hotel.

Troy would be the northernmost point on his walk up the Hudson. Here he could cross the Union Bridge, an eight-hundred-foot covered span built entirely of wood in 1804 and later elegantly lined with glass windows. It supported train tracks, plus room for walkers and horses and even cars destined for the resorts of Saratoga Springs. (The bridge burned and collapsed into the river just two months after Weston walked over it.) From here, Weston would turn west and head toward the setting sun, to western New York, Ohio, and Chicago.

Weston took a less-than-direct route west, he explained, as a favor to a pair of friends. He didn't explain much more, but it's likely that those friends had lined up paid lectures for him in cities along the way, which would have generated welcome income for him and his friends. (Community lectures were what one went to before movies were the movies; people were always happy to pay a modest fee for an evening's diversion.) By 1909, Weston was coping with growing financial strains—by no means an unusual situation for him. And by walking first to Troy before heading west, he would now be able to retrace his steps along a route that had earlier brought him tremendous fame. He'd walked between Portland, Maine, and Chicago in 1867—his first high-profile match against time—and he'd duplicated that feat just two years before, in 1907. He would now be striding through towns where everyone knew him by reputation, staying at hotels where proprietors reserved his favorite room and served his favorite meal.

"More people know me every trip," Weston said. "Makes a fellow feel good on a lonely road. . . . Bless the people! I've tramped the country over many a time—they've been good to me."

So Edward Payson Weston at last started walking west, striding into his own past.

CHAPTER 3

I SIT,
THEREFORE I AM

*We are becoming too much of a sit-down animal. We sit
down when we are at work and when we are going from one
place to another even if it is only for a short distance.*

—**EDWARD PAYSON WESTON**, 1907

The La-Z-Boy Museum is located within the low, sprawling La-Z-Boy corporate headquarters in Monroe, Michigan. I arrived unannounced one fall afternoon and found the plate-glass front door locked. A woman in a rust-colored dress was sitting at the reception desk about thirty feet away, and she pointed to a phone on a low table to the right of the door. I picked it up. She picked up her phone. She told me that the museum, regrettably, was closed. It had actually been closed for several years—staffing had suffered from budget cuts. But I must have projected the right mixture of curiosity and fatigue, because she sighed and said, "Oh, come on in," and the door buzzed. Then she made another call and found out that the one-day-a-week employee named Michael who was in charge of the company archive happened to be in the building that afternoon and could spare a few minutes to show me around.

Michael came from the back and met me at the reception desk. He was gracious and didn't seem in the least resentful at my interrupting his work, which that day involved digging up archival ads featuring former football player and La-Z-Boy spokesman Alex Karras, who had just died; Michael wanted to post some images on the La-Z-Boy Web site. He then escorted me past acres of cubicles and a break room containing the most comfortable break room seating in the known world. The museum was in the back, in the original brick building, which had been more or less absorbed by the newer, midcentury construction. The bright, loftlike space was filled with overstuffed chairs, hundreds of them arrayed somewhat haphazardly, like conventioneers milling around an open bar. The designer Ralph Caplan once wrote that "a chair is the first thing you need when you don't really need anything, and is therefore a peculiarly compelling symbol of civilization." If you subscribe to his interpretation, the La-Z-Boy Museum is America's Louvre. It's a museum dedicated to sitting around and doing nothing.

The prototype La-Z-Boy was hammered together in 1928 by a pair of cousins from Monroe who were both named Ed. An early brochure referred to the "Recline-Relax-Recuperate chair." (It wasn't the first recliner; in the 1830s a pair of London upholsterers had patented a "self-acting" automatic recliner. And in the late nineteenth century, the craze for reclining Morris chairs in the Mission style demonstrated that owners could combine comfort and domestic tastefulness. The Barcalounger was introduced almost twenty years after the La-Z-Boy, in 1947, and dominated the trade into the 1960s.) The enterprising cousins used slats from orange crates and crafted a clever porch chair with a seat that, by means of a simple mechanism, slid forward as the back canted rearward. This was the first La-Z-Boy recliner. A version of the early model is displayed in a glass case near the entrance to the museum. It doesn't look as if it belongs in the same planetary system as the other chairs in the room. Compared with the more amply upholstered models, the stark original looks like a prisoner denied sustenance for many months.

Stylistically, many of the museum's chairs would fit in without much notice at your elderly great-aunt's, with antimacassars on both the headrest and arms and a bowl of hard candies nearby. But others were surprisingly hip, including colorful, plush chairs designed by the cast of *Friends* for a fund-raiser. Even more out of place were the *Jetsons*-style chairs designed in a shape the architect Morris Lapidus called a "woggle"—sort of like a swooping, kidney-shaped pool—upholstered in bright Naugahyde and dating to 1961. Michael went over and showed me a little troll-like doll sitting on one of the chairs; it was called Nauga and was a mascot and giveaway from the chair's fleeting space-age era.

La-Z-Boy was the first to make an integrated footrest that rose as one leaned back. That was in 1952; in 1961, it rolled out the Reclina-Rocker, which, true to its name, both reclined and rocked. This proved to be a breakthrough based on marketing research that had noted that women like to rock and men to recline. This discovery helped boost annual sales from $1 million to more than $50 million within a decade. In 1999, La-Z-Boy produced a chair with a built-in refrigerator suitable for keeping beer at hand, so those settled in for a game would be spared the trek to the kitchen during the commercials. A more recent and highly popular line of chairs and sofas was inspired by the gauzy, nostalgic paintings of Thomas Kinkade.

Staying ahead of consumer desires is a constant struggle, but Michael told me that focus groups as of late had been sending one message: Chair sitters want power. Early model La-Z-Boys required pushing back on the seat; later, this could be done by pulling a lever that hoisted the leg support as it reclined. That's old-school. Customers now want chairs that plug in. Chairs that recline at the push of a button. Chairs that let you ease back to nearly supine without expending a single excess calorie. One of the company's most popular chairs today is the La-Z-Boy PowerReclineXR, which, the company immodestly claims, represents the "future of reclining." The latest incarnation is the PowerReclineXR+, which "gives you all the benefits and customized movement of PowerReclineXR but takes your comfort to the next level with the power-tilt headrest and power lumbar [support]. Limitless comfort and easily adjustable with the handheld remote."

A chair with its own remote may be the newest sensation, but the very concept of a chair is relatively new in the long, historical panorama of leisure. The engineering of immobility and comfort is essentially a modern advance. Furniture pieces like chairs have long occupied a place in the world of elites, but were all but unknown to the common people until the Renaissance in Europe. The Egyptian Old Kingdom (2649 to 2150 BC) aristocrats had low chairs, but these faded from use after Egypt was overrun by Arabs, who were ground and floor sitters. They preferred pillows for luxury (and contributed the words *divan* and *ottoman* to our lexicon). The Japanese sat on mats; the Chinese started with low stools that gradually grew into chairs and tables for the affluent. Much of the world then, as now, relaxes not by sitting on stools or chairs, but by squatting on heels and haunches.

In America, the recliner transitioned in record time from a chair suitable for the medically unwell to an essential anchor of the modern television room. By one estimate, one-quarter of American homes now have a recliner. In an early incarnation it was promoted as a heart saver; it quickly became more associated with weakening one's heart through inactivity.

Walking through the La-Z-Boy Museum, with nearly a century of sitting technology and history on display, I got the distinct sense that our chairs have been evolving to gradually encase us, like trees that imperceptibly surround and engulf a strand of wire over the course of a decade or two.

That's not just metaphorical—there's also something physiological at work. As technology historian Edward Tenner has noted, "The technology of chairs, even those scientifically designed for comfort, promotes a self-sabotaging technique. As sitters become accustomed to the support of a backrest, their back muscles weaken and they must recline even more. The chair is a machine for producing dependency on itself."

Daniel Lieberman, an evolutionary biology professor at Harvard, notes that people often like to fault evolution for their back pain and believe we were poorly engineered to stand upright for long periods. But he points out that if being upright were to blame, natural selection would have ensured that bipedal hominids would already be extinct. "What is more likely is that many people sit in chairs all day, get no exercise, and thus have weak backs," he told the *New York Times*. "We did not evolve to sit in chairs all day."

We are, in short, being eaten by our chairs.

———————

March 19, 1909. Displaying his trademark vigor and briskness, Weston left the Hudson River valley and walked into the low, rolling hills of western New York. His route largely followed the old Great Genesee Road (a turnpike dating to the late eighteenth century), which ran alongside parts of the Erie Canal and would take him through forested hills and agricultural lands dotted with an archipelago of villages and ornate Italianate homes.

In 1909, the aptly named Empire State was flourishing amid its own golden age and boasted the largest, most vibrant economy in the nation. The Erie Canal had opened the state to commerce in 1825; in the eight decades since, it had served as a sluice that brought great flows of cash into a once economically arid region, allowing towns to blossom along its length. Money flowed to laborers maintaining and working the canal and its feeder system; to manufacturers, which could make and easily ship goods of copper and leather; and to nearby farmers, who raised apples, grains, dairy products, and meat, much of which was loaded on barges destined for the hungry metropolis at the mouth of the Hudson.

Weston walked briskly from one prosperous village to the next over the course of a week. He passed near or through towns with regal classical names—Troy, Ilion, Utica, Rome, Manlius, Cicero, Syracuse, and Scipio—lingering evidence of a time when the fledgling nation was looking to the classical past for inspiration. America strove to imitate the glory and democracy of ancient Greece, and secretly aspired to the grandeur that was Rome.

The landscape may have been lovely and welcoming, but the weather was anything but. If he regretted choosing his seventieth birthday for a departure date—or regretted having been born in March—he kept those thoughts to himself. Winter conditions plagued Weston: Deep snow and a blustery wind often forced him to lean into the wind and shorten his stride as he buttoned up his outfits to quell the flapping. In Utica, after arriving several hours behind schedule and exhausted, he tumbled headfirst into bed within ten minutes of walking through the hotel's front door late on a Saturday night.

The first Sunday of his walk followed, and so he was rewarded with his first full day of rest. Sometime after the Civil War, Weston began a lifelong refusal to walk professionally on Sundays. (He would at times undertake Sunday walking excursions for pleasure while on his long walks, but would return to where he started.) His mother never approved of his walking career, fearing he would slip into a life of sin and gambling. Weston acknowledged that people bet on his walking, and so he pledged to his mother that he wouldn't walk on the Lord's day. This allowed him to demonstrate that he was a good Christian and a good son, with the bonus of being able to rest up and recuperate. He was looking forward to his day off in Utica, he said, as he had fond memories of "the great hospitality tendered me by the Johnson brothers of the Baggs Hotel" during previous trips. He also noted that here he enjoyed "the best coffee . . . that I ever found in any hotel." (Weston was an early and avid practitioner of product placement.)

He also had a chance to take stock of how his walk had progressed in the first week. His verdict: "For the first time in my public career of forty-five years I am amazed at myself and what I have accomplished during the past week," he wrote in his dispatch to the *New York Times*. (No one ever accused Weston of excess humility.) Admittedly, he'd had a grand week. In the six days—five and a half, really, given his late start from Manhattan—he'd walked 275 miles, averaging nearly 46 miles per day. And he did this while trudging through miserable conditions of both weather and road.

During his day of rest, Weston caught up on correspondence and wrote his dispatch for the *Times*. He also fended off visitors of marginal interest. A man named Lansing Bailey sent an imploring note to Weston requesting five minutes of his time. "Let me assure you that I am not an agent for any foot ease powder or any rubber heels, and have no corn remedies to advertise," he assured Weston, "but for purely personal reasons I would like to have the pleasure of greeting you again." It's unknown if Weston received Mr. Bailey.

Restless and eager to get going after a day of repose, Weston resumed his walk, as he often would on this journey, well before the sun rose on Monday. At five minutes past midnight, with a cold, groggy crew roused and following by automobile, Weston left Utica, one step at a time. Traveling by headlight where he could and by lantern where he couldn't, he followed what he considered a "splendid" road to the town of Oneida Castle; when daylight came, he trekked over "execrable" lanes to Syracuse. "I struggled over a road composed of the stickiest red clay I ever struck," he wrote. "It was like mucilage, and whenever I pulled out a boot it sounded like a cow's hoof coming out of the mud."

People continued to stream from their homes and nearby villages to watch Weston walk past, which he found gratifying. A reporter wrote that swelling masses "had gathered as swift as a storm upon his walks." Weston himself noted that "the crowds were so great at Little Falls, Mohawk, Ilion, and Frankfort that they impeded my progress." But, he added magnanimously, "I am willing to forgive them."

At Syracuse, an excitable mob shouted, "Here he comes!" when he and his chuffing entourage came into view at the crest of the hill outside the city. The crowd grew more uncontrollable as he approached, and one of the two cars following him had to move ahead to part the crowds so he could maintain his pace; policemen in blue uniforms soon came in and took up positions in front and on either side of him. Weston moved "with the zest of a boy" and with his "silvery head up like a grenadier's, white mustache militant, his hat swinging easily in his hand," wrote an observer. A "sharp staccato crack of clapping hands" followed him as he "walked on, a rebuke to senility, a triumphant foe of years, the breathing embodiment of iron will."

That night he addressed a large crowd that had gathered to hear him speak at a church, and then he set out for dinner. "I ask your pardon for being so 'dopey,'" he told his dining companions. "It's the wind. Fifty-five miles from Utica and wind every step of the way. It makes you drowsy." He consumed steak and vegetable soup. ("Vegetable soup?" he told a local reporter. "You bet. Is there anything like vegetable soup? It puts new life in you.") "Renewed by the food and his favorite beverage of coffee," the newspaper reporter added, "the old gentleman looked ready to take to the road again."

And on he went. More crowds awaited him when he arrived in Buffalo on Friday, March 26, having again slogged through ankle-deep mud after leaving the village of Bergen. He arrived at 11:30 at night, muttering, "I hope I don't strike anything as bad as this between here and the coast."

He did. Weston left Buffalo at dawn, striding into a pouring rain streaked with snow. "The roads are heavy," the newsman sent to cover him reported. Outside Chaffee, New York, he soldiered through a blizzard and navigated roads of frozen ruts. Outside Olean at nightfall, his day brightened: He was besieged by an eager, swarming crowd and accompanied by a boisterous brass band. "Were it not for the police and the combined efforts of the Olean Snow Shoe Club members," Weston wrote, "I don't know that I would have reached the hotel in safety." A good night's sleep, and on again early the next morning toward Jamestown, where he again arose before dawn and then tramped through Clymer and Wattsburg and into Pennsylvania, arriving at Union City that evening. Here, he made one of his rousing speeches about the glories of foot travel, then danced a brief jig to prove that the ankle he'd sprained earlier in the day was just fine. The headline the next day: "Dances with Hurt Ankle."

Your mother was right: You shouldn't just sit around all day. But that's what Americans do; by one estimate, the average American adult spends about 70 percent of each day just sitting—at home, at work, in a car. In the last few decades, we have become an impressively sedentary people.

In 1950, Americans holding high-activity occupations that involved being upright and mobile and using large muscle groups (telephone lineman, farmer, milkman) narrowly outnumbered those with low-activity sitting jobs (telephone operator, accountant, insurance adjuster). By 2000, twice as many Americans had low-activity jobs as high-activity ones. Agricultural jobs, for instance, dropped from just over 12 percent of the total labor force in 1950 to less than 2 percent a half-century later.

While more of us sit at work, all of us sit at home, and we sit more than ever. Consider television, the most studied stand-in for sedentary time. "We become what we behold," media critic Marshall McLuhan wrote. "We shape our tools and then our tools shape us."

Until the late 1940s, the television was a novelty. In 1950, only one home in ten had a television; now you'll find a television in ninety-nine homes out of a hundred. And the television is an aggressively invasive species, spreading throughout households. The average American home now has 2.24 televisions, and two homes out of every three have three televisions or more. Depending on what statistics you believe, the nation may currently be home to more televisions than people.

And the amount of time we spend with our glowing screens has increased at about the same rate that the screens have increased in acreage. For years, American television watching has grown steadily by about 1 percent annually. Since television entered our homes, every decade we've added about thirty-six more minutes of television to our daily media diet. According to a 2009 Nielsen survey, the average American watches about 151 hours of television a month, or about 5 hours every day. And technology allows us to shift time, giving us the ability to automatically record shows and watch them later at our convenience. Television technology first conquered space by bringing distant people and places into our living rooms; it has also adeptly conquered time by allowing us to tailor television broadcasts to fit our schedules. Some 40 percent of American homes have digital video recorders, a number that's steadily growing.

Traditional television viewing—that is, watching a show, whether recorded or not, at home on a television—has recently bucked the long-term trend, according to Nielsen, and declined slightly in both 2010 and 2011. But that may well be because we're watching more nontraditional television by streaming classic and recent episodes on laptops, or replaying clips of last night's *The Daily Show* on our smartphones or tablets. We can easily link to our home televisions via a remote viewer, allowing us to sit and watch our regular cable network shows on our laptops in a hotel room in Mumbai or Munich. Indeed, Nielsen reports that we've added six hours a month of television viewing on gadgets, with that number sure to swell as tablets become cheaper, the technology easier to use, and a new generation grows up believing that the normal way to watch television is on a small screen held in your hand.

Americans are also living with an interesting paradox: We move more while we move less. We are a free-range people; we travel farther from home every day than our ancestors. Yet we tend to be less physically active in doing so. That's thanks to the automobile and jet, of course. We have in the last nanosecond or so of our evolutionary time line figured out how to be immobile while significantly increasing our range and expanding our horizons. Cars and planes, essentially, provide us with the empty calories of mobility.

The average American spends about 190 hours a year commuting, according to Gallup. That's to say, the average American now spends more time in his or her car traveling between work and home each year than that same average American gets in vacation time. On top of commuting, we deliver kids to soccer, run to the hardware store for a wrench, go out to dinner and a movie at the megaplex, and carry out other errands. The average American makes four trips each day in a personal vehicle, traveling a total of twenty-nine miles and averaging about fifty-five minutes of moving about in a car.

Although "moving" might be overly optimistic. We're being slowly ossified in traffic, like flies caught in slow-moving sap, as more cars vie for a limited amount of road. Traffic congestion in urban areas has swelled over the past few decades—the average American was delayed in traffic for about seven hours annually in 1982, a figure that nearly quadrupled to about twenty-six hours by 2001. So we spend, on average, one full day out of every year stalled in traffic.

Thankfully, it's a comfortable day. Cars have been described as living rooms on wheels, and that's never been more apt. Automobile sound systems are often better than those we have at home; the large industry that develops mobile entertainment systems assures this. (The United States Autosound Competition—"the loudest sport on earth"—has a 180-club roster for car sound systems that can top 180 decibels, or some 50 decibels above the threshold of pain, and louder than a stun grenade.) Seating, likewise, is often more sophisticated than at home, with seats that warm up with one flick of a button, firm up lumbar support with another, and adjust the height and tilt with yet another. Add to that an array of electronic gadgets that keep the kids amused and plush, oversize armrests fitted with cup holders sized for a thirty-ounce soft drink, and you've got a sophisticated shelter to convey you from here to there. Think how far we've come: When Weston was walking, some car drivers still wore leather helmets and goggles to protect themselves from kicked-up pebbles and inclement weather.

And those kids in the backseat? They're often being driven to school. In the nineteenth century, of course, everyone walked to school, since buses didn't exist and school districts were designed around neighborhoods. That changed, but more slowly than you might think. In 1969, about half of all schoolkids still walked to school; 41 percent of all students lived within a mile of their school, and 89 percent of these students walked.

Then school districts consolidated, suburbs expanded, the classrooms moved farther from homes. More parents started driving their kids, which led to a downward cycle for walking: With more cars on the road around the school, even parents living close to schools started worrying about the safety of their kids on foot, and so they starting driving their kids the few blocks to drop them off. Today, only 13 percent of America's children walk to school. Instead of exploring the world, burning calories, gaining independence, and socializing with friends along the way, kids are cocooned in cars, earbuds in place, watching screens on their laps or screens that have descended from the thickly padded ceiling of the car.

————————

Darwin wants us to walk; everything in our evolutionary history has proven it. And yet we do the opposite and sit all day—at home, at work, in cars—fighting the results of natural selection. Some researchers call what's happening "progressive sedentariness." That's a top-shelf way of saying that we have sitting disease. And sitting is, quite literally, killing us.

At least, several recent studies have arrived at that conclusion following different avenues. One British sports medicine journal published the findings of a survey of some twelve thousand Australian adults that linked the amount of time spent watching television with life expectancy. After controlling for various factors, the researchers concluded that, after the age of twenty-five, every hour of watching television reduced life expectancy by

21.8 minutes, which seems a pretty poor return on investment by any measure. Watch six hours of television a night throughout your allotted eight decades or so, and you reduce your life expectancy by about five years. (This was the case even if television viewers made a point of getting to the gym regularly between bouts of television watching.)

Another 2012 study, this one published in the online medical journal *BMJ Open,* reached a slightly less alarming conclusion for chronic sitters, but nothing anyone would cheer as good news. The study concluded that Americans in aggregate were dying two years prematurely as a result of sitting too much. By reducing the amount of television watching to just two hours a day or less, they'd potentially add 1.38 years to their lives.

These and other reports—including a 2012 meta-review of studies that found that those who were most sedentary had a 49 percent greater chance of dying prematurely—provoked some disgruntled murmuring from critics, who noted that many other factors could be fouling the outcomes. For instance, it could be that people who are unhealthy for any number of reasons, like poor diet or unfortunate genetics, simply sit around more, so these sitters are naturally more likely to perish ahead of what the actuarial table predicts. It can be hard to control for such factors in studies.

It's also virtually impossible to carry out a lifestyle trial of sufficient length and scope to reach a firm conclusion. In any event, it would be considered unethical to instruct one study group to spend the next few years sitting around and another group to walk more if researchers reasonably believe (as they do) that the former will reduce life expectancy. "We are just starting down the road of causality with sedentary behavior," one researcher told the *Wall Street Journal.*

More detailed studies focusing on the benefits of walking have been cropping up because of one simple advance: the small, inexpensive pedometer. The old-school pedometers were clunky and hung from one's belt and mechanically clicked with each step. The new digital models, about the size of a modest pocket watch or smaller, just clip on a belt or slip in a pocket or go on a wrist like a watch and unobtrusively track how many steps the wearer takes over the course of a day. These are being used in more studies, as they're easier and more reliable than asking someone to compile a nightly journal of his or her activity.

These unobtrusive tools are allowing us to learn more about walking and its effects. With pedometers, we've confirmed what people have long suspected: Children walk more than adolescents, and adolescents walk more than adults. Men (especially young men) walk more than women. Australians and the Swiss walk about the same amount in a day, which is nearly twice the distance the average American does.

But the pedometer hasn't helped in one area: understanding how far our parents and grandparents and even more remote ancestors walked.

Have we actually abandoned walking after millions of years of evolution pushing us toward upright mobility? Or are we walking the same amount and have simply swapped long treks across the savanna for long treks across shopping mall parking lots?

Coming to a reliable conclusion on this is harder than you might think. Early hominids found that by moving upright they could go farther in a day, and thus could find more food at less cost in terms of energy expended. But how far did they roam in their gathering of food? Studies draw various conclusions. One noted that contemporary hunter–gatherers in primitive environments, free of modern conveniences, typically walk an average of six to eight miles each day in search of food. Perhaps our early ancestors walked a similar distance. Other studies suggest that this estimate could be low. A 2002 study concluded that the typical American expended only 65 percent of the energy each day that their Paleolithic forebears did.

A report from 2005 examined the energy output of active hunter–gatherers in the Kalahari Desert and Burkina Faso. From this, they estimated that for modern humans to duplicate the energy output of early *Homo sapiens* "prior to the time when modern tools, labor saving devices, and social organization reduced the needs for food gathering and defensive activities," we would need to walk 5.7 hours each day "over fields and small hills" in addition to our usual activities. So that's some seventeen or so miles of walking daily.

With some extremely nonscientific, seat-of-the-pants averaging of these and other studies, it seems that Paleolithic humans walked around eight to twelve miles a day. Or roughly four to six times the distance the average American walks today.

Of course, the Paleolithic era is so, well, Paleolithic, and data from that era are fraught and flimsy. But what about a century ago? How far would the average American have walked on an average day in, say, 1900? That must be better documented, right?

Actually, no. The technology to track daily walking wasn't commonplace, and walking was such an unexceptional part of daily life that it didn't attract much scrutiny. But we can hazard some guesses based on information gleaned from contemporary studies. The most frequently cited is a 2004 study of Old Order Amish in Ontario. This is a group that has no truck with the machinery of the modern day, like cars and tractors and dishwashers. They still get around chiefly on foot and in horse-drawn carriages. Nearly a hundred Amish adults were recruited to wear a pedometer for a week. The average number of steps per day for men, it turned out, came in at 18,425—roughly nine miles—and for women 14,196 steps, or about seven miles. (The study also noted that none of the Amish men were obese, and just 9 percent of the women were classified as such.)

How much we walk today compared with our great-grandparents did may never be accurately known, but nobody to date has argued that we're walking as far as Americans did in the nineteenth century. As a species, we've spent five or six million years getting the hang of, and possibly even perfecting, walking—the very trait that has defined us as humans. Now we have chosen to abandon walking, and to abandon it both willfully and cheerfully. But the evidence suggests that giving up something we've done for eons hasn't come without significant costs.

Foremost among these costs is obesity. As we've walked less, we've put on the pounds.

You can't pick up a newspaper or magazine without finding an article warning about the obesity crisis. (A headline from the farcical *Onion* captures the tenor if not the precise truth of the issue: "National Institute of Health Study Finds Obesity May Be Caused by Too Little Sleep, Too Much Sleep.") More than two-thirds of Americans are now overweight; more than one in three are classified as obese. That's up from just one in ten obese Americans in 1960. (You're classified as obese when you're more than 20 percent over your ideal body weight relative to your height; someone who's five-foot-eight, for instance, is considered obese at 197 pounds.)

Just because the decline of walking has tracked the expansion of our waistlines doesn't prove that one is necessarily linked to the other, however. Consider the timing. Americans overall were more fit in the 1950s and 1960s, when the car culture was hitting its stride. It was a time when families would pile in a car just to go a block or two, because cars were big and fun and had tailfins and there was little traffic and you could always find a place to park. Yet Americans were far less overweight then than they are now.

One might also note that our decline in walking is merely part of a bigger and broader decline: our outsourcing of everyday labor to machines. The management of the home was given a hard look in the October 2003 special issue of *Obesity Research*. Household tasks have "been automated through the use of dishwashers, clothes-washing machines, and vacuum cleaners," the authors of one paper reported. "Each of these tasks has resulted in 'labor saving' and increased sedentariness." In marshaling evidence, the authors pointed out that reenactors living out bygone days in Old Sydney Town, Australia, a theme park of history, showed 60 percent higher physical activity levels compared with their modern-living counterparts. For their own study, the researchers recruited volunteers to use stairs instead of elevators and to wash dishes and clothes by hand rather than by machine. The results? When it came to washing, "the subjects showed significantly greater energy expenditure . . . while performing the domestic tasks by hand compared with using the machines." And riding an elevator meant "significantly less" energy was expended compared with walking the stairs. Their conclusion: "Domestic mechanization is a likely environmental force in the obesity epidemic."

Dwight D. Eisenhower established the President's Council on Youth Fitness in 1956 to get us moving more; First Lady Michelle Obama spearheaded the Let's Move campaign, as well as put a vegetable garden on the White House grounds and become an outspoken advocate for healthier diets. New York's former mayor Michael Bloomberg sought to cap the size of soft drinks sold in the city, flagging 400-calorie Big Gulps as a scourge. Other programs to encourage more activity are also making inroads. Inactivity is one part of the problem. But the chief battleground for public health advocates has shifted recently from how much we move to how many calories we consume, and the easy access we all have to these calories.

There's no denying it—a grocery store is a staggering storehouse of calories. Essentially every supermarket is an easily tapped oilfield filled with enough energy to fuel an infantry. The aisles of sugary treats and fatty meats would defeat even the most fevered imagination of the early *Homo habilis* wandering the land in search of a day's sustenance. Between the grocery stores, at interstate exit ramps, at urban intersections, along eight-lane boulevards are countless calorie outposts, like a line of modest fortifications against hunger. A study at Temple University showed that children stopping by convenience stores bought an average of 350 calories in snacks every day. It's never been easier to satisfy our appetites for high-calorie foods. And thanks to advances in industrial farming, we've figured out how to pack in more calories per acre, whether growing corn or raising pigs. Advances in food science, processing, and manufacturing have helped us figure out how to stuff more calories into ever-smaller and tastier packages, and to do it more cheaply every year.

These advances would be something to celebrate—widespread hunger, once common, is receding into the past for many nations—except for one problem: Our bodies were engineered millennia ago to retain calories for a possible future shortage. At the same time we were evolving to walk upright, natural selection was also taking place for genes that instructed our bodies to retain stores of fat. Accumulating fat is like hoarding batteries. We can run on active current most of the time by eating throughout the day. But if we get disconnected—if an early frost decimates the harvest and the larder grows bare—those who have reserves of stored fat are the ones who survive. In the words of one analysis, this ability is "a buffer between high energy turnover and variable food supply." Even someone considered to have a lean physique has two to three months of reserve energy they can tap.

Of course, the risk of an early frost or a drought depleting our supply of calories (at least in the developed world) carries roughly the same odds that you or I will swim to Antarctica. If your favorite fro-yo shop is out of double chocolate, you need only drive to the next strip mall. If Milky Way bars are out of stock at your neighborhood convenience store, you can move one yard to your left and resupply with Twix or Hershey's bars.

As we evolved, our ancestors generally enjoyed a natural balance between energy inputs and energy outputs. The food they ate on an average day was enough to give them energy to complete the physical tasks required, and during harvest season, perhaps to store a bit for a rainy day. Energy in, energy out, with a net balance of zero. But evolution has lagged as advances in food production and technology have galloped ahead. Our genetic makeup is essentially the same as it was ten thousand years ago; we haven't evolved to burn more calories per task, or to reduce our appetites. Modern Americans are accumulating vast surpluses while also eliminating avenues for spending these surpluses.

As a result, more and more Americans now have their pockets filled with several hundred extra batteries, and we keep accumulating more. Never mind that the odds of our being disconnected from our power source are vanishingly remote. As a 2002 paper in *Preventive Medicine* put it succinctly, we're falling into the gap "between 'Stone Age' genes and 'Space Age' circumstances."

If every American started walking ten or twelve miles every day, it still might not solve the obesity epidemic, because so much high-calorie food is readily available and so many other factors are also at play. Walking's effectiveness is further hindered by its efficiency. Of course it's efficient—that's why we started moving about upright in the first place. It's a remarkably low-energy way of covering long distances, and it's why we had an evolutionary advantage over apes and other early hominids. If you weigh 170 pounds, walking for an hour burns some 342 calories. That's approximately seventeen Triscuits. We get pretty extraordinary mileage; you essentially can travel a mile and half on a venti Starbucks Pumpkin Spice Latte made with whole milk. On the downside, even if you walk a few blocks and take three flights of stairs between the coffee shop and your office, you won't offset that midmorning coffee-and-pastry trip. The batteries accumulate.

Given its inherent efficiency, it's hard to conclusively indict society's abandonment of walking as the most likely cause of the epidemic of weight gain over the past century.

Yet there's this: Study after study shows a link between walking more and weighing less. A 2001 study by the National Institutes of Health found that participants who spent 150 minutes a week engaged in some physical activity (walking, for the most part) dropped 7 percent of their body weight in one year. Another study tracked middle-age women for fifteen years and found that those who walked for at least an hour a day maintained their weight; the more sedentary put on the pounds.

Studies of walking, which often note the connection between walking and weight loss or weight control, commonly float a disclaimer: Correlation is not causation.

"What does that mean, no causation?" asked Caroline Richardson during a two-mile walk we took through Ann Arbor one cool fall morning. She's an associate professor at the University of Michigan Medical School and a researcher with the Department of Veterans Affairs. Among her specialties is setting up programs using pedometers to encourage her patients to walk more. "No causation? Just ignore that. It's not that complicated. People make it really complicated, but it's not. There's an incredibly strong correlation between cross-sectional step counts and body mass index."

Keep it simple: Walk more. Weigh less.

People who met Weston often commented on his athleticism and wiry frame, and observers noted that he often appeared even more robust and vigorous when on long walks. A reporter wrote of one early walk, "since his march commenced, his calves . . . have increased in size until they resemble young cows."

Following his 1861 walk to Lincoln's inauguration in Washington, Weston appeared destined to return to a life of obscurity. But not just yet. The adoring attention of crowds along his long walk appealed to him, not to mention the attention of important people—including a sitting president.

So in short order he offered up his services to the federal army, suggesting that he put his feet to work in support of the troops engaged in putting down the Great Rebellion, the first shots of which had been fired shortly after his Washington walk. The twenty-two-year-old was at last given an assignment. In late 1861, he set off with a batch of 170 letters addressed to Massachusetts and New York Union Army officers and soldiers then stationed in Washington, DC. The army had been having trouble delivering them: Confederates occupied territory in Maryland and were actively intercepting dispatches that could yield useful intelligence.

Weston would later refer to this as his Walk under Difficulties. He donned a disguise—Brooks Brothers gave him a set of clothes so that he would resemble a humble barge hand. (Those headed to Brooks Brothers today in search of a barge-hand ensemble will be disappointed.) The letters were wrapped in a waterproof rubber pouch, which was sewn into his clothing. He then took a train from New York to Philadelphia, and from there he continued on foot. He traveled mostly at night, during which time he would eavesdrop on conversations along the streets and on front porches to learn of Southern troop positions. That's how he was apprised of the "large crowd" guarding the Conowingo Bridge over the Susquehanna in Maryland, the group having gathered there to repel Pennsylvanian soldiers and ferret out spies. Weston thought better of trying to bluff his way across and headed upriver, where he found an unguarded crossing.

When Weston wasn't walking, he slept—in the crooks of trees and in haystacks and occasionally in the bedrooms of friendly acquaintances. He sometimes accepted rides from farmers with horse carts. Playing the fool, he would cajole rebel sympathizers into revealing helpful information. He passed for younger than he was, telling one farmer he was but sixteen and that both his mother and father had recently perished. ("Had I possessed an onion at that time, I could have made the answer more effective," he said.) When questioned by people he met along the road, he replied that he was from Goshen, Maryland, a place none had heard of for the simple reason that he made it up. He strolled into Baltimore without incident, and there lodged with friends. The next day he departed late at night, slipping past several sentries, including a pair slumped asleep next to bonfires at either end of a bridge they were supposedly guarding.

Outside Annapolis Junction, Union troops halted him with a sharp "Who goes there!" He jocularly replied, "Never mind," and continued on, but the guards insisted on the countersign, and when he was unable to provide it, the situation grew serious. Revolvers were leveled at him, and soldiers escorted him to the officer on duty. His captors were the Sixty-Ninth Regiment of New York, to whom Weston explained his mission, even extricating the letters from his coat lining. The soldiers still suspected him of subterfuge and tossed him in what he called a "nasty, filthy" guardhouse with four other captives. After a few hours he was recognized by a Union officer who had seen him on his walk to Lincoln's inauguration, whereupon he was detained in the more civil environs of the officers' quarters, although still not free to go. (He became "very irritable" at one point, and grumbled that he was "tired of being hauled around by an . . . Irish regiment," adding an "unflattering name" for good measure. Soldiers of Irish lineage tossed him back into the squalid guardhouse.) His stealth mission was finally confirmed via telegram to New York. At last he was allowed to continue on his way, and he delivered the letters to the intended troops.

He then returned home to New York and went in search of a job that would involve something more cerebral than putting one foot ahead of the other. "He hopes soon to enter a more laudable business than pedestrianism," Weston wrote in 1862, referring to himself in the third person, "but as *his heels* are the only things which he has to rely upon at present, he considers it his duty to allow them to serve him, when *all else fail* [italics in the original]."

All else did fail, and he was back on his heels soon enough. He completed a walk of 510 miles in ten days, a slightly longer distance than the Washington walk, perhaps to knock that chip off his shoulder about not making it to the inauguration in time. And in 1862, as he had promised President Lincoln, he again attempted to walk between Boston and Washington, DC, in less than ten days, this time heading north. He set off from Washington and reached the Susquehanna River, but was injured in a fall during a storm. He abandoned the rest of the trip and the spotlight moved elsewhere.

A few years passed. In November of 1864, when he was twenty-five, he married Maria Fox, one year his junior, in a ceremony in Boston. (Little is known about her, though one cannot help but speculate that she must have been a tremendously patient woman.) They moved to a small town just north of New York City. Weston worked in Manhattan, taking a series of newspaper and publishing jobs. Although they lived eight miles north of the city, Weston typically walked to work, and then walked home. He said he could beat the horse tram by twenty-five minutes. He found a job as a messenger for the *New York Herald,* and soon was promoted to police reporter. His gift as a walker proved a boon, allowing him to beat out competing reporters in getting to the scene of a crime and back to the newsroom again. As one account put it, "He could bring a story down from the Bellevue morgue faster than all the horse-cars. He was the best 'leg man' in the history of journalism." In 1865, he and Maria had a daughter, whom they named Lillian. (Two years later they had a second daughter, Maud, and another two years later a son, Ellsworth.)

By 1867, Weston had once again accumulated large debts, although exactly how and how large is unknown. (His great-granddaughter said Weston had a lifelong penchant for get-rich-quick schemes, none of which resulted in his getting rich, quick or otherwise.) His friend George K. Goodwin concocted a way for Weston to get out from under his financial burdens. It would involve once again returning to his heels. "My private reasons for undertaking this walk were, of course to relieve my family from pecuniary embarrassment," Weston later explained.

Goodwin arranged a large wager on the long walk. Backed by a Maine sporting club, Goodwin put up $10,000, betting that Weston could walk twelve hundred statute miles within thirty consecutive days. The bet was accepted by one T. F. Wilcox of New York. Weston's race against the calendar would begin in Portland, Maine, and would end—if all went well—one month later in Chicago.

October 1867. In late October 1867, Weston took a steamship north to Maine and commenced his high-stakes walk to Chicago. The size of the $10,000 wager attracted attention, which led to tumultuous crowds along the route, including many who'd made side bets with associates or neighbors. They lined the streets to see Weston peg by as he tried to maintain a pace of 126 steps per minute. (An enterprising reporter had calculated that his entire walk would require 2,589,312 steps.) Some on the route started out walking alongside him and then pulled ahead and outpaced him to some mark of their own determination. They would then jubilantly announce to friends and family that they'd beaten Weston in a competition, albeit a competition of which Weston was unaware.

A small entourage accompanied Weston on this walk, most riding in a carriage that carried his supplies. This included trainers, a carriage driver, and two witnesses for each bettor, who were along to guarantee that he walked the entire route in the allotted time and without aid. Weston had drafted a letter of instruction to his witnesses, noting that he would eat food and drink liquids only if they'd been first overseen by his trainer, a Mr. Grindell, and that all should be courteous to postmasters, who had provided him with information about distances. Also, he noted, "you may expect to come into contact with all classes, and some may use offensive language to you." He urged them to remain calm so that "we may proceed quietly on our journey." Hotel stays had been arranged, and when he'd arrive, often late at night, his mission was chiefly to avoid the milling crowds, who at times tried to barge into the lobby or his room, or at the very least would press up against the window to gawk at the famous walker as he rested inside. (He often attracted swooning young girls despite his married status, including one young lass who managed to force her way into his hotel room while he was undressed. The Rochester paper reported that "the California Lunatic Asylum is rapidly filling up with young women who have fallen in love with him.")

On Sundays and his infrequent free evenings, he'd read through the large stacks of mail and telegrams awaiting him at each stop. He'd find his way to the dining room with his companions and eat staggeringly large amounts of food. (He weighed just over 125 pounds when he started from Maine, and had managed to actually gain a pound two weeks into the journey.)

As on his previous walks, he slept little—just a few hours each night. As soon as he'd wake up, he'd have his circulation revved up by one trainer, who "scrapes him vigorously with a chip until he is of a bright magenta color, while another feeds him from a bottle." His feet would then be washed and shaved (presumably the tops of his feet and above the ankles, to reduce chafing), after which he would dress and take to the road.

One of the challenges for his attendants was to keep the crowds at bay so the pedestrian could avoid being slowed by spectators. Walk organizers sought to keep the exact route secret to prevent crowds from congregating too densely and blocking the road. Even so, people knew he'd invariably arrive via the post road and would gather at the edge of town to await him. "All the standing places on the Rochester road for three miles out had been taken up two days previous by the Buffalonians," a reporter noted. "It was a beautiful sight to see them in two rows, all with telescopes pointed down the road, like two ranks of the militia aiming by right and left oblique."

When walking through populated areas, Weston was both preceded and followed by attendants who maintained what he called a "charmed circle" of ten feet in diameter. Weston wanted this to ensure that he could maintain speed, but also to keep saboteurs at bay. He lived in fear that someone would surge out of the crowd and stomp on one of his feet to throw the wager to Wilcox. (His paranoia extended beyond the crowds. According to one account, his shoes were "of the regular army pattern . . . and made to shed rain. They were made expressly for Mr. Weston who, to prevent any foul play, sawed the wood and cut the pegs himself, and passed them out separately to the manufacturer. The leather was cut from the outside skin of a favorite ox belonging to Mr. Weston's father—this was also done to prevent foul play.") The "charmed circle" didn't always hold; crowds surged in both Pawtucket, Rhode Island, and Norwalk, Ohio, knocking him down and overrunning him, leaving him, in Ohio, "nervous and excited."

In Rochester, to his surprise and small confusion, no crowds lined the route to greet him. Empty streets were an anomaly. An explanation soon followed. Evidently a fellow named Whyland had dressed himself up like Weston, ridden in a carriage to the edge of town, and then, followed by the carriage, walked briskly down the road waving jubilantly at the assembled hordes. Satisfied that they'd witnessed Weston amid his labors, the spectators gathered up their children and headed home, leaving Weston to enter what appeared to be an abandoned city.

Weston's carriage escort always followed behind him (under no circumstances was it to precede him), and he used a small whistle to communicate with its occupants. One short blow on the whistle: Which road? One long: What time is it? Two short: Call for Mr. Gower. Three short: Bring the bottle filled with water or cold coffee. Four short: Call for Mr. Ingalls. Four long: Whiskey for my shoes. Several "rattling blasts": Dogs present, or general alarm.

Most of these requests are easily understood, although one invites further explanation. "A dram of whiskey is frequently given [to his shoes], being poured into them by means of a small funnel inserted at the side," a reporter noted. "This is done to keep his feet from chaffing or swelling, and is said to be an excellent preventative."

His walk to Chicago also involved a sub-wager: He would walk one hundred miles within a twenty-four-hour period while en route. This was spelled out in the articles of agreement between the two parties. If he didn't manage to meet the second part of the bet, he'd forfeit 60 percent of the wager. So if he made it to Chicago within the allotted time but failed to walk a hundred miles within twenty-four hours while doing so, he'd be paid $4,000 rather than $10,000. He was allowed five chances at making a hundred-mile day within the month-long journey.

His first attempt came in Connecticut. He gave it up when he had thirty-seven miles to go, acknowledging that he couldn't do it in the six hours remaining. His fifth and last attempt came in Indiana, when he walked either seventy-six or eighty-six miles (there was a dispute over the day's distance), then gave it up. The closest he came was in Ohio, when he abandoned the attempt at 91 miles with three hours still to go, doing so on the advice of his trainer who feared that his "swollen feet" would hobble him for the rest of the route.

His failure to beat the sub-wager, especially on his last attempt, when it seemed wholly within reach, was a source of public skepticism and grumbling. Rumors abounded, among them that a group of his friends were betting against his success on the sub-wager. Another was that the famed bare-knuckle-fighter-turned-sporting-gentleman-turned-US-congressman John Morrissey had bet $100,000 that Weston would fail to walk the hundred miles; just to make sure, Morrissey was said to have agreed to pay Weston $20,000 to throw the bet. By Ohio, people along the route were hollering at him, "Have you sold the race?"

Weston vigorously denied it. A writer from the *Buffalo Commercial Advertiser* who interviewed him along the route reported there was "nothing about him in the remotest degree resembling the 'sporting man,' or gambler; no slang, no profanity; his language and manner being that of a respectable, well bred gentleman." He denied shenanigans to the end.

Weston arrived at the Chicago post office at 10:36 on the morning of November 29, beating the deadline by several hours. It was a leisurely stroll into the city; he'd spent the night before in Hyde Park, just six miles south of the Chicago post office. His arrival was marked by "a scene of the wildest enthusiasm," with a crowd estimated at about fifty thousand on hand to cheer his accomplishment. Spectators swarmed in to witness his arrival from as far away as Milwaukee, "like a pack of asses to a thistle field." (The *Chicago Journal* suggested that its readers "make [their] own estimate" of the crowd along the route, based on the observation that the crowd was a hundred feet wide and three miles long.) Another reporter noted that Weston was "feted and lionized like a French count."

Weston was all but pushed through the mob to the finish line. "The police had some difficulty in making a way for him," noted the *New York Tribune,* as "the crowd were so impatient to give him a welcome." The *Chicago Tribune* wondered about all the commotion. "If the most admirable archangel in the skies had flown down and 'lit' on the Court House dome, and blown his blessed horn for twenty-four hours, he could not have created any more sensation than Weston."

After placing a hand on the post office to mark his arrival, Weston noted that he'd just rendered twelve hundred miles of train track of little practical use except, he grudgingly admitted, "for the transportation of freight." The *Tribune* noted that "not Grant nor Sherman, nor any of our country's heroes, were ever made the subject of more ardent curiosity on the part of our citizens than the hero of the thousand-mile walk." (This account was not entirely laudatory, however, as the paper went on to call him "the hero of the moment, a sixty-second idol.") Another paper wrote that "his arrival assumed the shape of a sudden tornado which swept over the city for a few hours and then subsided into a sudden calm leaving the majority of the people in a kind of mystified wonderment as to what it really meant after all."

He'd won the main bet, but lost the sub-wager, and so pocketed four thousand dollars. He earned less than the ten grand he'd hoped for—any secret agreement with John Morrissey notwithstanding—but accounts suggest he used his promotional skills to turn a nice secondary profit by hawking souvenirs of his walk. He'd printed a photograph of himself, standing poised and slightly tense, looking to his left and holding a riding crop, which one of his associates sold to bystanders for a quarter apiece. At a table set up to hawk pictures in front of a Buffalo hotel, a newspaper reported, "the sale was as rapid as the most ambitious speculator in such wares could possibly desire." By one estimate, he'd sold sixty thousand photos even before arriving in Buffalo (and doubtless more afterward), bringing in additional revenue of at least $15,000.

His walk, it turned out, was just the beginning of a new career. *Harper's Weekly* reported that "this walk makes Weston's name a household word, and really gives impetus to the pedestrian mania which has become so general."

Today, distance walking has gained a popular if ironic association with illness—hardly a weekend goes by when a walk isn't staged to raise money for a cause like Alzheimer's, leukemia, breast cancer, or multiple sclerosis. Yet the idea that regularly talking a long walk may be a route to one's own well-being seems curiously ignored.

Health benefits accrue from walking; that's been proved by study after study. One extensive meta-analysis of studies in a 2002 issue of the *Journal of Applied Physiology* found that the consequences of being physically inactive was about as common a theme in the medical literature as courtly love was in medieval literature. Those who were more active were shown time and again to be less susceptible to a wide variety of diseases.

A few examples: A large study of nurses conducted by Harvard researchers found that the risk of coronary disease and stroke was reduced by 30 percent among those who walked briskly (three miles per hour or faster) for at least two and a half hours every week. Other positive results were found for hypertension, type 2 diabetes, gallstone prevention, immune dysfunction, adult-onset asthma, arthritis, and osteoporosis.

Then there's cancer. A 1999 study of women ages thirty to fifty-five found that over a sixteen-year period, those who walked or similarly exercised for seven hours a week had less risk of getting breast cancer. A study of twenty-two thousand men ages forty to eighty-four found that moderate daily exercise cut in half their risk of getting colon cancer or polyps. Other studies found a positive correlation between being more physically active and preventing colon cancer, pancreatic cancer, and melanoma.

The benefits of walking are particularly noticeable in middle age and beyond. In 2001 the *New England Journal of Medicine* published a study of seventy-four thousand women over the age of fifty that showed that taking regular walks was just as effective as running in reducing one's risk of heart attack or stroke. Walking helps people maintain bone density in their hips as they age, meaning they're less likely to experience crippling falls. And walking (when combined with an improved diet) does more to stave off diabetes than the preventive drug metformin. Another study found that regular physical activity reduced the incidence of erectile dysfunction.

The ultimate and encouraging conclusion: If you walk more and sit less, you live longer. A study of more than four hundred thousand residents in Taiwan, published in *The Lancet,* showed that those who engaged in an hour and a half of moderate exercise weekly (walking, jogging, bicycling) increased their life spans by roughly three years. In another study, a review of previously published research concluded that walking briskly for thirty minutes five times a week reduced an otherwise sedentary person's risk of dying prematurely by 20 percent.

If walking is salutary for health, you might make the logical leap that running must be really good. Yet this doesn't pan out. Studies have found that doubling down on exercise—running farther, faster, more frequently—doesn't add to longevity, and in many cases subtracts from it. "If anything, it appears that less running is associated with the best protection from mortality risk," Carl J. Lavie, a cardiac specialist in New Orleans, told the *New York Times.* "More is not better, and actually, more could be worse."

That walking reduces one's chances of getting sick is by no means a new discovery. Weston preached the gospel of walking loudly and often. The day he left New York, he told a reporter, "I will feel that my life work has been completed if I can prove to the young men of the country that God made them to walk and that if they'll walk they'll be healthy."

Other fitness proselytizers active in Weston's era frequently echoed that theme. In 1897, essayist James Henry Rice wrote that walking "will make the sick man well, but it keeps a sound man in good health [and] renders him tough and able to resist disease." Columnist Edward Nye in 1909 observed that "man was built to go as a walking machine, and when he walks, he best performs his natural functions," with the diaphragm kneading the organs, circulation increasing, and the pores of the skin opening, and a walking man will "never be troubled by a sluggish liver." A year later, Bernarr Macfadden of the Bernarr Macfadden Healthatorium in Chicago wrote, "On many occasions in the past we have referred to the very great value of walking as an exercise. We have stated that it increases the endurance, adds to the vitality, and prolongs life. That, furthermore, it will keep one young, full of the live cells that are a part of youth."

While the connection between walking and disease resistance is a common and ancient preoccupation, the mechanisms behind this connection have only recently begun to attract serious study. It's often suggested that the link might be best understood if we think of our bodies as organisms programmed thousands of years ago to work under very different circumstances—for instance, amid a land of scarce food where hard work and abundant competition were required to secure it. The human genome—that is, our overall genetic blueprint—was more or less locked in at least an ice age ago and hasn't altered much since. "Modern *Homo sapiens* are still genetically adapted to a preagricultural hunter-gatherer lifestyle because the overall genetic makeup of *Homo sapiens* has changed little during the past 10,000 years" was the conclusion of four experts in the 2002 *Journal of Applied Physiology* meta-analysis mentioned earlier. (The paper's title tells all: "Waging War on Physical Inactivity: Using Modern Molecular Ammunition against an Ancient Enemy.") Our genetic blueprint was established "when physical activity was obligatory for survival," and those genes are now operating "on a background of inactivity as seen in the present-day sedentary lifestyle."

The result? Less than encouraging. Genes designed to function in active humans appear to go rogue and run haywire in humans who've embraced inactivity, and this may be contributing mightily to the wide array of chronic diseases that are increasingly afflicting us.

These problems, the authors assert, are compounded by a medical establishment that consistently "underpractices primary prevention" and "undervalues the importance of understanding the cellular, molecular and genetic bases of diseases" caused by inactivity. "The bad news," they conclude, "is that exercise and exercise biology appear to be the least-used weapons in our arsenal."

Weston's frequently delivered messages of moderation—drink sparingly, eat lightly, walk instead of run—have proved prescient. It's the message increasingly emerging from academic studies, and echoed in the popular press.

That's both good news and bad, however. Moderation is hard to market. It's essentially at odds with the American ethos. "Work hard, play hard" read the T-shirts and bumper stickers. Where does walking fit into that formula? Simple: It doesn't. Walking is the semicolon of activities—not quite the full stop of a period, and not quite the fleeting pause of the comma. It's the amorphous in-between, not really exercise, but not quite being sedentary either.

In 1987, *New Scientist* magazine wrote about walking as "America's fastest-growing fitness activity," but noted some difficulties in getting more to participate. Part of that was recognition for one's endeavors. While everyone recognizes a committed jogger ("panting, red-faced and sweating"), walkers remain undistinguished, practically invisible. "A man in a tracksuit walking is a man in a tracksuit walking, nothing special." And we all want to be special, and recognized for making an effort.

Not walking has been, at the least, an interesting experiment. But few who've taken the time to study the results would dispute that it's an experiment on its way to failure. We're fatter, we're less healthy, we have less energy. In the late nineteenth and early twentieth centuries, walking was a learned art, with Weston one of the chief practitioners and educators. Walking methods were taught in magazine articles and manuals. In a 1903 guide elaborately titled *How to Walk: Describing the Whole Art of Training without a Trainer: Full Instructions and Hints for Those Who Intend Entering Walking Contests Either for Short or Long Distances, and a Special Chapter on Walking for Women,* the connections between health and walking were clear. "Walking is a cumulative pleasure," the author wrote. "Quite apart from the sporting aspect it is a recreation that never palls. It clears the head, keeps the entire body healthy, and permanently abolishes that feeling of lassitude that most city dwellers are subject to."

"Walking is the sweet spot," Michelle Segar, a behavioral sustainability and motivation scientist at the University of Michigan, told me recently.

We walk because that's what we were born to do.

April 1, 1909. Somewhere near the New York–Pennsylvania border, Weston became separated from his support vehicle. It had last been seen stuck in the mud not far from Jamestown. Reports of an engine breakdown soon followed. Weston noted, "This was rather unfortunate for me as my beef extracts, clothing, shoes, etc., were being carried on the automobile, and the absence of these necessities inconvenienced me greatly and to some extent impeded progress."

But not enough to impede him from pushing on through northwestern Pennsylvania. He lamented a lack of police protection in some towns where thousands came out to cheer him on, but he was undeterred; in only one instance did he divert his plan, when his scheduled lodging was surrounded by a rambunctious crowd. This was a barricade he deemed unwise to run, so he headed to a quieter hotel nearby and spent the night.

Then, on to Ohio, crossing the border near Sharon, Pennsylvania, and walking on to Youngstown (where he remained through a Sunday of rest at the elegant Tod House on the town's square, addressing "several thousand" from the hotel's balcony). The roads hereabouts continued to be all but unnavigable—"of a most aggravating character," he wrote. One foot would slip back in the deep mud six or eight inches, while the other foot "would try to slide off into another county, leaving me to look after it."

He gave some thought to detouring a hundred miles to the south and east to Pittsburgh, based on the urging of friends and no doubt to earn some cash by lecturing. But the city was in throes of excitement over an upcoming marathon hosted by the athletic club. Being a fan of moderation, Weston did not approve of these. "I am against these heart-rending marathon races and would certainly say something against them had I gone to Pittsburgh," he said. Having nothing nice to say, he steered clear.

Early Monday he set off for Canton, and he arrived after a single-day march of fifty-six miles. (His car had been repaired, but lagged 138 miles behind him by now; he hired a horse and carriage as a support vehicle in the meantime.) This was followed by thirty-eight miles to Wooster, which actually seemed longer than the previous day, he reported, as he dealt with steady rain, "very heavy" roads, and a fierce headwind that knocked him all around and brought him at times to a standstill. "Twice it blew me under a rail fence," he reported. This was followed by a day of forty-three miles and another of fifty-three, and thence into Toledo.

A glance at a map will show that Weston's route west was shaped not by expediency and directness, but by his past and the demands of his lecture circuit. Just as he walked across New York State because it was familiar to him and he to the residents, ensuring full lecture halls, previous experience also determined his route through Ohio. Weston chose to detour south, through Youngstown and Canton and Wooster, before veering north toward the lakeshore and Chicago. This was not because he wanted to visit those regions as much as it was that he was looking to avoid another. "He will avoid Cleveland as he has no use for the people of that city," the *Mansfield News* reported.

Because the management of crowds was critical to Weston, his opinion of that city had soured during an earlier long trek, when he had walked from Portland, Maine, to Chicago at the age of sixty-eight to mark the fortieth anniversary of his great walk of 1867. On that trip, he walked into downtown Cleveland shortly after 8 o'clock one morning, and the spectators "became a wild surging mob." He was trailed by a massive Stearns tractor to serve as a shield against the following throngs. But the crowd—some ten thousand, packed "curb to curb"—surged around the sides and front of the tractor, and he was "pushed and crowded until he was in danger of being trampled down." The sixty-eight-year-old Weston had "received his only injury of the whole trip, a boy treading on his foot, which caused him severe pain for the following two days." He had to rest up for a couple of hours, and then departed for Elyria with a pronounced limp, although now protected by a phalanx of sixteen young men he'd recruited to create the ten-foot charmed circle around him. He nurtured a long-standing grudge against the city.

By the end of the second week of April 1909, Weston had made it across Ohio and most of Indiana, walking on post roads through Goshen and South Bend and New Carlisle. ("Every farmhouse I passed the entire family was out at the gate to greet me.") He went on to Hobart, not far from the Illinois border, capping a fifty-three-mile day, and after a good night's sleep, he was up and on the road, crossing the Chicago city limit on the morning of April 17.

It was a fine day, and he was walking on what he called "the best roads that I have encountered on my trip." He'd had good police protection through Hammond, and at the Chicago line an escort of a dozen policemen greeted him to create a mobile shield as he walked into the city. Only one incident marred the day: An eleven-year-old boy following Weston on a bike got distracted and ran headlong into an automobile moving slowly in the opposite direction. "There was a scream, a crash of metal as the bicycle was smashed to bits and the boy disappeared under the auto," wrote a reporter on the scene. Weston heard the commotion, stopped his walk, and dashed back twenty yards to ensure the boy was all right. (He was, save for some sadness about his bike.)

As they had been in 1867, the city streets of 1909 were lined with tens of thousands of applauding admirers as Weston arrived. A former alderman and championship walker, Joseph Badenough, joined him toward the end and walked with him to the Illinois Club, where he was greeted by a surging crowd waving club flags. "The marvelous endurance and efficiency of the human machine were striking, demonstrated to an automobile riding, horse burdened, street car infested, railroad haunted Chicago when a little white haired old man strode jauntily up Michigan Avenue," a newspaper reported.

It was a very good day to be Edward Payson Weston.

"Just say for me that the worst part of my trip is now over," he announced in Chicago, having competed about one-quarter of his cross-country journey. "I am 108 miles ahead of my schedule. . . . You can bet that I'll finish this trip on time."

PART II

Mind

CHAPTER 4

BRAINCASES

*The business or professional man who takes his daily
constitutional in the right way will be well repaid in health
and ability to resist disease; nothing is better for the relief of
the tired brain and the promotion of a healthy appetite for
wholesome food than vigorous walking in the open air.*

—**RICHARD NELLIGAN,** assistant professor of hygiene
and physical education, Amherst College, 1908

Weston didn't invent pedestrianism. It wasn't even an especially new sport in the late nineteenth century. Large-scale walking contests with formal rules and cheering spectators were recorded in the early 1800s in England and Europe (whereas informal walking contests no doubt first surfaced in prehistory). Walking matches were often staged by pubs, which turned profits by selling refreshments to spectators. The United Kingdom thus bred its own stable of early walking celebrities.

Foremost among them was Captain Robert Barclay Allardice, a Scotsman born in 1779 who started taking up walking challenges at age fifteen and is generally credited with popularizing early British pedestrianism. His feet (and feats) were legendary; most famously, he walked one mile every hour for a thousand consecutive hours in Newmarket, taking about six weeks to do so and winning a bet of a thousand guineas. (Some hundred thousand pounds were reportedly wagered on the outcome by others.) Several others had attempted this seemingly simple challenge before, but the mental stamina and determination it required were immense. All had failed.

Walking spread to the United States in the first half of the century, in part carried by a wave of emigrants from England and Ireland. The craze was further aided by the more precisely measured, better-maintained roads that were now snaking their way across the landscape. Accurate, relatively inexpensive watches were also more common, making it easier to train and easier to stage a race against the clock.

But this was all but a prelude to the golden age of walking in the late nineteenth century. The allure and popularity of walking matches in post–Civil War America is hard to overstate, and a large share of this mania was attributable to the public infatuation with Weston and his walking. *Harper's Weekly* was right: Weston's 1867 Chicago walk added fuel to what was already a budding craze. "We hear of erratic pedestrians rushing across this continent in every direction," the *New York Times* reported in 1867, "just as the recent meteors traversed the heavens."

After reluctantly taking to his heels to earn money in the post–Civil War years, Weston soon full-heartedly embraced his new career and fame as a walker. He accepted one bet after another as to whether he could achieve some feat of prodigious walking within a certain amount of time; later he took on challengers directly in competitions for a purse, not unlike thoroughbred racing. The sporting life was just then starting to hit its stride. Prior to the Civil War, newspapers and magazines, including the New York City–based *Spirit of the Times: A Chronicle of the Turf, Agriculture, Field Sports, Literature and the Stage* (founded in 1831) and the *New York Clipper* (1853), were established to cover sports and endurance contests; both served as billboards where walkers publicly challenged others to matches. The war itself contributed to walking contests indirectly; soldiers often spent extended periods in camp between battles, and impromptu competitions— wrestling, horse racing, running, sparring, baseball, and walking—would fill the downtime. After the South surrendered at Appomattox, both Union and Confederate soldiers headed home zealous for their newfound pastimes. In countless villages, baseball boomed, and it was the era of the track at Saratoga (which opened in 1863) and bare-knuckle fights in rings (terms of engagement were codified in England in 1867 under the Marquess of Queensberry rules).

While the actual physical competition appealed to many, the betting on such events drew an even broader swath of America. If something moved, the odds were pretty good someone would place a wager on it. Steamships raced up rivers against one another while passengers and observers bet on the outcome. Fighters on board those ships slugged it out for a purse, and gamblers sat around tables playing faro and a new game called five-card stud, winning and losing colossal pots. The popularity of ancient games of billiards, especially pocket billiards, or "pool," surged in the late 1870s, chiefly as vehicles for wagering.

Challenges and competitions evolved toward the arcane. Head-butting contests were popular, involving two thick-skulled men who would run at one another at full speed; spectators would bet on who would crumple first. A young soldier stationed on the lower Mississippi River accepted a bet that he couldn't pull a sixty-five-pound sulky six miles around a track within an hour—and did it in fifty-nine minutes and thirty-five seconds. H. G. Varner of Boston issued one of the more rococo challenges of the era: "I will match any man in the United States, for $50 or $100, to pick up 50 eggs, placed a yard apart, with my mouth, and deposit them in a bucket of water; making the separate trip for each egg, and having my hands tied behind, and not touching my knees to the ground; and pick up 50 stones placed in the same manner with my hands, run 1 mile, walk 1 mile, walk 1 mile backward, all at one start, or will match against time, doing all in one hour. Match to be made within six weeks."

Then, of course, there were the pure walkers. A typical setup at a tavern or saloon would feature a board track some three feet wide and from fifteen to forty feet long. In a typical contest, a walker would stride back and forth upon this without rest for one hundred hours. Patrons would bet on how long the walker would last or on how many miles he might accomplish in that time.

More traditional long-distance matches were also ascendant. Young, fit men took up walking over hill and dale, or around a track, to win a purse established by bettors. A facile walker endowed with some stamina could take home more winnings in a week than a young man without connections might expect to earn in a year of dreary labor.

Among Weston's most persistent challengers early in his career was a man named Dan O'Leary, an Irish immigrant who lived in Chicago. The city embraced O'Leary as one of its own and celebrated his victories after he gained notice by beating Weston in a head-on walking competition in 1875. Indeed, O'Leary made as strong an impression on the city of Chicago as Weston did on the small towns through which he walked, and all of Chicago suddenly seemed to take up walking. "The sidewalks are now crowded with hurrying pedestrians," one paper recounted, saying of the streetcars, "if they contain any passengers at all they are cripples, weak and infirm old people, or shop boys with heavy bundles." Newspapers reported that residents across Chicago were imitating O'Leary's walking style: "People dash through the streets with heads thrown back, chests thrown out, elbows drawn backwards as if fleeing from some terrible danger, or as if in answer to some important summons." Women's fashions were altered to accommodate those who wanted to step it up, with dresses cut more loosely to allow "free use of limbs," parasols abandoned, "high heels . . . dropped, and the easy, roomy shoe [being] the correct thing." One newspaper reported that "there is every prospect that pedestrianism will rival base-ball in popularity, and that ladies will devote themselves to it to the exclusion of croquet."

———————

Weston had the great advantage of having escorts to clear the way through crowded city streets. Most of us don't. As it is, walking is a matter of nearly absurd complexity as a physical endeavor, requiring coordination of the contraction and relaxation of muscles to swing the leg pendulums just so, then working with gravity to maintain forward momentum in order to stay balanced and upright while flexing the ankle fore and aft and side to side, like a gimbal, to remain level when crossing uneven terrain.

And that's only the physical bit. Walking is also an intricate matter involving constant visual and auditory scanning to provide the data for a dizzying array of mental calculations that allow one to navigate through rough terrain. The process can be daunting both physically and psychologically.

"The individual as pedestrian," wrote Erving Goffman, the preeminent sociologist of the sidewalk, in *Relations in Public: Microstudies of the Public Order* (1971), "can be considered a pilot encased in a soft and exposing shell, namely his clothes and skin." When in adequate condition, our vehicle is astoundingly mobile and agile, able to stop or reverse quickly, ascend rough trails, get over low fences designed to block other mammals. And it constantly adjusts and adapts to the environment it passes through. As Goffman put it, "Pedestrians can twist, duck, bend, and turn sharply, and therefore, unlike motorists, can safely count on being able to extricate themselves in the last few milliseconds before impending impact." When driving, there's no eye contact permitting interpretation (headlights all have the same vacant thousand-yard stare), there's no pulling back the shoulder an inch or so to avert the clipping of another. To depend on this would be to invite repeated collisions and mayhem. That's why so many rules have been put in place to regulate traffic. Social cues have to be swapped for turn signals, lane markers, stoplights governing traffic, police officers at rush-hour intersections, and the like. It becomes even more complex when the interaction is between pedestrian and driver, each of which are following different rule books—one attuned to social interaction, the other following more rigid guidelines. (More on that in a later chapter.)

When walking, our piloting is nonstop. We scan from side to side ahead of us to look for possible obstructions or lower-friction routes, but we also look up and down, processing information as it comes into view. Studies prove walkers' common sense: We look downward at a sharper angle whenever the terrain is uneven (think broken or cracked sidewalks, curbs, and curb cuts). Further studies—by sociologists H. L. Golson and J. M. Dabbs in 1974—found that women look downward more frequently than men, possibly because they walk slower or "to avoid the gazes of men who are looking at them." (The authors also suggested that the footwear favored by women may require that more diligence be paid to the walking surface.)

But as we move our gaze downward, the broader environment blurs into background. So we have to look up again to reorient ourselves. Up and down, back and forth, processing information like an air traffic controller, eyes and ears always scanning, trying to guide the vessel to its destination. All the while, we're also busy analyzing both micro- and macro-navigational data, asking ourselves such questions as what block we are on, where we are within the block, and where we are relative to our destination.

And all this fails to take into account the more subtle social interactions we encounter when walking through an urban landscape. Sociologists, who for unexplained reasons took a keen interest in sidewalk behavior in the late 1960s and 1970s, found that we tend to "stream"—that is, to fall in behind others walking in the same direction, like fish—creating a flow that interweaves with the counterflow instinctively set up by those heading in the opposite direction. (Americans are socialized to move to their right under most circumstances, a move that also reduces the overall sidewalk friction. British pedestrians, it's interesting to note, have an inclination to walk to the left on sidewalks, mirroring driving patterns, but it's a weak inclination, and studies suggest that they just as often veer right and in general eschew the minnow-like linear schools of walkers that form in many other nations.)

Goffman notes that our scanning patterns continually shift as we walk. "The scanning area is not a circle but an elongated oval, narrow to either side of the individual and longest in front of him, constantly changing in area depending on traffic density around him." Typically, Goffman writes, someone walking down the sidewalk maintains a scanning range of "something like three or four sidewalk squares," rendering snap judgments on whom to pay attention to and whom to ignore based on the approaching person's speed and walking direction.

Goffman singles out two special moments that occur when pedestrians encounter each other. The first is when one sends out "a critical sign" to alert the other to the route they intend to take to avert a collision. This can be extremely subtle, such as a slight dip or twist of the shoulder or a slight shift in the direction of their gaze.

We subconsciously process a lot of cues when approaching someone. In one Finnish study, published in the journal *Psychological Science* in 2009, three researchers had test subjects (mostly students in their early twenties) "walk" a computer-simulated city street, in the course of which they were approached by an animated male figure. Using a response pad, they had to choose which way to go around him. The chief difference in the experiment's iterations was the direction in which the approaching avatar looked—either left or right, or switching from one to the other. The results showed "how humans flexibly make use of other people's gaze direction for guiding their own visual attention and selecting collision-free walking paths during simulated locomotion."

Not surprisingly, if the figure approaching looked to his left, the test subjects veered to their left, and if the avatar looked to his right, they veered to their right—that is, in the direction opposite to his gaze. (The avatar, frankly, was creepy-looking, all the more so as his eyes mechanically averted, making it deserving of a very wide berth.) The researchers therefore determined that people perceive a walker's gaze to be a sign of intent, which is important to know to avoid somebody oncoming, and also to send one's own signals. Essentially, when someone says, "Why don't you watch where you're going?" we would do well to take that literally, directing our gaze at our intended route, thereby sending oncoming walkers a clear signal and avoiding the awkward dance.

Goffman's second special moment is the "establishment point," when both parties have exchanged the "critical signs" on which direction they intend to veer. These signs aren't always conveyed flawlessly (even after tens of thousands of years of practice, and especially when we're visiting unfamiliar countries where the sidewalk dance might be conducted differently). This impasse—the extrication from which often involves self-conscious sidestepping—is ordinary enough that many have felt the need to coin a name for it. Contenders have included "concrete quadrille," "sidewaltz," "shuggleftulation," "faux pas de deux," and the "sidewalk shuffle."

Assuming we've communicated the critical signs and are at the point of passing one another, we often engage in another minor minuet, which was dubbed the "step-and-slide" by sociologist M. Wolff in 1973. How this plays out depends on the environment; on a crowded sidewalk, two people might brush past one another and nearly touch, each twisting slightly at the shoulder at the last moment in order to slip past. Typically neither pedestrian is willing to concede all of his or her space, but is willing to give up half of it if the other pedestrian will do the same. Every time you pass a pedestrian on a crowded sidewalk, it's like Yalta all over again. If both execute the give-and-take flawlessly, a clean pass results. If not, what those who study pedestrian behavior call a "brush" occurs with the upper body, and the contact can be either light or jarring. A 1975 study in New York City instructed coconspirators to walk straight toward strangers on a sidewalk and not yield. How many collisions resulted? None, as the subject being approached always sidestepped or twisted at the last minute. However, there were a large number of brushes, which the authors hypothesized "serve to remind the offender of a failure to yield just a little." Brushes involve shoulders, upper arms, and elbows; researchers have observed that most people simultaneously bring in their hands as they twist. No one apparently wants flesh-to-flesh contact with a stranger.

The step-and-slide and brush tend to be executed most commonly between those of the same sex; those of an opposite sex tend to be given a wider berth. Another study in 1975 found that "'beautiful' women were given more space than 'unattractive' women," groups of pedestrians were given more room than individuals, and, generally, men were given more space than women. The authors concluded that the simple act of walking down the sidewalk was anything but.

And all this is *still* only part of it. Research shows that as we walk down a sidewalk, we often glancingly study the faces of those walking toward us; they serve as rearview mirrors, with their inquisitive looks alerting us to anything going on behind us that we should be aware of. All of this is done almost seamlessly and without conscious thought.

Sidewalk sociologist Jon Wagner reported in 1981 that an intricate division of labor occurs on a sidewalk, much as with a line of ants marching to a food source. If you're walking on an empty street and you reach a crosswalk, you'll quickly and quietly scan for several sources of information: the walk/don't walk sign, the stoplight for cross-traffic, and approaching cars. But if groups of pedestrians are gathered at the corner, we tend to automatically divide up tasks among specialists, like a small, impromptu platoon: Those on the "front line" watch the lights, and another group scans for approaching cars. "The person in the backfield does not look at the signal or the traffic conditions," Wagner noted, "but looks straight ahead at the back of a front-liner," awaiting the signal to cross.

"The back-fielder often relies completely on the judgment of a front-liner," Wagner wrote. "In the roles of light-watcher, street-watcher and backfield, anonymous individuals have worked out a collective solution to one small part of their common fate."

Movement and mind are intimately connected. As neurophysiologist Rodolfo Llinás put it, "Thinking is the evolutionary internalization of movement." Just as our bodies evolved to walk upright and became adept at covering ten miles or more a day in search of food, our brains evolved as well, helping us to navigate and make sense of the world through which we moved.

April 19, 1909. Weston spent an additional day in Chicago, aggravatingly stationary. He had arrived on Saturday afternoon, and taken his usual Sunday off. But then he remained in the city through Monday night in order to spend the day finding and hiring a new car, driver, and attendant. (This involved some sixty phone calls, he groused.) Weston had at last grown exasperated with the companions who had accompanied him from

New York. They had a propensity to get stuck in the sand and mud and appeared wholly unconcerned whenever they led him astray. (One day in Ohio they sent him off on an unneeded detour of fifteen miles). Both the "interesting chauffeur," as Weston called him, and Weston's valet were sent packing. He found and employed a new driver and valet, saying they would be subject to more discipline and hoping they "would give me a little attention" and could "do something besides eat and sleep."

Declaring his Chicago stay nonetheless as "among my most pleasant experiences," Weston was up and off just after daybreak on Tuesday morning, walking westward out of downtown Chicago. By all accounts, he was optimistic and cheerful. Two hours later, his new supply vehicle was mired in tenacious black mud. It took twenty minutes to pull it out with the aid of two horses that had been uncoupled from a passing beer wagon.

Walking west, he entered more open, less populated terrain; it had little in common with the familiar Northeast. "It seems desolate all along the road with nothing but an occasional burying ground in sight," Weston wrote. Fewer adoring crowds came out to meet him as he walked through small towns (despite, thanks to the rise of the telephone, communities getting advance notice of Weston's arrival; he found it gratifying when families walked out as far as three miles from town to escort him in). Alas, his new valet continued the streak of ineptitude, losing the two new hats that had been sent out from New York and adding a mile to Weston's route one day by misinforming him about his hotel's location. "I tell you right now walking is the easiest part of this task," Weston said.

As one would assume by now, walking conditions went from bad to worse. The road outside Joliet was at first unpleasantly muddy, then flooded. Weston slipped under barbed wire seeking a way around the floodwaters, but without success. He had to return and wade through water up to his knees but had regained his composure by the time he reached Coal City. He walked so fast now the crowd behind him tried to keep up in a "laughable and uproarious run."

———————

If movement requires a brain, does our brain also require movement to function optimally? Theories regarding the evolution of the complexity of our brains have come and gone, like the now-embraced, now-dismissed theories of bipedality and the evolution of our limbs. New evidence begets new ideas, in which a new generation of scientists finds flaws and then develops a more convincing set of notions.

But one thing everyone now agrees on: We walked upright well before our brains expanded to their current size. In other words, we didn't figure out how to stand upright because we had bigger brains. (This was a common assumption in Victorian times and persisted among those who wanted to believe that our mental capacities, not our bipedalism, define us as human beings.) We now know that what happened was quite the reverse. We stood upright for efficiency in our search for food and territory, then some time later our brains started to grow and expand.

But why, and how much later? A compelling early narrative was that the brain grew because we now had hands and arms available for doing things other than locomoting—making tools, catching slow-moving animals, and eating insects, among other things. So evolution gave us more firepower to figure out exactly what we should be doing and how to do it well.

It's a pleasing, simple theory, but flawed and largely discarded; a horde of findings by paleoanthropologists suggests that several million years passed between early hominids standing upright—thereby freeing their hands for other uses—and the expansion of our brains. Indeed, it's also believed that millions of years elapsed between our first use of stone tools and the expansion of our braincases. That's a suspiciously long lag time to imply a cause-and-effect relationship.

It's now generally accepted that human brain size expanded gradually for thousands of generations after we started walking upright. In other words, the growth of our brains generally mirrored the overall growth in our body size. Then something dramatic happened: Long after we started walking about and using crude stone tools and causing alarm among species we deemed delicious and nutritious, our brains suddenly and terrifically ballooned in size, allowing our early ancestors to undertake more complex tasks and create more complex tools. (Whether this happened 2 million years ago or as recently as 200,000 remains a matter of some squabbling among paleoanthropologists.)

Why did this happen? Some theories: Our minds grew in order to manage ever-more complex social relationships. That is, evolution selected those who had the capacity to work together to obtain food and shelter, creating an increasingly interdependent species. Relationships required more mental capacity to manage on a day-to-day basis.

Another notion: The greater quantity of animal protein—mostly meat—in our diet as a result of our increased mobility allowed us to evolve from passive gatherers into more active hunters. This, in turn, established a sort of positive feedback loop: The meat gave us a more concentrated fuel, allowing our brains to grow evolutionarily (brains are extremely "expensive" energy-wise). Also, meat, especially that cooked over a fire, was easier to digest than whole grains. Thus our digestive tracts evolved to become less complex and energy intensive, which allowed our brains to use the excess fuel to expand.

In 2012, a new theory emerged, put forth by two American anthropologists, David A. Raichlen and John D. Polk, and published in the *Proceedings of the Royal Society B: Biological Sciences*. It suggests that our rapid brain growth was fueled by the more mobile lives of our ancestors. At some point, we evolved to favor long-distance trekking and endurance running, which opened new territory and allowed us to chase down mammals that were very fast in short sprints but unable to sustain speed over long distances. That aerobic activity, in turn, manufactured natural proteins within us that fed our minds and fueled brain growth. In other words, they posit, it wasn't just the greater cognitive demands of an increasingly complex life that led our brains to grow. Rather, our increase in intelligence may have been "a by-product of improved athletic performance."

The understanding of the links between mobility and the evolution of our brains is in its infancy. But the long and short of our understanding right now is this: Our braincases and the cauliflowery tissue within them expanded long after we started walking upright; all those complex firings of synapses and linkings of neurons were built upon a foundation of upright walking and movement—probably long-distance walking. We walked, and only after we'd done this for some millennia did we gradually start to think more complex thoughts. We began to rely less on instinct and more on logic and other forms of rational thought.

As previously noted, our bodies likely are genetically encoded to walk a certain amount each and every day. Without that walking, our bodies have slyly turned on us, becoming more susceptible to disease, accumulating fat that leads to health problems, and atrophying our backs, knees, and feet.

Why would we think the process was otherwise for our minds? Our brains evolved to their present size and level of acuity in people who walked a lot more than we walk today. And so, one might reasonably surmise, *not* walking could very well impact our minds as much as not walking has impacted our bodies.

So, what occurs, physiologically speaking, inside your mind when you extricate yourself from the La-Z-Boy and start to walk?

A lot, as it happens. For starters, your circulation amps up, and your blood flows more freely. More oxygen makes it to your head. You instantly become less tired. You gradually start to develop a general feeling of well-being thanks to endorphins, a group of substances manufactured by the body (in the pituitary gland and spinal cord, among other places) that produce effects that opiates, such as morphine, try to mimic. Endorphins are often found in the blood of long-distance runners and are thought to be the source of that much-vaunted runner's high. Debate continues over how much of a high, or the process by which endorphins affect us (some researchers assert that endorphins are barred by certain mechanisms from entering the brain, where receptors are awaiting them). Yet there's plenty of anecdotal evidence to support the idea that exercise has a direct impact not only on our physical health, but also on our sense of well-being. Bottom line: When you walk, you start along a path toward feeling more upbeat, owing to natural chemicals circulating in your body that you otherwise wouldn't produce when, say, you're encased in a car and not using your major muscle groups.

These benefits aren't just theoretical. Studies corroborate the fact that life is better when one is on a walk. A clinical study conducted in 1999 at Duke University showed that for people ages fifty and older, moderate exercise (walking briskly or jogging for thirty minutes three times a week) was just as effective at reducing the symptoms of depression as sertraline (Zoloft). And as Harvard Medical School professor John Ratey notes in *Spark: The Revolutionary New Science of Exercise and the Brain,* an excellent survey of recent science, "Human beings are social animals, so if you're depressed, it would be ideal to choose a form of exercise that encourages making connections and that can take place outside or in some environment that stimulates the senses."

Clinical studies also have shown that exercising regularly results in a 50 percent drop in the prevalence of symptoms of anxiety experienced by patients with coronary heart disease. Two Louisiana doctors who've looked into this, Carl Lavie and Richard Milani, said of one study on the treatment of anxiety with medication and psychotherapy that they were surprised "that there is no mention of exercise as an additional means of treating anxiety." Physical activity works—Lavie has published eleven papers on the topic, and in every one he concludes that exercise reduces anxiety.

Walking and exercise aid not just endorphin production and short-term relief of symptoms of anxiety and depression—briefly lifting you up from a dreary afternoon—but also appear to benefit the brain in the long term. And this is where science is treading into new territory almost daily. Normally reserved researchers have even permitted themselves some unacademic enthusiasm about what they're finding.

One study, published in the *Proceedings of the National Academy of Sciences*, tracked 120 healthy but generally sedentary older Americans, in which one group walked around a track three times a week (for up to forty minutes at a stretch) and the other group engaged in less rigorous activities, such as light workouts with resistance bands or yoga. Each participant submitted to a brain scan before the trials began, and then again after a year. The result? Those who walked showed an average growth in the hippocampus of the brain of about 2 percent. That was in contrast to the other group, where hippocampus size dropped by about an average of 1.4 percent.

The conclusion: "Physical activity, such as aerobic exercise, has emerged as a promising low-cost treatment to improve neurocognitive function that is accessible to most adults and is not plagued by intolerable side effects often found with pharmaceutical treatments." Other studies conclude that those who exercise regularly have better memory retention and show more aptitude in learning skills. (What kind of exercise? As Ratey notes, "Many of the most convincing studies use walking as the mode of exercise.")

The precise mechanisms for these improvements are still matters of debate, but some promising avenues have opened up.

For starters, as suggested above, it's been shown that exercise maintains the health of the hippocampus, the part of the brain essential to memory. (It's also the first part of the brain to show signs of damage as Alzheimer's disease sets in.) As we get older, the hippocampus loses tissue mass, much as our bodies lose muscle mass. Our memory skills start to diminish. Yet that rate of diminishment can be slowed with exercise.

Relatively new research—much of it done in the past decade or so—also suggests the force at work is something cumbersomely called brain-derived neurotrophic factor, or more commonly, BDNF. Ratey has zeroed in on this in his writings, and he calls it "a crucial biological link between thought, emotions, and movement." More memorably, he's referred to it as the "Miracle-Gro for the brain," a Twitter-length description that's stuck.

BDNF is a protein that your body naturally produces when you're moving and exercising. It binds to receptors on your synapses, which connect the neurons in your brain and allow you process and remember data. It essentially increases the voltage of your brain—the phrase "firing on all synapses" is actually appropriate here—making the synaptic signals stronger. In laboratory tests, BDNF applied to brain cells in a petri dish showed that they sprouted more structural branches, producing the same structural growth that makes for stronger, better connections and increased memory and learning.

What's more, BDNF triggers action inside the cell that allows it to manufacture even more BDNF, which in turn leads to more cell production within the hippocampus. The hippocampus thus grows larger with exercise. The common notion that brain cells follow a one-way path—that they die rather than regenerating—has been soundly rejected in recent years.

The relationship between movement and the brain was encoded in us starting three to six million years ago, and it's been fine-tuned in the last half million or so. By choosing to not move and get exercise, we're inviting a needless disruption of and imbalance between body and mind. As Harvard's John Ratey puts it, "If you get your body in shape, your mind will follow."

April 22, 1909. People who met Weston and shared their thoughts about him invariably commented on his spryness, his evident youthfulness, his light humor, and, even at age seventy, his nimble mind. His memory was said to be fearsome. He often recalled passing through small villages forty years earlier, accurately remembered whom he met when there, and even what he ate for breakfast while there. ("They treated me in princely style," he said of one hotel in upstate New York.)

Moving past Chicago, he would have no memories to draw upon, but instead fresh vistas as he pushed west. The roadways between towns in 1909 were as poorly tended in the West as they had been in the East, if not more so, and Weston was further plagued by a continuing onslaught of poor spring weather. The mud and the tracks of horses and wagons turned the lanes into miserable mires. He moved to the railroad tracks, which were relatively level and well maintained, although they had their own hazards. He tripped over switches along the tracks, and without the shelter from trees, he was buffeted by winds from across the open plains. Stiff gusts succeeded in knocking him down repeatedly, and he occasionally injured his hands and arms bracing himself in falls on gravel, tracks, and cinders.

But more often than not, the railbeds were a godsend, elevating him above the mud on firm, well-drained ballast. "The Chicago and Alton has the finest roadbed I ever saw," said an advertisement quoting him in the *St. Louis Times*. "The foregoing testimonial was unsolicited and comes from him who is better acquainted with the physical conditions of the various railroads than any living man," the ad went on. It also boasted that passengers would find "No dust. No dirt. No smoke. No cinders."

Anyone who's walked along a railway knows doing so is not a simple feat: The ties are spaced to hold the tracks in place, not to allow for a steady and comfortable gait. They're placed too closely together for a long, elastic stride, but too far apart to double up and hit every other tie. Weston avoided this by sticking to the ballast along and between the tracks, generally not always walking on the ties themselves. This likely would have become easier as he moved westward. The farther west the tracks led, the more expensive the heavy, solid ballast—like granite—was to find, and rail lines often cut corners by using packed dirt. Still, as Weston noted several times both during and after his walk, considerable exertion was required to keep up his favored pace of four miles per hour if he had to constantly cross and recross the tracks to angle for the smoother route. He calculated that this ate up two to four minutes each mile, reducing him to an effective speed of three-and-a-half miles per hour.

When on the tracks, he could hear the steam locomotives chuffing from a distance and could clear out of the way by stepping off to one side or by walking on the opposite track if they were in pairs. A passing train was a good thing: Passengers and crew would always lean out and shout encouragement, which he found heartening. When a Chicago and Alton Railroad car motored past, he was hailed by a group waving handkerchiefs and cheering him on. One tossed a newspaper to him, with a singularly uninspiring exhortation penned in the margin: "You are doing fine; go ahead." A casual information network had been set up to keep the trains apprised of Weston's whereabouts, with telegraph operators at train stations having been instructed by Union Pacific to let their dispatchers know when Weston passed through and to have the dispatcher inform him of scheduled trains.

This put Weston's mind partly at ease, but not completely. Near Glasgow, Missouri, Weston had to cross a train trestle spanning the Missouri River. It was a mile long and as high as 150 feet. He started off confidently, having been assured no trains were scheduled, and, in the end, no trains came. But the trestle's length and height and lack of a practical exit made him increasingly twitchy and agitated with every step. "I was very nervous and was getting dizzy," he later reported. After he managed to cross without being hit by a train or plunging to his death, he said that he was "thoroughly weakened." (The next day he wrote, "I walked that trestle again in my sleep," a dream that left him so debilitated that he delayed his day's start by four hours.)

Walking long distances rarely involves derring-do, as in trestle walking, but rather is more a matter of sheer stamina, of mind over malaise. In the six-day walking races of the 1870s, contestants who started out strong in the beginning were often wobbly and weak by the end, with each and every step forced and tentative. (The bleachers were often packed to the point of mayhem during the final days and hours, with spectators arriving by the wagonload to watch disoriented walkers on the verge of hallucination and collapse.)

And in 1909, Weston's stamina was set against the backdrop of his advanced age. At seventy, he had long passed his expiry date; life expectancy for males was about thirty-eight when he was born, and a child born the year of his transcontinental walk could expect to live to about fifty, though these numbers were both skewed by the high infant mortality rates of the times. Yet here was a seventy-year-old striding on confidently and indefatigably, day after day, often maddeningly cheerful, at a pace that would challenge walkers a half-century younger. This phenomenon naturally attracted considerable attention.

"Were Weston forty years younger it would be a feat worthy of arousing wide attention," noted the *New York Times*. "Now, at the age of 70 years, when a man's active career in athletics particularly, is supposed to be at an end, Mr. Weston is preparing to eclipse all of his other achievements."

Indeed, Weston was walking headlong into the nascent field of gerontology and upending the debate over assumptions about how to live out one's advanced years. Society was just then starting to turn its attention to the aging process—what it meant, how to manage it, how to come to terms with it.

―――――――――

Just a few months after Weston started off toward San Francisco, several men gathered at the house of G. Stanley Hall, president of the American Psychological Association, in Worcester, Massachusetts. Present were three well-known psychologists: William James, Sigmund Freud, and Carl Jung. No one thought much of this high-octane get-together at the time, least of all the participants. The sixty-seven-year-old James evidently didn't esteem the fifty-three-year-old Freud but hit it off very well with the much younger and (then) much less well-known Jung.

While the science of psychology had been around for some time—the first laboratory of experimental psychology had been founded in Leipzig in 1879, and James was considered a pioneer in the field—gerontology, the study of aging, had only recently arisen, with the term itself coined in 1903. Harvard historian Jill Lepore has referred to Hall as the founder of gerontology, and among the first to understand that senescence—the opposite of adolescence—was a period worth studying on its own. "Old age takes everyone by surprise, and no one ever really comes to terms with it," Lepore wrote. "Hall thought this was because old age is the only stage of life we never grow out of, and can never look back on, not on this earth, anyway."

Others had given thought to aging, of course—ancient Arabs had various special treatments just for the elderly—but no one person had drawn as much attention to theories of aging at the time as the McGill University–trained doctor Sir William Osler. Osler was the chief physician at Johns Hopkins Hospital in Baltimore for fourteen years, but his notoriety could be captured in a subhead on his 1919 *New York Times* obituary: "'Chloroform at 60' a jest."

Osler had found unwitting global fame in 1905 after making an offhand comment during his Johns Hopkins valedictory address before repairing to England to teach at Oxford. Osler spoke of the "comparative uselessness of men above 40 years of age" and made an apparently jocular reference to the Anthony Trollope novel *The Fixed Period,* which averred that man's work was done by age 40 and that he ought to be "chloroformed at 60."

Ironic comments sometimes fail to travel with their quotation marks. Osler spent much of his remaining years on the earth insisting that, no, really, it was all a joke and that he actually didn't believe people over sixty should be done in. (He was fifty-five when he made the speech. His *Times* obituary pointed out that "he reached the age of 70 himself, and his last ten years formed a period of great activity and of his greatest influence.")

During Weston's 1909 walk, Osler's accidental controversy was far from extinguished, and Weston was happy to see his walk prompt the debate to flare anew. Weston's jaunt became part of a national discussion about age and the usefulness of the elderly. This debate took place in newspapers and drawing rooms and among knots of people gathered along the roads to watch Weston pass by. Most had to agree that he looked healthy and active, and his life and vigor provided a welcome alternative to a lethal rag and eternal sleep. With his pluck and dauntless walking style, he demonstrated what those of advanced years can accomplish if they put their minds to it.

"Edward Payson Weston is a living example of what open air, temperance, exercise, and healthy mindedness will do for the human race," one newspaper trumpeted just days after he'd departed New York. "His example is worth a hundred sermons. He is embodied disproof of the Osler theory."

"Many physicians, of this city at least," reported the *New York Times,* were watching his trip closely. "Their interest is not excited alone by the nature of the feat, though all hold it marvelous that a man of Weston's age is capable of even attempting it; they are looking deeper, watching for the effect which this example will have in renewing the lost interest in walking as a pastime and an exercise, and for the effect they believe it will have in countering the theory they condemn—the theory that at the age of fifty or thereabouts a man is 'down and out.'"

A column in the *Dallas Morning News* admitted that many considered Weston's walk from ocean to ocean "foolishness" and "an idle waste of time." But, the writer asked, was it "preferred to the needless senility into which far too many men begin to drift at the period of three score years and ten?" The writer chastised those who chose inertness when their working days were over, "lounging about in the sort of aimless apathy which benumbs the soul and closes up all the channels of sensation." He went on: "Remember that there is mighty little excitement of divertissement in shuffling to town twice a day 'for the mail,'" and that lapsing into indolence was "far more foolish and ill-advised than it was for Edward Payson Weston to start on his seventieth birthday, to walk from New York to San Francisco."

Around the time of Weston's walk, exercise at an advanced age was typically regarded in poor favor, as if practitioners were involved in a zero-sum game: If you exercised too much, you sacrificed mental agility. A "nerve specialist" from New York named J. Leonard Corning said in 1909 that he was opposed to "excessive exercise," which was what he believed Weston's attempt to be. He thought that with the "over-cultivation of the physique the mentality suffered."

Corning wrote during a period when experts widely believed that brain cells didn't regenerate. As a result, graceful aging was in large part a matter of learning to cope with gradually diminishing brain capacity. Modern science has shown that's not the case; we do generate new brain cells throughout our lives, although the process can become increasingly imperfect and less efficient with age, as it does with much cellular activity.

But staying active helps. One study of older rats suggests that running for a total of just eleven to fifteen minutes four times a week for four weeks led to healthy developments in the parts of the brain associated with memory; these rats then performed better than sedentary rats did on spatial memory tests. That's proving true in human testing as well. One of the largest studies ever conducted is on a group of 122,000 nurses, who, starting in 1976, have been surveyed on a wide range of their health and lifestyle habits. The survey has been repeated every two years. This has established a trove of valuable information, which public health researchers have been fruitfully mining since. Among them is Rush University assistant professor Jennifer Weuve, who studied the data collected on 18,766 of the nurses, who were then ages seventy to eighty-one, to unearth connections between exercise and cognitive ability. The results, published in *JAMA (The Journal of the American Medical Association)*, suggested that those who exercised the most—the group that maintained a median level of walking for six hours a week—were 20 percent less likely to show cognitive impairment than those who exercised the least.

Other long-term studies also show that even modest exercise can serve as a bulwark against dementia. A study started in 1989 with 299 elderly volunteers in the Pittsburgh area tracked mental acuity and exercise habits. The subjects' brains were assessed by MRI two to three years later, and then again in 2008, when the first of two measurements of their cognitive function was also performed; the second of these took place four years after that. The results, published in the journal *Neurology*, were sweeping and conclusive: Those who walked the most cut in half their risk of developing memory problems. The optimal exercise for cognitive health benefits, the researchers concluded, was to walk six to nine miles each week. That's a mile to a mile and a half a day, without walking on Sundays if you're inclined to follow Weston's example. (This study concluded that walking an additional mile didn't help all that much.)

A study written up in the *Archives of Internal Medicine* in 2001 tracked nearly six thousand women ages sixty-five and older for six to eight years. The women were given a cognitive test at the study's beginning and end, the results of which were then correlated with how many blocks they walked daily. Those who walked the least had a drop of 24 percent in cognition. Those who walked the most still showed a decline, but of a lesser degree: 17 percent. The results were clear: "Women with higher levels of baseline physical activity were less likely to develop cognitive decline." Given the aging of much of the US population, we'll no doubt be seeing more research along these lines.

Peter Snyder of Brown University's Alpert Medical School, who studies the effects of aging on the brain, recently told National Public Radio that "what we're finding is that, of all of these noninvasive ways of intervening, it is exercise that seems to have the most efficacy at this point—more so than nutritional supplements, vitamins, and cognitive interventions. . . . The literature on exercise is just tremendous."

Indeed, a twenty-year study in 2010 found that walking just five miles per week "protects the brain structure" over a ten-year period in people with Alzheimer's disease and in those who exhibit signs of mild cognitive impairment. "The findings showed across the board that greater amounts of physical activity were associated with greater brain volume," the researchers concluded. Another study, from 2012, supported those findings, also concluding that even moderate walking helped stave off further deterioration among elderly people in the early stages of Alzheimer's disease. That study tracked 104 Alzheimer's patients, who were classified as either active or sedentary. Among the active group, those who walked for more than two hours a week showed significant improvement in scores on tests of their mental abilities, whereas the more sedentary patients showed marked declines.

While different studies arrive at moderately different conclusions via various routes, the recent research of dozens of scientists more often than not converges at a single intersection. And that consistently suggests that if you exercise, your brain will be fitter than if you don't. This applies to the young, those in the prime of their days, and especially to the elderly.

The twenty-year 2010 study mentioned above, results from which were released by Cyrus Raji of the University of Pittsburgh, followed 426 older adults, including healthy people along with those showing mild cognitive impairment or the actual onset of Alzheimer's. Across test subjects, more walking was shown to result in greater brain volume. "Unfortunately, walking is not a cure," Raji said. "But walking can improve your brain's resistance to [Alzheimer's] disease and reduce memory loss over time."

═══════════

April 29, 1909. By late April, nearly a month and a half after he'd departed, Weston was bit by bit falling behind his ambitious schedule, and there was little he could do about it. Constant winds from the west continued to torment him, forcing him to lean into the gusts and slow his steps. (He claimed to have tromped through seventy-mile-per-hour winds in Missouri.) He was also plagued by bitterly cold days, with temperatures below freezing—some days he was hard-pressed in "getting up a pace sufficient to keep me from freezing." These would be quickly followed by sweltering days "simmering under the sun that so nearly caused an attack of lumbago." Other complications arose: He had a falling-out with his replacement valet and fired him; then some "tilt" arose with the provider of his new car, who evidently didn't think its provision was generating enough publicity for him. Weston went one way; car and driver went another.

Weston was now alone, with only the moral support of his manager keeping in touch by telegram and phone from his base in the east. He hired the occasional horse and buggy as a support vehicle, but more commonly would send his baggage ahead by train to be deposited at the next station. Trip conditions, he wrote, were "the most annoying and the hardest to overcome." He did find small cheer along the way: The station agent at one rail depot turned out to be a fan and gave him extra milk and bread. But overall, he was off to a poor start in the post-Chicago leg of his walk. In the week since he'd left, he'd managed a meager 220 miles, only about half of what he'd planned, putting him at least 200 miles behind schedule.

CHAPTER 5

KNOWING WHERE YOU ARE

We are apes who have been designed by evolution to roam the savannah at a leisurely 5 to 10 miles per hour or so. Yet here we are, at the start of the 21st century, guiding vehicles around the congested roads of the developed world at speeds far in excess of that—and most of the time not colliding with each other or the scenery.

—**GRAHAM HOLE,** *The Psychology of Driving,* 2007

Weston mapped out his routes in impeccable detail well in advance of his journeys, using atlases and information obtained by writing ahead. Once his journeys were under way, he nearly always followed these predetermined routes, generally guided by assistants when he wasn't firing them. In the west, where long-distance roads were fewer and poorly maintained, he mostly followed train tracks, and so had to make directional decisions only when he came to junctures in rail lines.

When calculating distances between points, Weston relied in large part on postmasters and other employees of the postal service. Mail carriers were generally considered the arbiters of the nation's distances, with the Post Office Department, the predecessor of the US Postal Service, employing a staff to maintain charts showing the exact mileage from one post office to the next and the lengths of the roads around town to plan mail deliveries. The data weren't infallible: at times, the post office calculated distances based on the rail lines, which put Weston at a disadvantage when walking on nearby roads. He often said he didn't get full credit for the distance walked. "This is caused by the roads winding and curving so as to go through towns, avoid hills, etc.," Weston groused in the *New York Times*. "A railroad, as a rule, goes straight by many towns, passing a mile or so on the outside." He estimated that during his Portland-to-Chicago journey of 1907, he may have walked a hundred miles in excess of his advertised total because of the gap between claimed and actual distances.

So Weston knew where he was most of the time, thanks to copious notes and maps and the occasional helper. But his instincts that told him he may have walked farther than the data said came from somewhere else: Like all of us, he was possessed of an innate sense of space and locomotion and direction. Today, some of the more fascinating modern studies on motion and navigation—knowing where you are—are emerging from virtual reality research. Video games are now a $93 billion industry worldwide, and, depending on which figures you trust, that industry is either outpacing Hollywood in gross revenues or rapidly advancing upon it. *Grand Theft Auto V* was released in 2013, and within twenty-four hours grossed $816 million worldwide, easily eclipsing the top weekend grosses of hit movies like the 2002 *Spider-Man*, which brought in $115 million its first weekend. Other video games—*Halo, Call of Duty*—also post stunning numbers. Virtual environments aren't just confined to video games. They're becoming standard tools in major architectural commissions (allowing clients to "walk through" a project when it's still just a concept). Faux worlds are also created for training policemen and soldiers how to best respond to hostile situations.

A video game played on a flat screen television typically involves a complex environment of buildings and hallways or canyons that you move through by operating a joystick. You imagine that you're walking, but it's more like floating. Virtual environments are not limitless spaces, where you can just keep going and going, as in the real world. These are more like a baseball field, where there's an infield, an outfield, a warning track, and then you literally hit a wall. With a joystick or trackball or some other device, you can move through corridors and doors and gates and perhaps leap over chasms or onto platforms above you (depending on the game), at times running into dead ends that require you to backtrack.

Yet game designers have found that players often lose their bearings and find it hard to retrace their movements and to figure out shortcuts. That's not necessarily because of flaws in the game design or player incompetence. It's simply because one learns by physically walking, possibly employing a wholly different set of neural pathways to anchor oneself spatially. "People navigate every day in the real world without problem," wrote the authors of a 2011 study of this phenomenon, "however users navigating [virtual environments] often become disoriented and frustrated."

Researchers have found that something interesting happens if gamers are equipped with a virtual reality headset and then allowed to walk normally through a maze as they search for targets or their progress is impeded in some way. According to the 2011 study, "participants traveled shorter distances, made fewer wrong turns, pointed to hidden targets more accurately and more quickly, and were able to place and label targets on maps more accurately" than when navigating with a joystick or wearing a virtual reality headset and walking within a circumscribed space.

Since the early 1990s, game developers have been advocating for treadmills to help players establish more sophisticated internal maps when exploring virtual worlds. But therein lies a problem: Basic treadmills typically only allow a user to move forward or backward in a linear direction; they don't provide for rotation or changing direction, which studies suggest is essential to understanding our location. To date, real walking while virtually exploring is used chiefly under laboratory conditions, where researchers can configure a warehouse-size empty space or lease an expensive omnidirectional treadmill for tests requiring headset walking. (The CyberWalk treadmill, a platform that allows walking in any direction and is housed at the Max Planck Institute for Biological Cybernetics in Tübingen, Germany, weighs approximately twelve tons.)

In one experiment, thirty-six subjects wearing virtual reality headsets were instructed to make their way through a rudimentary virtual maze that measured, in virtual space, about fifty by fifty feet. The subjects moved by one of three means: using a joystick, walking in place (moving their feet up and down, which was translated into virtual forward movement via optical sensors), or wearing a headset as they navigated through an open space. The physical space was about twenty-one feet square, less than half the size of the virtual maze, so each step was magnified. But they could turn and walk at whatever angle they wanted. The study confirmed the researchers' longstanding hunch that "real walking is critical for navigating [virtual environments]." When actually walking, "participants were significantly better at navigating" virtual environments than both those walking in place and those navigating by joystick, the authors found. The difference was "the stimulation of the proprioceptive system," and while walking in place does partly stimulate this, forward motion while walking does so more accurately. In short, we navigate with our bodies just as we do with our minds.

We're all hardwired with navigational skills. Studies have shown that, unlike some animals, humans don't instinctively know which way is north by sensing magnetic fields, despite persistent beliefs to the contrary. But we've developed a sophisticated system for understanding directions and our location based on things such as landmarks and the position of the sun or stars overhead. And this navigation is aided by physical movement. When we're not actually moving, we're less certain of where we are.

May 6, 1909. Eleven miles outside Kansas City, in unseasonably chilly weather and with a low mist obscuring the landscape, Weston was met by a delegation from the Kansas City Hiking Club, along with a convoy of about twenty cars filled with passengers who had ventured out from the city to witness his arrival. He greeted his greeters enthusiastically and then walked on, trailed by a growing rabble. He briefly stopped by a high school in Independence, where he was warmly received by 250 students; they gave him a loud cheer and he set off again. The ten miles between Independence and Kansas City, Weston said, were "one continuous ovation." Then, seven miles outside the city, five mounted policemen met him to form a guard to part the crowds for the remainder of the walk; along the way, three more schools emptied out to cheer him on. "I was greatly pleased with the enthusiasm displayed," Weston wrote. He arrived downtown just before two in the afternoon, and thousands came out to hail him as he walked to the Coates House Hotel. He was feeling more chipper than usual, and added, "I am confident that I have not overrated my ability and will finish my walk in the allotted time of 100 days." The Midwest was agreeing with Weston. "As a matter of fact," he said, "the air out here is so invigorating that it has proved the best and most satisfactory since the start."

After he arose at four the next morning, Weston attempted an experiment. He had oatmeal and a pitcher of milk sent to his hotel room at 4:30, and after eating he set off at five, hoping to get seventeen miles under his belt before tucking into a full breakfast at the first sizable town. The experiment was not a success—he was famished after three hours, and one of his local walking companions volunteered to go ahead to scavenge a breakfast for him along a rural lane. A "good Samaritan" was found who agreed to prepare him a full meal. Weston spent forty-five minutes gorging before continuing on.

Like eating, walking involves a combination of natural instincts and skills we learn and remember. But researchers have also concluded that the physical activity of walking is innate to our bodies, bypassing our brains. That is, we might be able to stand and move about even if we had our brains scooped out of our heads like flesh from a melon. In other words, we may very well be able to put one foot in front of the other without applying our brains at all, although it would be movement without motive or direction.

This theory hasn't been tested on humans, for reasons that don't require explanation. But with a little searching you can turn up a YouTube video of a cat walking on treadmill demonstrating three different gaits (a walk, trot, and gallop) as the treadmill speeds up. The cat is, in technical terms, "decerebrate." That is, it's a cat whose spine has been surgically severed from its brain. (Some descriptions of the experiment refer, incorrectly, to a "cat without a brain.") It's evident that some basic sensory stimulation triggers a response in the cat when the treadmill starts to move. The cat knows how to walk. And trot. And gallop. And it can do so without its brain telling it to do so. Indeed, starting in the early twentieth century, studies found that our spinal cords contain primitive neural networks (or "central pattern generators") that control basic locomotion (like walking and swimming). We may believe that we can control everything with our minds, but parts of the complex act of walking may not be among those things.

When we walk, our bodies and minds are performing a number of remarkable tasks, although so easily and seamlessly it doesn't seem very special. Specifically, we're creating new cognitive maps. And we're following old ones.

What is a cognitive map? It's mostly a convenient metaphor; it's not as if we're actually drawing up blueprints with routes and intersections and filing them away in long mental tubes. But we're encoding information we gather and storing it in our long-term memory, and doing it in such a way that we're able to quickly retrieve and reassemble it into complex networks.

One researcher defined cognitive mapping as "internal representations of experienced environments." But it might be more simply defined as "knowing where things are, even when we can't see them." How we create these maps has been the source of considerable debate: Do we know these routes because we remember individual turns in sequence? Or are we following a broader, more comprehensive network of routes in our minds?

This is more important than it may seem on the surface: How we map the environment around us can define how we arrange and process our other thoughts. Mentally mapping space is likely the oldest form of human cognition. We learned how to navigate space before we developed verbal and analytic capabilities. As Canadian researchers Ian Spence and Jing Feng have put it, "There is much reason to believe that spatial cognition was an essential foundation for the development of these more recent cognitive capacities."

Knowing where we are and where we should go are among our central tasks. It's high on our list of things to learn after we're born, when we start moving about and exploring the world around us.

We know *how* to walk by the time we're six weeks old. But we lack the muscle tone and coordination to actually do much about this, and so we kick and then we crawl until we figure it out. Then, at about a year, we take our first steps, whereupon several complex processes unfold, starting with a long negotiation with gravity. We stand clinging to an adult's pant leg, then release and start to pitch forward. One leg swings out, and then the other, and—*whoa!*—we lurch a step or two. Fall, repeat. Writing in 1863, the polymath Oliver Wendell Holmes's description of walking sounded like ad copy for a new video game: "Walking is a perpetual falling with a perpetual self-recovery," he wrote. "It is a most complex, violent, and perilous operation, which we divest of its extreme danger only by continual practice from a very early period of life."

Once we work out the basic mechanics of forward motion, walking aids our cognitive development. We explore and find things. We learn about landmarks and anchoring. We develop our working memory, since it's essential that we keep our destination and route in mind as we navigate the Scylla and Charybdis of multiple distractions. We learn to stay focused, to navigate past the television with its kaleidoscope of colors and mesmerizing sounds, and past the sleeping dog upon which we have thrown ourselves before to interesting effect. Eventually, we stay on task and get to the kitchen and explore that fine aroma, which past experience suggests is freshly baked cookies. And then we know how to get back to where we started.

Up to the age of two, among our main tasks is figuring out that a gap exists between ourselves and the world around us—although we're loath to give up that supremely egocentric worldview. From ages two until about seven, we begin to assemble our own universe from the flotsam of the world we encounter as we move about. From seven or eight years old onward, we exploit a new capacity: using knowledge to construct and understand a larger universe—the world we cannot see but now assume to exist—that lies beyond our immediate experience.

Independent movement plays a critical role in our social and emotional development. It's in part how we learn about formulating and carrying out our own plans, of learning to be ourselves. A number of studies have arrived at a similar conclusion: Independent mobility doesn't just coincide with dramatic changes in our behavior. Walking actually causes our behavior within and thoughts about the world to change.

The father of cognitive mapping was Edward Chance Tolman (1886–1959), a psychologist born and raised in Massachusetts. Tolman conducted numerous experiments that involved watching rats find their way through mazes. His goal? Figure out the processes used in determining and recalling routes. In effect, Tolman oversaw the wedding of cognitive psychology with the space around us.

Tolman's 1948 paper, "Cognitive Maps in Rats and Men," summarizes several of his studies. (Tolman also demonstrated that academic studies needn't be dry. "Most of the rat investigations," he wrote, "were carried out in the Berkeley laboratory. But I shall also include, occasionally, accounts of the behavior of non-Berkeley rats who obviously have misspent their lives in out-of-State laboratories.")

Tolman's paper takes a long look at what he calls our "central office" (that is, our brain) and finds elements of both "a map control room" and "an old-fashioned telephone exchange," with the former being the more prominent.

The "telephone exchange" approach to wayfinding is essentially connecting one point with another and then another. This might best be summed up by a *Star Trek* comic strip from the 1980s. It depicts the crew of the starship U.S.S. *Enterprise* following Spock as he leads them out of a complicated maze. When someone expresses astonishment at the ease with which he guides them, Spock shrugs it off, replying: "When we were headed here before, I observed 128 turns, some left, some right . . . a simple binary code." (Thanks to Michael Hill for flagging this in his book *Walking, Crossing Streets, and Choosing Pedestrian Routes.*)

Following a simple binary code is sometimes also referred to as "strip mapping"—tracking a linear route of sequential turns that connect points and eventually create a map. This is in contrast to a more comprehensive "network map," which includes these points and routes but also presumptive linkages between previously unconnected routes.

Tolman believed that we use both types of mental maps depending upon the situation. We might follow a mental strip map when attending a conference at a large hotel. This allows us to get from our guest room to the downstairs meeting rooms quickly and repeatedly, without cluttering our minds with thoughts about what lies down this hallway or that. But we're likely to lay out a more sophisticated mental map of the space between our home and the convenience store six blocks away. We might stop by when driving home from work, or walk a roundabout route on a sunny day, or bike a direct line that incorporates an alley or two. We compile an inventory of routes in our heads, and from this we can create new routes within this complex network.

Cognitive mapping studies have progressed considerably in the six decades since Tolman watched how rats get from point A to point B. Researchers have added to the body of knowledge, including looking at socioeconomic influences on cognitive mapping. (It's been found, for instance, that poor people in dangerous neighborhoods create cognitive maps that vary from those in affluent areas. One study found that the poor tend to have far more restricted maps, sometimes limited to a nearby intersection, or even an apartment complex. This may reflect more limited mobility, but it's also been suggested that people in some groups choose not to "see" adjoining territory they view as belonging to other groups.) Other researchers have posited gender differences: Women, it's believed, depend more on landmarks for navigating, while men rely more on internal maps. As a result (if you subscribe to the gender theory), men are more aware of ordinal directions at any given moment; for landmark-driven women, which way is north isn't assigned as much weight as the location of an anticipated gas station or bridge. This disparity of course fuels the hoary comic staple of a couple getting lost. The woman, seeing no familiar landmarks, says, "We're lost, let's ask someone." The man says, "I know where we are." As it happens, both may be right. And studies have shown what we already know: that individuals inherently have different skills and capacities in cognitive mapping. Some people are just more cartographically minded and thus more accurate in their cognitive mapping than others, just as some possess more acute hearing or sight.

As these fields evolve, disagreements arise. Factions among cognitive mappers include "anchor point" mappers (who believe that we use landmarks as anchors and construct our spatial understanding around those, like the growth of salt crystals) and others who believe that views of landscapes or cityscapes trump landmarks as the elemental units in building a cognitive map.

Researchers since the early 1990s have largely agreed that Tolman was fundamentally incorrect in one essential way: Few now believe that each of us has a "map control room" containing intricate mental maps. This rejection arose in large part following a series of tests with rats and mice using something called the Morris water maze. Unlike a traditional maze, with its open and dead-end hallways, the water maze is a swimming tank equipped with a small platform for a rat to stand on to rest. The platform is hidden just below the water's surface by one of several means that make it invisible, such as dying the water. A rat is released from varying points in the tank and then watched to see the length of time and route it takes to find the platform. In the meantime, visual cues—such as distinct geometric shapes—are applied along the tank's edges to provide navigational cues. These can then be moved and manipulated, and parts of the tank can be blocked off to create areas that are as yet unmapped in the rat's mind. By running rats through this maze repeatedly with different variables, researchers determine how they use knowledge gained during earlier trial-and-error explorations to navigate within an unfamiliar situation.

Among the conclusions: Rats don't follow internal network maps; instead, they rely on point-to-point navigation. Similar tests in environments other than water tanks have been performed with bees and ants to track the directness of their routes when landmarks are changed. The results were similar: They seem to draw on stored snapshots that help them recall how to get from one spot to another.

Other studies involving humans, MRIs, and spatial recognition in the late 1990s produced similar results. It turns out we may not be all that different from rats, ants, and bees when it comes to plotting a route. We take a series of visual snapshots as we make our way through the world, store them, and then recall them as needed when we return. The reliability of this process can be uneven. Some studies have shown that we often learn the end of a route first and have the hardest time with the middle, so that's where we tend to make wrong turns. We do this consistently enough that police generally know to start searching for someone who's lost at the midpoint of their journey, not at either end.

In certain ways, driving a car is more like moving through a virtual environment with a joystick than exploring on foot. Drivers control their vehicles' movements by slight fore and aft tilting of our ankles and the occasional smooth, power steering–assisted movements of our hands and arms. Passengers do little other than lean slightly when the car goes into turns to offset the centrifugal effect. We don't use our large muscle groups to get from here to there, and we don't gain any proprioceptive knowledge from our muscles, joints, or tendons about direction or distance.

As noted earlier, we learn about where we are using input from multiple neural routes, including visual understanding and muscle memory. Traveling by car yields a rich harvest of visual information, and we collect snapshots as we go. Driving also provides "vestibular" information, which helps us define distance and space using mechanisms in the inner ear that assess acceleration and changes in gravity.

Yet the worlds of the walker and driver have about as much in common as the worlds of wolf and wasp. To start with the obvious: Walking is slower than driving, and that invariably shapes our perception. "An environment comfortably stimulating from a car becomes monotonously boring on foot," writes architect and architectural theorist Amos Rapoport, "while what is interesting on foot becomes chaotic in a car."

But is the way one views the world—how we translate what we see to what we think—fundamentally altered by mode of travel? Do our thought processes change? This was a question that cropped up not long after the emergence of the automobile. In 1928, author Walter S. Hinchman wrote of "the advantages of mental pedestrianism." He conceded that "the pedestrian mind doesn't get very far in one day, to be sure." But on foot the mind has "ample opportunity to see where it is going. It proceeds slowly enough to observe and record." And this was when cars were traveling at far slower speeds along rougher roads; what would Hinchman think of freeways and seventy-mile-per-hour cruise control?

It's often remarked that distances appear to shrink when we travel faster—our cities, our nations, our planet have all become seemingly more compact with rapid transport. Of course, distances don't shrink. A mile traversed by foot is the same mile traversed by car, just as a pound of feathers weighs the same as a pound of lead. But because we naturally link distance with time, our perceptions of space are shaped by speed. What took several weeks of travel by sailing ship or wagon now takes several hours by jet, and so one would expect that our idea of the space traversed would accordingly adjust.

But it may not adjust in the way you'd think. While the broader world may be perceived as smaller as you speed here and there, the more immediate distances around us may actually appear to be farther.

The urban planner Melvin Webber explored this as early as the 1960s, developing the concept of the "elastic mile." He noted that one's perception of what constitutes a mile varies depending on the speed of travel. So it turns out it's not just the actual exertion of walking a mile that dissuades many from taking to foot, but that they have also developed the belief that a given trip is far longer than it actually is.

For instance, a study conducted by the University of California Transportation Center asked people at a Los Angeles shopping mall to estimate the distance from where they stood to city hall. The respondents were classified into active travelers who walked or biked, transit riders who traveled chiefly by bus, and passive travelers reliant on cars. The active travelers estimated that city hall was 11.1 miles away. (It was actually 9.2 miles by car, or 10.5 by transit.) The transit riders estimated 17.3 miles, and the car passengers, on average, said 26.1 miles.

What's more, our perception of distance is also elastic depending on the motivation behind our walk. Studies have shown that we're inclined toward shorter walks when we're errand oriented—on a mission to pick up a half-and-half for coffee or the like. When we're out walking for recreation, on the other hand, we'll willingly walk farther, and the distance doesn't seem as long. A mile to the convenience store is, subjectively speaking, not the same as a mile through a leafy park. It's longer. In this context, and given his belief that he was on his life's errand, Weston may have seen his forty-mile days en route to the West Coast as little more than afternoon strolls.

May 8, 1909. Weston made his way into Topeka, Kansas, under the escort of several cheerful young men who'd come out to accompany him. In town, a sizable rabble had gathered to greet him at his hotel; inside, off the lobby, he found a reception room "filled with ladies." After he enjoyed an early dinner with newspaper reporters, he set off again in midafternoon, but soon faced a double setback: A mile out of town, heavy rain moved in, and at the same time a walking companion suddenly took quite ill. They sought refuge from the storm at a house "owned by colored people," and when the rain let up, retreated back to the hotel in Topeka, where Weston could spend the remainder of Saturday and Sunday at rest and his companion could recuperate. His mileage for the day: a mere eighteen miles, a sad bookend to his tremendous sixty-eight-mile day the previous Monday.

But after more than a full day of rest, he made up the shortfall the next Monday, making seventy-two miles by striding on through Manhattan, Kansas, to Junction City. (Still, these long rests were sometimes hard to recover from. Leaving just after midnight from Topeka, he was, one observer noted, "so stiff that he was compelled to walk down the stairway backward.") Limberness regained, he was now hoofing through the rolling Flint Hills, where the frequent rains had their benefits. "The fields of wheat and potatoes show healthy signs of big yields," Weston noted.

He marched on, mostly by day, but sometimes at night to avoid the strong sun and rising heat of late spring. At night, though, he was still buffeted by strong winds that sent him tumbling onto the tracks. One night the persistent wind blew out his lantern, which he was unable to relight. He continued on cautiously even though the "darkness was dense" and he could average only two miles per hour. On another Kansas evening, he was caught in a "small cyclone" and took shelter under a railroad bridge, where he found "enough cornstalks and grass to make it quite comfortable." He was initially joined by "a covy [*sic*] of quail, a snake, and a rabbit," but all fled.

The emptiness of the open plains was at times offset by fleeting company. A contingent of Elks came out to hail him in one town, and outside another he was joined for parts of his walk by an eager young man, then by "a prominent druggist" near yet another. Two young women joined him for three and a half miles at one point, and at Victoria, Kansas, he wrote, he "was met by the entire population." Near the town of Hays, he walked with the editor of the *Free Press,* plus a twenty-one-piece band.

In giving his evening lectures, something he often did after a long day's walk, Weston drew from a fairly narrow range of topics. One favored lecture was titled "The Vicissitudes of a Walker," which mixed anecdotes of travel on the road with advice on how and why one should take long walks. "Walking as an exercise is something I wish to see encouraged—something that I think will benefit the youth of America—will benefit the youth of any land," he'd say. "It is an exercise, not only healthy, but it is a pleasure, at times, and as good an exercise as man can take."

Among Weston's themes was how to live a healthy lifestyle. This involved being moderate in all aspects of life and walking every day in lieu of driving about in motorcars or slouching onto streetcars. "Weakness is the result of indolence, and I regret to say that there is too much indolence," he said in one of his talks. "The infants of today are reared in the hot-house and the youth is taught indolence, the mother of vice." Weston "looks at the trolley cars speeding over the landscape and thinks that the race is growing effeminate," reported the *San Jose News* in 1909. The new subways in New York whisking New Yorkers from Times Square to City Hall were "foolish," he believed, best reserved for old women and children in arms. Everybody else could walk.

In the first decade of the 1900s, and in part owing to the interest in old-fashioned pedestrianism Weston had generated, new walking clubs sprouted up. Weston himself was involved in organizing the Weston Walking Club in New York, in which he would lead packs of boys and girls on marches for several miles. On one walk, some four thousand children showed up to walk two miles with him, mostly boys, some girls, and more than a smattering of old-timers who wanted to see if they still had it in them to keep up with Weston. "The good he is doing in arousing a liking for pedestrianism has been far-reaching," noted Oregon's *Coos Bay Times* in 1909.

Weston's commandments for healthy living also involved abstinence from certain indulgences. Among the things to be avoided was smoking. Weston reserved a special distaste for cigarettes. ("Smoke cigars or a pipe if you must," he allowed.) His dislike may have arisen in the 1870s, when he often competed in indoor walking races on tracks surrounded by smoking spectators. Weston complained bitterly about having to make his way through the foul miasma. He liked to say that more people were ruined by cigarettes than by the demon rum, which was not a common sentiment leading up to Prohibition in 1919. As for liquor, he was fond of pouring whiskey into his boots, as noted earlier; he occasionally let a taste of wine or whiskey breach his lips; and he admitted in 1909 that enjoyed a bit of beer when playing euchre with friends. But for the most part, he didn't care for the effects of alcohol. "When you hear anyone hammering at human nature he's a poor old grouch," he once told a reporter in Syracuse. "He probably drinks too much."

In other matters, Weston's instructions for prolonging youth as one headed into old age were not terrifically complex: "Eat prunes daily; take a cold sponge bath each morning; walk to and from work; don't keep late hours." As simple as walking itself.

Onward Weston pressed across the open plains and low hills of Kansas, keeping to train tracks that seemed to forever converge in the distance. A silo might appear on a horizon and grow marginally larger, then disappear over the course of an hour. A farmhouse might do the same. He was keenly attuned to the conditions of the road (mud one day "was of a new variety—black, greasy, very sticky"). In the broad, uncluttered spaces, clouds became his principal landmarks, shifting and moving constantly, but offering no sense of scale or distance. ("The clouds are gathering in the west, and it looks very much like a storm is coming" was one typical observation.) His surroundings had devolved into something like a sensory deprivation tank, with little to entertain or distract him other than "an occasional burial ground."

Weston had a somewhat melancholy reaction to this unfamiliar landscape. The sheer novelty of the land may have triggered this in part, but it might have reflected something deeper as well. It raises a question: What sort of landscape best fulfills human needs?

———————————

Some have postulated that the ideal landscape for humans is a mixture of terrain combining savanna and forest. This has been characterized as the "prospect" and "refuge" landscape. The thought is that we're consistently drawn to environments that have a combination of both distant views (to spot prey and potential predators) and shelter or protection (to hide swiftly in the event that we find ourselves suddenly vulnerable).

The theory suggests that humans are drawn to this sort of mixed environment—more than, say, to the middle of a dense jungle or the Great

Plains—because we all share the same basic genome, the essentials of which were established when our ancestors were still living in central Africa and fine-tuning the mechanics of walking upright.

Evidence of this is spotty but intriguing. Cross-cultural studies suggest there's a widespread human preference for a certain kind of tree: one with a dense canopy and a trunk that bifurcates close to the ground. In other words, a tree that's easy to ascend and take cover in.

Two artists, Vitaly Komar and Alexander Melamid, discovered a similar aesthetic proclivity in the early 1990s when they commissioned survey takers to find what qualities people in ten countries preferred in their paintings. Then, like police sketch artists, they painted those preferences. Most landscapes looked like European calendar art. This project was meant as a sly commentary on market-driven creativity, but inadvertently demonstrated what appears to be an innate attraction to vistas of meadows and trees.

Is that preference truly embedded in our genes? Some, including the art critic Arthur Danto, doubt it. Danto suggested that these general preferences may more accurately be a demonstration of the pop-art industry's influence over global tastes. The art on calendars doesn't reflect an innate preference for the savanna, that is, but rather creates the longing.

We don't gravitate to this sort of landscape only in art and calendars, it turns out, but also in the real world. The savanna-and-tree landscape hit its apogee in popularity in the eighteenth century under famed British gardener Lancelot "Capability" Brown (1716–1783), who was renowned for designing grassy, open fields studded with randomly placed clumps of wide-crowned trees. He designed some 170 parks in Great Britain and is essentially the patron saint of the suburban backyard. Credit (or blame) him for the ubiquity of lawns edged with small stands of Japanese maples or crape myrtles, a sort of bonsai version of the African savanna.

So that may be the static landscape we prefer to gaze upon. But what about when we're in motion? Is there an archetypal walkway that we're hardwired to be drawn toward when in motion?

If a preference does exist, it may be the linear equivalent of the savanna, or what's been called a "keyhole pathway." These are straight or slightly curving routes overarched thickly with tree limbs and creating a tunnel effect, offering protection from light rain (and harsh sun) along with a distant view (if slightly obstructed). It's also permeable along the sides, allowing those on foot to quickly duck and cover if a threat arises.

One person who understood this sort of landscape was Lucy Maud Montgomery, a contemporary of Weston's who grew up on Canada's Prince Edward Island and wrote the immensely popular novel *Anne of Green Gables*, first published in 1908. Overarched pathways were common features in her stories and at times served as a powerful metaphor—in Lover's Lane, within the ring of birches of Idlewild. They were places of both transit and transition. Montgomery was also an accomplished amateur photographer, and many of her best prints featured, in the words of one biographer, "bends in roads, distant circles or keyholes of light, and archways made by curving branches, all carefully framed to capture a way of seeing as well as a sight." She felt at home in these places. "I always feel better after a stroll under those green arches where nature reveals herself in all her beauty," she once wrote.

Striding along a keyhole pathway, a walker feels pulled along, often captivated by what lies ahead, curious about how that fragment of the view ahead fits into the whole. As geologist and writer N. S. Shaler put it in the *Atlantic Monthly* in 1898: "In general, the more the scene has to give, the narrower the range of vision which can profitably be applied to it."

A keyhole pathway meshes with our innate desire for a story: there's a beginning, a middle, and an end, with a gradual unfolding of episodes along the way. Compare that with crossing a plain or desert, where one knows the whole story before a single step. A keyhole view edits and condenses while establishing a mystery. On a forested pathway, we keep walking to see what the vista around the next bend or over the next rise will bring.

Architectural historians have noted that the stout columns lining the naves of great cathedrals aren't simply structural, keeping the roof from colliding with the earth. They also mimic the trunks of mighty trees and lend the aspect of a path through a still, ancient forest. The central cities of early European and Latin American cities were often lined with long arcades, which could feel like forested pathways cut in stone. Bologna, Italy, has about twenty-five miles of covered walkways. Paris had shopping and dining arcades that bisected stout buildings, like shortcuts through a grove. Taking a less formalized approach, nineteenth-century urban walkways in the United States were often partially covered by balconies or galleries, or by retractable awnings in dense streetcar suburbs in the early twentieth century.

After five million years of perfecting the skill of walking upright, we've lost the battle in maintaining the spaces that feel like home, spaces where we feel welcome to linger and relax. And this undoubtedly contributes to our walking less. "Landscape design" has the sound of something effete and precious, an art practiced by the overeducated for the overcompensated. But it's not. In fact, it may be among our central survival mechanisms.

―――――――――

How we plot and find our way through our world and how we perceive distance are influenced by how we travel. But even more, our relationship with the land around us is shaped by the stories we craft from objects of both natural and cultural history, our connections to our society's past, our understanding of links between places. Aborigines in Australia are fabled for their songlines, those long walking routes in which landmarks such as hills and gullies become parts of intricate, sung stories that capture and explain their cultural history. It's hard to imagine such stories being woven by Americans today from a landscape sculpted of corporate interests and transportation policy decrees, which often emanate from hundreds of miles away.

Consider the lullaby of the freeway. Driving down an on-ramp to merge onto a four-lane roadway, it's as if we're entering a day nursery for adults, devoid of detail and subtlety. As traffic theorist Tom Vanderbilt has suggested, the high-speed driving environment resembles a toddler's playroom: It's all basic colors and simple geometric shapes. A red octagon means stop. Green means go. An upside-down yellow triangle means "Watch out!" You strive to keep your colorful car inside the fat white lines, as if it were a crayon at use in a coloring book. We push on pedals and turn a big wheel. We communicate with others by blaring a horn that plays a single note, or by employing a hand signal that involves a single finger.

Automobiles are the Plato's caves of the modern world. From them we see only shadows, the rough outlines of our existence. The map of this world is drawn with fat, cartoonish markers rather than finely sharpened pencils. The detailed lines of the etchings around us are lost, replaced with hulking shapes whizzing by at sixty miles per hour, vague and often amorphous forms, save for the jaunty and startlingly blue Best Buy sign and the inquisitive yellow eyebrows of the McDonald's arches jutting over distant rooftops.

But choosing to move freely outside those lines, to get off the constructed highways and explore a world painted with a camel-hair brush, seems to bind us more tightly to the land. Exploration of such a detailed environment yields a complex education, and it's a technique that appears to be hardwired in us, at least when we're younger. Children have been observed to avoid simplicity when choosing routes. A 2004 study looked at how adults and children, each traveling solo, plotted their walk between home and school. The result? "Elementary school children as a group took much more complex routes than their adult counterparts." They tended to make random turns and would move parallel to or even away from their destination for brief stretches. It's postulated that this behavior reflects the learning process, and that this "environmental manipulation" is an essential part of personal growth to develop personal competence and a sense of space, and to feel soundly anchored in the world. Children who are chauffeured everywhere in sealed cocoons sidestep these essential catalysts of development.

———

Walking at its most elemental is purely transportation, going from one location to another, like using the mind only for coming up with a solution to a problem. But walking can also be like the best sort of daydreaming, a way to explore without direction. The art of the long, aimless walk was accorded uncommon respect and attention across the Atlantic in the nineteenth century. The flâneurs—from the French word for "one who strolls"—filled a strange ecological and cultural niche. Flâneurs were a distinctly European invention, specifically Parisian, and they once occupied avenues and boulevards. (Although the tendencies of the flâneur were first identified by American Edgar Allan Poe in his short story "The Man of the Crowd.") Flâneurs walk. They observe. They read the cityscape as they are moving discreetly through it. They favor walking *lentement,* and spend considerable idle time at outdoor cafés simply observing. The flâneur is a man of the crowd (and almost always a man), but isolated from the masses: He moves, he observes, he does not participate. He's become an icon of the city; his typology did not exist before the modern city emerged. The flâneur was "a scientist of the sidewalk, a detached observer, dissecting the metropolitan crowd," wrote urban historian P. D. Smith. The art of flânerie was most concisely described by Honoré de Balzac as "the gastronomy of the eye."

Walking by oneself through a city brings solitude more than isolation:

You are alone, but with others. You are encased within a bubble that travels with you. That's the essence of the flâneur: being a part of life while being apart at the same time.

Many Americans appear to have a hard time emulating the world of the flâneur (although some urban hipsters may have rediscovered it of late) not only because it's slow, and not only because the built environment often resists it. (What can one gain from a stroll through parking lots, across divided highways, and down unpeopled culs-de-sac fronted with impassive garage doors?) But also because our language lacks the vocabulary to describe it, and so the concept can seem alien and cumbersome. "English has no positive word for lingering on streets," wrote British transportation consultant John Whitelegg. Writer Jay Griffiths expanded on Whitelegg's point: "In English, slowness in general is often treated with pity (a slow learner, retarded), with derision (sluggish) or with suspicion (loitering). . . . Latin yields the wisdom of slowness—*festina lente* (make haste slowly); Italian dignifies it with *largo* or offers the radiant serenity of *dolce fa niente* (literally, sweet doing nothing); while French provides the subversive flirtation of the *flâneur,* the dusky-eyed pauser, stroller and observer."

And what words have we contributed to describe our public space? "Gridlock," "underpass," "road rage," "frontage road," and "left-turn lane."

If the nineteenth-century French made walking and observing an art, their twentieth-century inheritors sought to convert it into a science. They dubbed it psychogeography, and their laboratory was the city; their apparatus of discovery, their feet.

Much of this push was driven by those associated with the Situationist International, a revolutionary group founded in 1957 in (yet again) France whose influence peaked during the 1968 student riots in Paris. This small, rather intellectually opaque group advocated for a world that rejected the advanced capitalist system, in which they believed spectacle (that is, the mass media and its emphasis on consumption) was manufactured to distract everyday people from their unfortunate state of existence. The movement called for creating temporary situations in which one could more clearly analyze and understand one's true desires and separate these from the faux desires manufactured by a corrupt, manipulative system.

One such situation was the *derivé,* which is French for "drift." "The derivé was an act of urban (and self-) exploration, best conducted under the influence of alcohol," wrote P. D. Smith. The Situationists believed that the derivé was "the key to unlocking the city's secrets and revealing the imaginary, and even the ideal, city." One walked, one observed, one sought out authentic experiences.

Balzac—who inspired the flâneur—was replaced in the hero's pantheon by essayist Thomas De Quincey (1785–1859), the author of *Confessions of an English Opium Eater* and an inveterate walker of city streets. De Quincey wrote of his long rambles through gritty nineteenth-century London under the influence of opium. When he reversed course to return home, De Quincey often opted for an unmapped, desultory route—or, as he put it, he sought "a north-west passage, instead of circumnavigating all the capes and head-lands I had doubled in my outward voyage." This led him farther into "terrae incognitae" through alleys and "a sphynx's riddles of streets without thoroughfares." At the time that De Quincey was exploring London, sailors were seeking an Arctic shortcut to the treasures of the Orient, and the only way to actually find it was to enter into the ice and wait to see where you came out. Death and cannibalism might (and occasionally did) await, but it was the only route to discovery. This became a metaphor for psychogeographers who felt that aimless rambling, of setting off into the unknown—the derivé—was the way not only to explore the northwest passage of one's own consciousness, but also to understand the actual life of the city (with prescient additional benefits: More recent studies suggest regularly trying new routes between, say, home and work helps maintain brain health and strengthen problem-solving abilities.)

The Situationists spelled out an admirably clear and straightforward definition of psychogeography: "the study of the precise laws and specific effects of the geographical environment, consciously organized or not, on the emotions and behavior of individuals." Unfortunately, that's where clarity ends. Much of the Situationist writing then drifts into an ice field of jargon and self-referential babble, where it finds itself frozen in place with a setting sun bringing on darkness. In one document, the Situationists insist that situationism is "a meaningless term . . . obviously devised by anti situationists." Cue the cannibals.

French Marxist Guy Debord (1931–1994) was among the founders of the Situationist International and a leading advocate for psychogeography. He insisted that it was a hard science, like chemistry, and that someone skilled in psychogeography could identify what amounts to the chemical makeups of varied urban environments and their effects on humans. How?

This was accomplished via the random walk. As Merlin Coverley explained in his concise overview of psychogeography, "Emotional zones that cannot be determined simply by architectural or economic conditions must be determined by following the aimless stroll." From this, one devised "a new cartography characterized by a complete disregard for the traditional and habitual practices of the tourist." Or as Greil Marcus put it, moving at random by foot allowed "the physical town [to be] replaced by an imaginary city."

You drift. You daydream. You find De Quincey's "north-west passage" into your subconscious, where the city's structures of past and present speak to you. The random walk, in theory, can help us reconfigure our cognitive maps, rearranging assumptions and ideas as we relocate landmarks and lanes through chance discovery. Walkers are "practitioners of the city," as Michel de Certeau, the French scholar, put it.

Crafting a truly random walk takes some doing, since cities are designed with major arterials and boulevards to encourage directed movement, and culs-de-sac to discourage it. And we're conditioned to follow certain routes. One favored method is to bring dice and roll them at each intersection to determine whether to go right, left, or straight. Another method employed by psychogeographers was to explore London on foot by using a map of Paris.

Anyway. The central premise is that cities are meant to be walked, just as words are meant to be spoken.

———

Weston was the accidental companion of flâneurs in the late nineteenth century. He spent several years in England, competing in high-profile walking races at the time they were drifting through the streets. Of course, he had little in common with the slow strollers and observing idlers; he would have regarded them as obstacles to be circumvented. In his writings he never mentioned the life of the city street as captivating or otherwise. Streets were something to be moved through swiftly and with as few stops as possible.

But he did evidently share at least one other habit with the flâneurs. He dabbled in mind-altering substances.

By the late 1870s and early 1880s, Weston was hailed as one of the greatest walkers in the world, but not universally so. The American press, in particular, took great sport in attacking him as an unredeemed humbug for failing to achieve his boastful goals. (Weston "nearly always succeeds in failing to do what he undertakes in the matter of pedestrianism, except in one thing—that of large announcements," a writer for a weekly paper groused in 1875.) Yet in England, he took up one challenge after another, and prevailed again and again. He beat William Perkins, a much younger local champion and eight-mile-an-hour walker, in a twenty-four-hour race at London's Agricultural Hall. (Perkins dropped out after 65 miles; Weston logged 109.) He trumped another younger competitor, Alexander Clark, in a forty-eight-hour race. (Weston topped 175 miles.) In both races, Weston's abilities of near-instant recovery were noted with awe. He often appeared beaten down and fatigued during a race, and more than one observer speculated that after Weston lay down to rest he would never arise to finish. But following a nap of fifteen or twenty minutes, he'd spring up and start walking circuits, looking no worse for the wear. ("He sleeps little, whether on a tramp or at ordinary times," wrote one person who'd spent time with him, "claiming that too long a sleep makes him heavy and lethargic.")

Yet to some watchers, something seemed slightly amiss in England. In those first two British matches, Weston was seen repeatedly and mechanically chewing on something, and observers noted that his lips were stained brown. As it happened, he was being observed more closely than usual this time. Doctors associated with the *British Medical Journal* keenly followed Weston on one race, taking detailed measurements of his inputs and his outputs in an effort to understand how nitrogen was processed in the human body. (The report noted, among other things, that his urine at the start of a race was amber, then during the race it was more "straw-colored.") Dr. John Ashburton Thompson wrote that the chewing and the stains "lead to the suspicions that he is refreshing himself with a quid of tobacco." But Weston was a strident opponent of tobacco and a well-known abstainer. He denied it. And as it turned out, he wasn't chewing tobacco. "That substance," the doctor wrote, "is the dried leaf of Erthroxylon Coca [sic]."

Coca leaves were at the time considered an object of benign curiosity, something used by South American Indians and brought back by explorers from the Andes. If Weston had been found to be chewing dried whale blubber from the Arctic, it might have provoked equal curiosity. It wasn't until late in the century that word of the addictive and potentially harmful properties of processed coca leaves—cocaine—would emerge.

But coca leaves had already been hailed for their beneficial effects, deemed useful by dentists, surgeons, and those afflicted with seasickness. Weston's biographers in *A Man in a Hurry* draw a series of intriguing links between Weston's behavior on the British track and the experiments then being conducted by Sir Robert Christison, president of the British Medical Association and one of Queen Victoria's doctors. Christison was fascinated by the purported powers of coca leaves. So he experimented on himself to gain firsthand experience (his son and some students also participated). During one test, Christison, a septuagenarian, climbed Ben Vorlich, a challenging Scottish peak of 3,224 feet. On the summit he skipped lunch and instead chewed coca leaves, then rested for 45 minutes. He stood and began his long trek back down. "I at once felt that all fatigue was gone," he reported, "and I went down the long descent with an ease like that which I used to enjoy in my mountainous rambles in my youth."

Christison's experience closely paralleled Weston's behavior in his first British races. Weston, too, showed remarkable powers of recovery, and continued to have a low pulse rate and body temperature, a vast capacity for repetitive behavior (step, step, step), and an increase in temperamental behavior.

The *British Medical Journal* noted, somewhat prophetically, "pushed to excess, coca is said to become a narcotic; and we shall, no doubt, hear a good deal more both of its use and abuse. Possibly we may be indebted to Mr. Weston for the introduction of a new stimulant and a new narcotic: two forms of novelty in excitement which our modern civilisation is likely highly to esteem." During World War I, British soldiers are believed to have been issued tablets made with cocaine, which were sometimes referred to as "forced march tablets."

Weston was unforthcoming about his secret ingredient, and slow to acknowledge his use of coca leaves. Eventually, he did cop to it, noting that it brought strength and made it easier to keep his mind on the task at hand. The public that had raised the issue of Weston's coca-leaf use moved on to other concerns, as apparently did Weston himself. No further reports of his use of coca leaves were published.

The flâneur's and pscyhogeographer's interest in getting lost, whether sober or soused, seems quaint today. In part, this is because the notion of getting lost is fading, like a buffalo nickel. Indeed, just as species of animals become extinct through predation, various forms of physical space can disappear. One of these is the Land of the Lost. Getting lost was once commonplace—pathways were poorly marked, maps were inaccurate, the sun would go behind clouds, disorienting us. Then came the predator, which took the form of a GPS unit in our pocket or on our dashboard.

As with so much else, we've outsourced to electronics yet another defining human task—that of staying found. "You are here" was once an arrow on a map mounted on a wall or kiosk. You looked for it, then put your finger on it and suddenly felt grounded. In an anti-Copernican reversal, the "you are here" spot on maps is now the red dot or the crosshairs on a moving electronic screen. We are always "here," and the world moves around us. We don't have to worry about where we are, and that gives us tacit permission to ignore the landscape around us. We don't need to note actual waypoints and landmarks—one of our foundational cognitive skills—because we needn't worry about finding our way back.

Geographic illiteracy is not a new issue. A longtime staple of wire-service news has been the survey piece focusing on how poorly Americans fare when it comes to locating places on maps, particularly countries and capitals abroad, but also landmarks at home. Nor is our map incompetence a new problem—thirty years ago a professor wrote of his rising concern about "the inability to read and draw meaning from simple maps used in history texts and teaching."

But map illiteracy seems to be galloping ahead at breakneck speed: More and more of those who've grown up with smartphones and laptops—the "digital natives," as education writer Marc Prensky has called them—see it as natural to have a map automatically center itself around them. There's always a little screen icon (a compass rose, or a little dart), which, when tapped, shows us where we are within a few dozen feet. Finding oneself on a paper map, lacking buttons or automation, is now practically relegated to the dark sciences, like reading entrails.

Research shows that how we perceive the environment around us depends upon how we get around. One study, published by a group of German psychologists in the *Journal of Environmental Psychology* in 2006, tracked test subjects navigating through a zoo. One group was aided with electronic GPS-style devices, the other used paper maps. They were tested

along the way about both their route memory and their "survey" memory, or what they noticed while walking. Both did well on route memory (although the electronic device users did marginally worse), but when it came to remembering sights along the way, the paper map users did a far superior job—or, in the words of the researchers, they were able to "encode, transform, and memorize spatial information" more effectively.

Being lost is an essential human condition, one that triggers profound reactions that take us briefly to a place of primeval terror. Working our way out of the Land of the Lost requires us to balance the hot emotions of help-lessness against the cool of rationality. ("Stay calm," reads the advice to Boy Scouts. "You can't use your brain well if you're in a panic. Breathe slowly and deeply. Drink some water, eat a little something.") Abandoning the experience of being lost is like losing our facility for empathy; it's a central part of what made us human, the bedrock upon which both mobility and mind were built. (Being lost and then becoming found is also the bedrock of Christianity.) Today, being lost comes about chiefly when the battery in one's smartphone dies and there's no place to charge it. You're disconnected from the world.

Some contemporary psychogeographers, who understand the allure and power of being turned around, have recently embraced the same technology that keeps us found. In fact, they've harnessed it to make us disoriented. One can now outsource to software the task of getting lost.

A smartphone app called Serendipitor is billed as "an alternative naviga-tion app for the iPhone that helps you find something by looking for some-thing else." This is not very helpful, but the Web site goes on to note, more helpfully, that "in the near future, finding your way from point A to point B will not be the problem. Maintaining consciousness of what happens along the way might be more difficult." The makers claim their app is "designed to introduce small slippages and minor displacements within an otherwise optimized and efficient route."

Toward that end, Serendipitor, using Google Maps as a base, plots for you an indirect route to a destination. Along the way, "small detours and minor interruptions" pop up, with instructions such as "Turn left on Chestnut Street and then follow a pigeon until it flies away. Take a photo of it flying." These suggestions may be ignored, but they do prompt observation.

We tend to think of street maps as two-dimensional objects extending north, south, east, and west to the edges, where that particular world ends. But as Bernard Rudofsky notes, "A street is not an area but a volume." It contains a third dimension. And you can't comprehend that volume by looking at a map or an aerial view or even by clicking your way through on Google Street View. It can be done only by moving through it physically, preferably by foot, with views unobstructed and muscle memory plotting where you are and where you've been.

Walking across the land also allows one to explore the dimension of time by, for example, observing the evolution of the landscape through history, whether it's a natural landscape in New England and the progression of dominant trees in the forest is from birch to white pine to maple, or a city, where buildings pass through functional and stylistic phases, from stern Greek Revival to elaborate Italianate to lean Modernism, each containing the kernel of a story of its era. "Walking is an activity in which one is not cut off, as one is in an aeroplane or when too busy or going too fast or not paying attention to one's surroundings," wrote anthropologist and author Allice Legat in 2007. "To walk is to pay close and careful attention to one's surroundings while thinking with the multitude of stories one has heard."

When walking, we are literally following in the footsteps of our ancestors. And we're not only absorbing the stories of the land, but telling those stories as well, just by being on the street and populating vacant spaces.

Weston was very much attuned to the world through which he walked. He would have seen and heard most everything around him, and gotten stories from his temporary companions. Although most of his dispatches focused on the wretchedness of the weather, the tenaciousness of the mud, and the enthusiasm of the crowds that greeted him, he also noted much else—like the bronze memorial statue to an earlier inhabitant in upstate New York, and "the most beautiful canyon in the world" near the border between Nevada and California. A reporter who interviewed him on his walk in 1909 found him "an intelligent observer" who was "aware of the great changes in the cities which he walks through."

Those on foot today, of course, have ways of isolating themselves that Weston could not imagine. This can be summed up in one word: earbuds.

We plug these into our ears, manipulate some controls on a scratch-resistant screen, and we've effectively locked out ambient sound as we create a new interior habitat that's often at odds with what's going on around us. We enter into a cinematic world, where the soundtrack can overpower us, making the information taken in by the eyes seem thin by comparison, both relegating it to background and changing it according to the emotional language of the music.

Walking while plugged in isn't full sensory deprivation, of course. While exterior sound may be blocked out, walkers still process information about sight, smells, and temperature as we walk. And we're harvesting vast amounts of proprioceptive information, our muscles informing us about where we are and how far we've gone.

If our gadgets were solely sound devices, it would be one thing. But the same gadgets that serve as conduits for conveying music and audiobooks into our ears are also complex portals to other worlds. Smartphones provide a virtual news crawl of information about where our friends are and what adult beverages they're drinking, about new restaurants that should be visited, about what turn to make at the next intersection.

"People used to walk with eyes to the sand and water" on a visit to the beach, MIT professor and author Sherry Turkle told the *New York Times* in 2011. "Now everyone walks with a device. No one is looking at the sand. . . . The technology which looked so good 15 to 20 years ago now looks like it helps us miss out on the complexities and grittiness and ups and downs of what real life has to offer."

The danger of texting while driving has attracted considerable attention nationwide—it's been shown to raise the chance of being involved in an accident to essentially the same degree as driving while drunk—while the hazards of walking and texting are just starting to attract study. But it's increasingly obvious that there's an impact. Anecdotally, there's no shortage of stories of distracted walkers wandering into traffic or tripping over sidewalk curbs or striding headfirst into utility poles. One woman made small news in 2012 after walking off a pier into Lake Michigan while texting.

Some studies have looked at the psychology of this in more depth. One, published in the journal *Gait and Posture* in 2012, took thirty-three test subjects, gave them a target a few dozen feet away, and then instructed them to walk there—some without any distractions, some while talking on a phone, others while texting. Those texting ended up walking 13 percent farther than the others and showed a "lateral deviation" of 61 percent. (Less surprisingly, texters also were one-third slower in getting to the target.) "These results suggest that the dual-task of walking while using a cell phone impacts executive function and working memory and influences gait to such a degree that it may compromise safety," the authors noted, adding that "texting creates a significantly greater interference effect" than talking on a phone while walking.

A society of walking texters also faces a more metaphysical danger than simple carnage in the roadways or violence on the sidewalks. That, of course, is the zombie apocalypse—armies of dazed people walking blankly through what might as well be generic space, passing through but not being part of the world around them. They are the opposite of flâneurs; they move through a world from which they are completely divorced. This world is now populated with people shuffling around airports or malls, identifiable by their persistent downward gazes and occasional forefinger flicks. They will stop abruptly to tap on a glass screen, and infrequently look up. When they do glance up, a brief squall of confusion often crosses their faces as they temporarily reorient themselves, then look down again and plunge back into their private, parallel worlds, scraping slowly onward.

Recent research published in the journal *Psychological Science* has shown that being constantly connected electronically can result in a marked decline in our ability—that is, in our actual biological capacity—to connect with other people in real life. Just as our muscles atrophy from sitting too much, researchers found that part of our cardiovascular system, the part that links mind and heart through the vagus nerve, can lose tone through lack of use. "If you don't regularly exercise your ability to connect face to face, you'll eventually find yourself lacking some of the basic biological capacity to do so," writes study coauthor and psychologist Barbara L. Fredrickson in the *New York Times*.

Others have concluded that we can lose the capacity to connect with the natural and built environment around us as well. "Just as over-reliance on air travel can undermine our sense of movement through space," writes Iowa State University professor of philosophy Joseph Kupfer, "so too can over-reliance on virtual, electronic connections erode our connection to actual physical places." He notes that connecting through electronic devices is not just telephone or television on steroids, but different in kind: "Our spoken and written communications are from anywhere to nowhere in particular." The "skills and habits" required to navigate a place begin to atrophy. "And even when somewhere, the place easily recedes into a blurry background," he writes. Places attenuate into pure, almost abstract volume wholly lacking detail—a wall here, a corridor there—as do the people around us, who become those faceless, Giacometti-like stick figures that populate architectural models, always walking, never arriving.

"Electronically produced experience is isolating," Kupfer notes with succinctness. "It isolates us from other people and from ourselves."

PART III

Land

CHAPTER 6

THE LOST GEOGRAPHY OF WALKING

The truth is I dislike cars. Whenever I drive a car, I have the feeling I have become invisible. People on the street cannot see you; they only watch your rear fender until it is out of their way.

—***THE MOVIEGOER,*** by Walker Percy

In 1994, an anthropologist named Cesare Marchetti published an observation that was at once simple and profound. Marchetti's Constant, as it came to be known, proposes that humans are willing to spend about an hour each day out and about, that is, traveling and unsheltered—a figure that Marchetti said has been reasonably consistent from prehistory to the present. The time our ancestors spent away from their shelters—starting in the treetops, then moving to natural caves and on to increasingly complex structures they'd built—has always been part of an elaborate calculation. We innately desire larger territory and the rewards that may come from it, but there's a price to pay: "It requires the physical exertion of moving over large distances, and [it] means [being] in the open, under the possible threat from enemies and predators," Marchetti wrote. Another researcher, Yacov Zahavi, a World Bank planner, had previously concluded that globally the "mean exposure time"—the amount of time humans everywhere spend outside—is approximately an hour. Marchetti built on that, calculating that at a walking speed of five kilometers an hour, a human's territory is effectively two and a half kilometers, or about a mile and a half.

Marchetti noticed that this innate preference subtly persisted around the world. But like fossilized raindrops, you would only notice this if you looked closely. For instance, Venice is exactly three miles across; indeed, the walls of virtually every city up until about 1800, from Rome to Persepolis, Marchetti noted, were three miles or less across, allowing anyone living on the margins to get to the center and back in an hour. Geographic studies in southern Germany show that as a group, small villages form essentially a honeycomb, with their centers about four miles apart.

The key here is that the constant isn't distance. It's time—the amount we're willing to spend in travel. The actual distance becomes a variable, which changes as transportation technology expands our range. First horse-drawn trolleys, then steam trains and electric streetcars and subways, and then cars and airplanes—our horizons are effectively widening as we remain in thrall to some dim message emanating from our genes, telling us an hour out and about is okay, but more than that, not so much.

In every early city, people first got about on foot. Owning a horse expanded the range for the more affluent, but horses weren't as common for personal transport—either traveling on horseback or being pulled in carriages—as we might believe from the movies. Horse-drawn omnibuses, however, became common in the first half of the nineteenth century and did expand the commuting range for the masses. But it was the arrival of the electric streetcar, railway, and subway that allowed urban residents to move beyond the walkable downtown core while maintaining Marchetti's imperative: They could still get to work within about thirty minutes, doubling the distance they might travel on foot. By 1850, Boston had some eighty-three commuter rail stations linked to its downtown. Manhattan expanded its effective range into the outer boroughs; Philadelphia, to Chestnut Hill; Chicago, to Oak Park. Streetcars pulled by horses linked other communities, such as New Orleans to Carrollton, and in 1888 the first large-scale public electric streetcar system began running in Richmond, Virginia, ushering in an era of faster and more efficient transit for daily commuters. Streetcar suburbs bloomed like forsythia on a series of attenuating branches.

Then came the automobile, and the mark humans left on the earth became more dispersed. Settlement patterns now looked less like flowers on a branch than like stars brought forth by a supernova, at least in those cities unbounded by oceans or lakes or mountains. As automobiles dropped in price, they swiftly shifted from being novelties to being workhorses, allowing early adopters to move farther from population centers' cores and establish homesteads far afield. Winding suburban lanes were incised upon what had been rigidly square farm fields, and strip malls were built along the heavily traveled routes between the suburbs and the downtown grids.

Eventually the economic importance of the downtown grids diminished; instead, shops were clustered first at shopping centers and then at malls amid vast parking lagoons. The same happened with the work environment, as office parks with abundant parking spaces cropped up outside the core near new retail villages, creating what journalist Joel Garreau lastingly dubbed "edge cities." Traffic went from a pattern of ebb and flow to a more chaotic bounding about, like overstimulated molecules in a solution; a growing number of people even chose to live in cities and commute to the suburbs for work.

In an urban setting, a car commuter can travel roughly six or seven times faster than a walker. That results in an effective city size roughly six or seven times as large as Venice, or about twenty-one miles across. That's about four hundred square miles, depending on the configuration of the city borders. Which is more or less the size of Indianapolis, Dallas, and Los Angeles. (American cities that were established when people chiefly walked tend to measure less than a hundred square miles and include Richmond, Virginia; Washington, DC; Baltimore; Boston; Providence, Rhode Island; and the borough of Manhattan. Some older cities that started out compact annexed suburbs and expanded their political boundaries in the streetcar and auto ages and now exceed their original sizes. These include Philadelphia, Atlanta, and New Orleans.)

US Census Bureau data appear to support Marchetti's Constant. The latest data (from 2009) show that the mean one-way commuting time in the United States is 25.1 minutes. This has been more or less unchanged since 1980, the first year the census started collecting this information. In 1980 the mean commuting time was slightly under 22 minutes; it then rose to about 25 minutes in 2000, where it's held steady. (Worth noting: About 2 percent of commuters, or more than 3.2 million people, commute more than 90 minutes each way to work, which undoubtedly is at cross-purposes with their genes and contributes to broad but deep-seated ill will toward all humanity, but especially the guy in the car directly ahead of them.)

New transportation technology has continued to expand the thirty-minute radius, especially in Europe and Japan. Twenty-four double-decker bullet trains operate on a sophisticated network within a hundred miles of Tokyo—it takes about fifty minutes to travel the sixty-five miles from Takasaki to downtown, with stops—creating a commuter shed that would have dazzled the Romans. And while you may not personally know anyone who commutes by taking a commercial flight to work, they're out there. In 2000, the *New York Times* profiled the growing trend of airline commuters, including about a dozen who commuted 250 miles by commercial jet from Rochester, New York, to New York City. (Most jet commuters do it weekly and bivouac locally before returning on the weekend; it doesn't make economic sense to fly daily, and also doesn't account for the aggravation of unpredictable security lines and weather delays.) The *Times* noted that in areas where real estate is exorbitantly priced, like Silicon Valley in California, it actually might make economic sense to buy a cheap home near a good airport and fly in regularly.

May 17, 1909. Weston spent Sunday in WaKeeny, Kansas, partaking of a "restful day and a most refreshing sleep." He napped in the afternoon and at 10:30 Sunday night ate a large meal before setting off at five minutes after midnight. He was accompanied by a small contingent of well-wishing men and women, most of whom kept pace with him for several miles out of town; one man remained with him for twenty-two miles, until they stopped for breakfast in Quinter. Weston was feeling "in excellent condition, not having pain or ache of any kind," and he pressed on through the small farming towns of Park, Grainfield, Grinnell, and Campus. "All along the route, whether early in the morning, or midday, I am met by enthusiasts who usually have some fresh milk or an eggnog for me," he wrote. In Grinnell, several Englishmen who had seen him walk in England some years before came out to meet him. He made sixty-six miles that Monday.

In the cities like Kansas City and Denver, Weston was walking though the golden era of urban transit, with trains and streetcars and horse-drawn trolleys. When Weston strode into a midsize town en route to San Francisco, what he would find was Main Street, USA. And that's in the trademarked, Disney sense.

Modern Americans may already have a good sense of what Weston saw architecturally in towns along his walk—much modified and sanitized, of course—if you've ever visited Disneyland or Disney World. When Walt Disney built Disneyland outside Los Angeles (it opened in July 1955), he made a conscious decision to have visitors enter by walking through a faux Main Street. He considered greeting them with a Wild West village, but discarded that notion, preferring to set a reassuring, nostalgic mood. "Main Street was calculated to correspond with one of the archetypes of the American imagination," Disney art historian Christopher Finch wrote, and "would establish the right ambience, so that visitors would be put in a receptive state of mind."

Disney picked an era he believed represented small-town America at its zenith—and it arguably was. Disney was quoted as saying of his Main Street, "Here is America from 1890 to 1910, at the crossroads of an era." He saw this as a moment of delicate balance, when the country looked simultaneously forward and back. Horses were still evident on the streets, but cars were starting to muscle their way into streetscapes. You'd find golden gas lamps here and bluish electric lights there, and sometimes both as cities transitioned from past to future. Main Streets tended to prominently feature Second Empire and Italianate architectural styles, whose detailing could be perfectly appreciated at a walker's pace. Granted, the buildings of Disney's Main Street, USA, are built at five-eighths scale, smaller than real life, making everything seem more compact, more intimate, more intense—more like brandy than wine. But all the elements are there.

Disney's vision was modeled in large part after his hometown of Marceline, Missouri, circa 1900. (In a Möbius-like twist, in the early 2000s Marceline revamped its Main Street, adding faux-historic street clocks where none had existed and dyeing the concrete sidewalks and scoring them with lines so they appear to be made of brick. In short, it remade itself to resemble Main Street, USA.) But Weston would have walked through towns that had been incised for foot traffic, with businesses clustered tightly and conveniently and homes just a block or two away.

The towns of Weston's America often had a defined edge, so residents knew where to gather to watch him arrive: either along the railroad or on the main road from the east, the one by which mail and essential supplies arrived via wagon and motor truck. These towns did not yet have multiple-lane highways, or left-hand-turn lanes, or overpasses, or frontage roads, or endless strips of repeating chain stores gathered at the city entrances. Weston no doubt saw some commercial repetition—by the time of his walk, more than a hundred F. W. Woolworth stores were scattered around the country as far west as Colorado—but mostly he would have passed by the small, independently owned businesses that populated the majority of downtowns. Sidewalks were broad, and shops used them as verandahs, cranking out awnings each morning to permit them to display their goods outside and also offering an inviting sense of shelter as potential customers strolled along. The towns were scaled for humans, and those humans were mostly traveling by foot.

Disney was right: The American town circa 1910 was on the cusp of sweeping change. Sputtering horseless carriages were motoring up and down streets in increasing numbers in cities and small towns alike. The more established metropolises had by then ossified into street grids, or had long-standing roads that followed hills and rivers. Alleys and sidewalks were already locked in place—it would have been far too expensive to tear them up and start anew when the automobile rolled in. Cities adapted.

So city streets began an evolution from anarchic public spaces equally home to cars and horses and cart vendors and pedestrians to more efficient traffic conduits designed for speed and linear mobility. (Pedestrians didn't roll over and abandon the sphere they'd occupied for centuries happily or without a fight; more about that in the next chapter.)

To implement the shift, a new vocation arose, that of the traffic engineer. This new class of professional approached cities like a plumber facing a house with leaky pipes and septic tank problems. He wanted to create systems to keep everything flowing without glitches or backups. These engineers started by separating cars and people. Streets were given over to cars, and sidewalks were designated as thoroughfares for walkers—they were no longer transitional zones between street and shop. The first one-way street in America was designated in Philadelphia in 1908, and others in Boston the following year. The first traffic light appeared in Cleveland in 1914, and the first painted lines appeared on streets around 1910. As George Herrold, city planning engineer for St. Paul, Minnesota, explained it at the time, "We do not attempt to pass water in two directions in a water main, nor to carry off sewerage in two directions through the same pipe." And so it would be for streets.

Herrold's is an apt comparison. Public streets were now viewed more or less as sewer lines, not as public spaces that belonged to those who used them, not as living and organic entities, but as components of a utility overseen by engineers who knew better than the public did how it should be managed.

In the process, one fragile urban ecosystem utterly vanished—the verge. This was the informal space that once occupied the soft zone between the sidewalks and the travel lanes for streetcars and horse-drawn carts. Sometimes this consisted of a buffer of grass; sometimes, dirt or macadam. Vendors parked their carts here and sold goods to passersby; chairs were pulled out of shops and set up. The verge offered both prospect and refuge and was a place that provided asylum from the movement along sidewalks and streets, yet was ideally located to observe the comings and goings of city residents.

But then came the cars, and places were needed to cache them while the operators went about their business. So the verges of the roadways were gradually taken over by inert automobiles—and cars in their dormancy still occupy an amazingly expansive and expensive amount of real estate in every city.

As it turned out, parked cars were too inert even for the merchants who originally were pleased that cars created a deeper pool of customers. Many drivers would park all day, preventing others from pulling up and shopping. Solutions were devised. Parking meters were patented in 1928, and first installed in Oklahoma City in 1935. They produced their intended effect: keeping drivers moving during the day. But they also had an unintended result: Now that cars were paying the city for the privilege of parking, driving advocates found they could make a larger claim on city officials when they argued for bigger budgets to accommodate cars, create more parking spaces, and pay for more engineering studies on traffic flows. It fed into a vicious cycle: More of the urban landscape was gradually devoted to cars, and less to those on foot. Pedestrians were losing their voice—and places to walk.

Cities changed, but not as dramatically as the quasi-rural precincts on the edge of town. Drivers, obeying Marchetti's Constant, moved outward, building their homes in fields where cows once provided milk or farmers raised produce for the city. (Trucks were more flexible than rail and more versatile than horse carts when it came to local transport, which meant that cities could now source their food from larger, more cost-effective farms situated farther away, giving rise to the term "truck farms." These made smaller farms within horse-carting distance of the city less essential, and their owners more amenable to cashing out when subdividers came knocking.) Land was cheaper beyond the downtown core, so home lots grew bigger, allowing more to live the dream of a bucolic country life with city amenities nearby. And the blueprint for the new communities was far different from the old city plans, where everyone depended on getting around on foot. The shift toward a car-centric landscape was not rapid and occurred over several generations. But in the words of historian Kenneth T. Jackson, this "represented the most fundamental realignment of urban structure in the 4,500-year past of cities on this planet."

The paving of the nation had begun. When Weston made his way to San Francisco, only 6 percent of the nation's roads were asphalt. And those that did get "macadamized" could, for the most part, thank bicyclists. (Macadam was named after Scottish engineer John McAdam, who pioneered a system for layering small stones to create durable roads in the early nineteenth century. Starting around 1902, tar or mined asphalt was added to seal the stones in place and keep down dust from the increasing numbers of motor cars.) With its founding in 1880, the influential League of American Wheelmen, a hundred thousand members strong by the end of its first decade, had started lobbying Congress to improve muddy roads. Bicyclists had been successful in macadamizing roads on the local level, but Congress proved far more resistant to a national program—the federal government was hesitant to involve itself in something as regional as road maintenance. (Although it didn't avoid national roads completely; in 1801 Thomas Jefferson authorized the first in several improvements to the Natchez Trace to connect to the Mississippi River.) Even after car manufacturers and auto advocates took up the crusade, arguing that a national road network was in the broader public interest, Congress continued to resist. As late as 1912, large-scale federal paving schemes were rejected as being only "for the benefit of a few wealthy pleasure seekers." Private enterprises took up some slack; the Lincoln Highway Association was established to create a coast-to-coast Rock Highway and started raising money for it in 1913. But Congress soon softened. Starting around 1902, oil companies swollen with the profits resulting from steadily growing car sales figured out how to make artificial asphalt from oil by-products, replacing naturally mined asphalt. They began pushing a paving scheme, with the backing of automobile clubs and drivers who clamored for better roads. By 1916, the federal government began to dabble in road funding, but it took more than twenty years for it to involve itself in more ambitious projects, which eventually culminated in the development of the Interstate Highway System.

Commuting distances grew, roads improved, the landscape changed dramatically. Weston's walk took place at the beginning of what was, at heart, the big bang of American transportation—an irrevocable change that exploded on the outskirts of towns, creating sprawling new residential nebulae configured not for the needs of people on foot but for those behind the wheels of automobiles.

After centuries of merchants, businesses, and homes being concentrated in tightly knit urban grids and village knots, the once-local world began to spiral outward and sprawl. And once this pattern was tentatively established, it became self-propagating, much like the reclining chair that produces a population more dependent on them. In the 1980s, urban planning professors Peter Newman and Jeff Kenworthy dubbed this "automobile dependence": the state we've arrived at through a self-perpetuating cycle in which drivers of cars successfully create a better environment for themselves—wider roads, fewer impediments, greater speed—which in turn encourages more people to drive, who then demand greater improvements, particularly relief from congestion resulting from the influx of cars, which then results in more and wider roads. And on and on.

At the same time, the incentives to walk began to rapidly erode. Merchants, grocers, and employers situated themselves in places designed for the upsurge in car travel and built new shops on cheaper land remote from other stores and residential areas. Each of those "improvements" for drivers chipped away at any allowances made for those on foot, like more sidewalks or wider crosswalks with more time allowed to get across safely, until walking became nearly unviable as a means of transportation. Our far-flung towns and suburbs became places where automobile ownership is now compulsory if one is to have any hope of being part of the modern economy.

Yet to this day, some either can't afford to drive or persist in walking because of a contrarian nature. It's not uncommon to see melancholy evidence of this subculture. Along arterials at the frayed edges of town, one often sees what have been dubbed "desire paths" parallel to roadways and angled though vacant lots. These are pathways worn by repeated walking through scruffy terrain. They are often five or ten feet from a shoulderless roadway, far enough to offer some protection from an errant auto, and then morosely decorated with tattered, windblown plastic bags caught up in thistles. Viewed one way, these paths are sad and depressing. Viewed another, these are the rutted overland routes of modern pioneers soldiering on, making their way toward their own fields of gold, real or imagined—in many cases, a minimum-wage job in a big-box or fast-food store.

May 18, 1909. In western Kansas, Weston met up with a "Glidden car." The Glidden Cup was sponsored by wealthy industrialist Charles J. Glidden starting in 1905 to demonstrate that automobiles weren't just rattling, noisy, unreliable toys for the well-off but rather practical tools for long-distance travel. The challenge had been established by the newly formed American Automobile Association and was open to anyone who owned a touring car. Each year, a starting point and a destination were announced. In 1905 it ran from New York City to Bretton Woods, New Hampshire, and back, for a total of 870 miles. The Glidden Cup wasn't exactly a race, but more a reliability challenge. Contestants started with a perfect score, then points were added for tire punctures, breakdowns, or falling behind schedule. The car that maintained the lowest score won. The tours generally featured daily legs of between 75 and 120 miles, and they attracted considerable press attention. (The Glidden Cup was fairly short-lived, however; the competition ended in 1913, the year all who entered finished, proving once and for all that cars were reliable for long travel across relatively rugged terrain.)

The Glidden car's driver, George Meinzinger from upstate New York, was puttering back east on his own after completing the 1909 Glidden tour from Minneapolis to Denver. Meinzinger had been a spectator when Weston headed west a month earlier near Schenectady. He'd heard the walker was still hoofing west and set out to find him from the opposite direction. He at last spotted him trudging down a long road under endless Kansas skies. "It was a pathetic sight," Meinzinger later recalled. "Or rather so it appeared to us to see the lone old man coming across the prairie." Weston had changed in appearance, Meinzinger thought, and when they stopped to talk, he was "a bundle of nerves [and] couldn't stand still for a minute, but kept shifting from one foot to the other as he talked." (Of course, Weston was falling behind schedule every minute he chatted with a well-wisher.)

Weston told Meinzinger something he hadn't mentioned in his dispatches to the *New York Times*: His support automobile had dropped out sometime after Chicago because the automobile company that had provided it had been disappointed by the amount of publicity the trek was generating. Now Weston was making his way west without a car to support him, and for long stretches without a human companion. Still, he seemed cheerful enough, Meinzinger reported, and Weston even boasted that on foot he could ford brooks and circumvent mud holes better than Meinzinger's car. They at last said their farewells, and Meinzinger continued east, promising Weston that at the next town, he'd call ahead to a farmhouse up the road, ensuring that someone would prepare for the walker a bite to eat. Weston requested two eggs beaten with sugar.

———

One of the great moments in the rise of auto dependency occurred thirty years after Weston's walk. It was the opening of the General Motors Highways and Horizons pavilion at the 1939 New York World's Fair in Flushing Meadows Corona Park. It featured *Futurama,* a vast and elaborate animated diorama depicting the automotive world of tomorrow ("tomorrow," in this case, being precisely defined as 1960), and huge crowds stood in long lines to get in. Once inside, they sat in small pods that carried them on a sixteen-minute narrated journey along an elevated track above the miniature landscape, as if they were flying slowly over the future. The diorama was based on a project created earlier by famed designer Norman Bel Geddes for Shell Oil. "A free-flowing movement of people and goods across our nation," Bel Geddes wrote, "is a requirement of modern living and prosperity." This model, he explained, illustrated "how a motorway system may be laid down over the entire country—across mountains, over rivers and lakes, through cities and past towns—never deviating from a direct course and always adhering to the four basic principles of highway design: safety, comfort, speed, and economy." The model city was riven with broad, multilane roadways and soaring ramps and cloverleafs—Bel Geddes was as smitten with the idea of speed and unbroken movement as Marinetti was in his 1909 futurist's manifesto. And, as it turned out, his vision wasn't all that removed from what was actually built under the federal Interstate Highway System, which was launched in 1956.

Bel Geddes's vision required a fundamental reshaping of the American landscape. The most radical element was segregation in modes of transportation, with cars moving at high speeds on one-way roads free of intersections and obstructions; in quieter parts of Bel Geddes's world, cars were restricted and pedestrians were allowed to freely move about, foreshadowing pedestrian malls. The *New York Times* was nearly rhapsodic, calling the concept a "pedestrian heaven." It was, the paper of record went on, truly a "city of the future where the pedestrian can walk without fear of sudden death and the motorist can always find a parking space."

No doubt, it *was* a seductive vision, particularly at a time when the fear of sudden death while walking was increasingly real, and motorists were growing aggravated by the rising congestion in the cities. Anything to improve the situation would be embraced. And so began the ascension of the exalted traffic engineer—a caste of furrowed-brow problem solvers who were all but worshipped for their skills in untying knots and achieving frictionless speed.

The history of traffic planning can be summed up fairly simply: Divide, then conquer. The public space was divided into discrete zones—you here, you there—and then those with lower standing would have their zones compromised and eroded over time, bestowing more room upon the rapid. It was survival of the fastest.

Miller McClintock was arguably the most influential figure in creating this strategy's policy underpinning. As part of a Harvard doctoral study of municipal government, McClintock wrote a thesis titled *Street Traffic Control,* which was published as a book in 1925. In it, he took a measured, sensible approach to moving people about, noting, among other things, the impressive economy of the streetcar, which could move large numbers of residents far more efficiently than cars strung out along the road, with each containing just one or two passengers. He wrote: "It seems desirable to give trolley cars the right of way under general conditions, and to place restriction on motor vehicles in their relations with streetcars." He went on to refer to cars as "the greatest public destroyer of human life."

His evenhandedness would not last. Within two years, McClintock had flip-flopped and was now a fervent advocate of making room for cars. (The fact that he'd been hired by the Studebaker Corporation to head up the Albert Russel Erskine Bureau for Street Traffic Research, which ultimately found a home at Harvard University, may have had something to do with this.) Now, McClintock became an evangelist calling for revamped cities designed to ease the way for automobiles. In 1938, *Life* magazine called McClintock the "No. 1 U.S. traffic expert." He espoused the merits of wider streets, elevated roads, and traffic lanes that restricted access. He pointed to "friction" points—notably, intersections and places where cars entered or left the road. He began to imagine a world in which pedestrians and streetcars were not part of the urban fabric, but hindrances to it. So under his tutelage and analytic cover, city streets began to tame the chaotic blend of multiple users and to become uncluttered conduits designed with free-flowing cars in mind.

Prior to the rise of the traffic engineer, local police departments typically advised municipalities on how city streets should be run and regulated. The police tended to be a conservative lot and generally sided with the old ways of doing things—pedestrians had always moved about freely, and so police tended to view automobiles as interlopers and called for them to behave in a way that wouldn't disrupt the old order. Streets were thus governed less by regulation and more by common sense. (Think of a crowded indoor shopping mall; there are no stoplights or yield signs—people just know how to act based on tradition and accepted behavior. That's what city streets were like for centuries.)

But the old order was falling apart: Cars were moving faster by the model year and were less nimble than horses or pedestrians. They were also rapidly expanding in number. In 1910, the nation was home to one automobile for every two hundred residents; just five years later, it was one in forty. In Newark, New Jersey, the number of cars doubled between 1912 and 1915. In Chicago, the number of registered cars rose tenfold between 1911 and 1921, when the city's overall population increased by about 25 percent. (At the same time, the number of horse-drawn vehicles plummeted nationwide; by the mid-1920s, only 3 to 6 percent of vehicles were pulled by horses in America's largest cities.) In 1909, one of the nation's first celebrity architects, Daniel Burnham, released his now-famous *Plan of Chicago* (considered among the first and best city-planning documents), which was a blueprint for "providing roads for automobility."

Not all planners and designers were caught up in the enthusiasm for reshaping cities for cars. "There has been a decided tendency on the part of official street planners to insist with a quite needless and undesirable rigidity upon certain fixed standards of width and arrangement in regard to purely local streets," wrote landscape designer Frederick Law Olmsted in 1910.

This, he noted, inevitably led to "the formation of blocks and of lots of a size and shape ill adapted to the local uses to which they need to be put."

The upshot of this urban upheaval was unsurprising: The pedestrian casualty rate spiked. By 1910, some city officials were talking of pedestrian deaths as a public emergency. New York City implemented the first traffic code as early as 1903 to try to get a grip on this, and new codes became commonplace over the next decade. Early on, the practice was to crack down on the newly arrived cars. When accidents occurred, police invariably found the motorists at fault. The median speed limit for cities nationwide in 1906 was just ten miles per hour.

But the growing number of drivers started to bristle at having their pace set by slow-moving pedestrians—anyway, they easily outweighed their opponents and could bully them when needed. In 1925, a traffic policeman wrote in *Scientific American* that he found the "extremely defiant attitude" of automobile drivers to be very irksome.

The slow speed limits for cars, the assumption of guilt in accidents, the constant series of obstacles put in the way of the new class of automobilists—this would not stand. The early adopters of automobiles were affluent and often powerful, and didn't hesitate to call in chits with their contacts at city hall. Favors were exchanged, and the police were shown the exit when it came to city planning and cars. As Peter Norton puts it in *Fighting Traffic* (2008), his fascinating history of cars in cities, "Police would remain important as foot soldiers, but engineers replaced them as the generals in the fight against traffic congestion."

Throughout the first decades of the twentieth century, traffic engineers expanded their influence and territory in tandem with the rise of the city manager. The city manager was a professional, business-inspired position that was swiftly displacing the traditional role of elected mayor around the time of Weston's walk. This new approach was swayed in part by Frederick Winslow Taylor, a mechanical engineer and author of the influential 1911 tome *The Principles of Scientific Management.* Municipalities everywhere now wanted to embrace a no-nonsense corporate approach, with a city manager as CEO and the city council acting as a board representing residents. Trained professionals were in demand for running cities by employing sound scientific methods. By 1918, nearly half of the nation's city managers came from engineering backgrounds.

The conservative, commonsense approach of city policemen to managing the shared space of cars and pedestrians was discarded as all too nineteenth century. Tradition was replaced by quantitative planning. Number crunchers fanned out through the cities, tabulating data. They started with simple traffic counts around 1910, but soon grew more sophisticated, compiling data sets that included speed, the number of turns, the movement of pedestrians, the incidence of accidents, and counts of through versus local traffic.

The numbers didn't lie: The engineers took these and convinced municipalities that they could make the streets safer and more efficient by restricting traditional activity and ensuring clear and unobstructed lanes of traffic—an approach as unimpeachable as removing roots choking sewage pipes. "This formalization of traffic forever changed the character of city streets," writes Norton. "Within a decade, streets and sidewalks—venues of myriad public activities as late as 1920—had largely been redefined as exclusive transportation ways, subject to regulation in the name of efficiency. . . . Engineers segregated traffic into lanes and imposed one-way streets, loading zones, through-traffic streets, and pedestrian sidewalks. They narrowed the functions of both the sidewalks and the roadway."

As housing developers followed cars to the edges of the cities and into the nascent modern suburbs beyond, the precepts of scientific traffic management moved with them. New construction across the country—in residential developments, in strip malls, along major arterials—embraced the scientific approach and was designed to maximize smooth, safe, speedy travel by car— wide roads, ample shoulders, curbs trimmed at corners to allow drivers to make turns without slowing unduly and causing backups behind.

Once the widening started, it fed upon itself. Engineers found that adding more open space on either side of the road—"recovery zones"—resulted in fewer damaging accidents because inattentive drivers could regain control and ease back into the travel lane before they plowed into something. So shoulders expanded accordingly, encroaching on any sidewalks that might have existed. Trees became less of an urban amenity and more of threat— they were solid and killed people when hit at a high rate of speed. So trees were leveled by the grove. This made it safer for drivers, but increased danger for pedestrians by taking out a natural barrier protecting them from cars. It also took out the welcome shade and that sort of natural, alluring tunnel that, as mentioned earlier, we may be genetically inclined to stroll along. And these highly engineered sewers moving traffic began their spread far into the former countryside.

With fewer people walking, sidewalks headed toward obsolescence; they were arguably an avoidable expense in building residential subdivisions, where many, if not most, residents had cars and garages. Along the commercial arterials, sidewalks were at times installed begrudgingly, then rarely used, thanks to the great distances between shops, the uninviting ugliness of the surroundings, and the lack of safety near speeding traffic. If sidewalks were installed, they were often quickly degraded: Utility poles were installed in the middle of them, they were pierced with frequent driveways and temporarily blocked by flashing signs on trailers seeking to divert the fickle attention of drivers speeding past. In the more absurd cases, sidewalks were required only under new code changes long after development had begun, so along one arterial you might find hundred-foot sidewalk segments that went from nowhere to nowhere, creating orphaned pathways, a place for pedestrians to pace back and forth in front of a new fast-food restaurant.

In both cities and suburbs, walkers were inconvenienced, and the traffic engineers no doubt understood that. Some may have regretted it. But pedestrians were stubbornly old-fashioned characters who refused to leave the nineteenth century behind. Sending these recalcitrant few on long detours—through rank-smelling underpasses, over bleak and exposed overpasses—was small price to pay as long as traffic could whisk along freely. Cars and trucks ensured the cogs of the economy kept moving. What right did walkers have to interfere with that?

"There are 26,000,000 autos and there will be many more," a Kingston, New York, newspaper editorialist wrote in 1929. "If they can't go where they wish to go, business will have to go where the auto can go in ease and comfort. . . . There should be both greater ease of movement through cities and greater opportunity for parking in them."

A few writers had the foresight to see that something was being lost as cities reshaped themselves around the automobile. Architectural critic Lewis Mumford was one: "The right to have access to every building in the city by private motorcar in an age when everyone possesses such a vehicle is the right to destroy the city," he wrote a half-century ago.

May 18, 1909. Weston was walking outside Sheridan, Kansas, when a massive thunderstorm appeared on the horizon, threatening to wash him away in a deluge. He spotted stockyard pens ahead—part of the Union Pacific Railway network—and scrambled beneath a platform that would offer refuge when the skies opened up. Just as he was getting settled, a wagon carrying a family pulled up—a man, two women, and two boys. They told him they'd been searching for him all afternoon. They'd seen that a fierce storm was brewing, insisted there was no waiting it out, and urged him to seek shelter at their ranch, about a half-mile away. Weston looked up at the rising and darkening storm clouds and agreed. The wagon went ahead with most of the family, and Weston walked with the head of the family, A. C. Overholtz, whom Weston would later call "that prince of ranchmen." They beat the storm and the sky opened up as they arrived at the ranch's gates, bringing cold winds and drenching rain. If it hadn't been for the rancher and his thoughtful family, Weston said, "I should certainly have been attacked with pneumonia or lumbago."

This wasn't the only act of generosity he'd enjoy in Kansas, and he would later say that in all his travels at home and abroad, he'd never met "such genial and hospitable people" as those in the Sunflower State. Every town and village, he dubbed "a paradise." While his description may have been characteristically overblown, his ability to tell people what they wanted to hear was, as usual, pitch-perfect.

Weston made himself comfortable at the ranch as the storm continued to lash the land with fury. At last, he gave up on continuing that night and took to a borrowed bed at eight that evening. Around midnight the storm moved on; the Overholtzes rose early and prepared him a full breakfast before dawn. At 4:50 a.m., the sky now clear, Weston bid his farewells and continued on down the freshly muddy roads, making it to Sharon Springs, twenty-five miles away, before noon. He wolfed down a huge meal at the Central Hotel, announced he was "feeling fine," and then walked out the door and onward, aiming to make it across the Colorado line by late that night.

His bad luck continued. "My first invasion of Colorado was made within two and a half miles of Cheyenne Wells, last night, when I was suddenly greeted with a downpour of rain which was entirely unlike any thunder shower in the East," Weston wrote. "I was drenched to the skin within three minutes." He made his way as fast as he could to a hotel, then stripped down and dried off, avoiding any colds or chills. He couldn't avoid the rain though—he arrived late on Wednesday and it continued through Thursday, forcing him to hole up and delay his departure until 6:20 on Friday morning. He had much ground to make up, and announced he would set off Friday on a fifty-five-mile day.

The open prairie landscape devoid of people and structures was certainly not upstate New York, with its well-spaced villages teeming with welcoming residents. He reported that here he had only prairie dogs, coyotes, and "the occasional rabbit" to keep him company. The grass was lush and verdant following the heavy rains, and the people who came out to cheer him looked "industrious and cheerful." Otherwise, there was room for improvement. "The towns are very small," he wrote, "and accommodations are not of the best."

Outside the tiny hamlet of Boyero, Colorado, the engineer of a passing train, a man with the excellent name of Levi Stoner, tossed Weston a pound of ice, which kept him cool and slaked his thirst for a couple of hours. He then met a couple of hoboes sitting along the track, and after passing by them he turned to find them, alarmingly, walking behind him and gaining. He stepped it up, assuming a four-mile-per-hour gait, but couldn't shake them. It may have been the slowest chase in history. Weston increased his speed a bit more and finally his pursuers dropped off, but not without a cost: In his fast walk, he'd torn a hole in a boot. Around noon he reached the town of Hugo, the county seat and a ranching and mining supply depot of a few hundred residents, which had been incorporated just that year. It wasn't much, but it would have to do, since he was obligated to stop here to get new boots. As it was now Saturday, he'd lay over on Sunday and resume on Monday. Denver was still 165 miles distant.

"I was over in Brooklyn the other day and I found to my surprise that the Brooklyn Bridge affords one of the best paths for walking I have ever seen in a long time," said Weston in 1907. "You not only have a good path, but can breathe the pure, fresh air. To those asking for routes, I would suggest that they try the Brooklyn Bridge."

If one were to seek out artifacts from the golden age of the pedestrian—as many look for remnants of the early auto age, like drive-in restaurants, drive-in movie theaters, and well-landscaped parkways—a leading contender for the most enduring monument of the walker's age would be the Brooklyn Bridge. Built between 1870 and 1883, it was designed to link two major cities, Manhattan and Brooklyn, soaring over two ports and allowing commerce to trundle across in wagons and carts and buggies (and between 1898 and 1950, various trolleys) without the time-consuming bother of ferries. It was a symbol of high commerce.

Yet, remarkably in today's context, walkers weren't ignored in the planning—indeed, they were rewarded with a spectacular elevated platform for the crossing. They got a broad deck with sweeping views, and it landed with flair and élan on the Manhattan side at its own landscaped plaza—it was as if the drays and beer wagons running beneath were an afterthought.

"This elevated promenade," wrote its first architect, John Roebling, in 1860 (a decade before construction began), "will allow people of leisure old and young to stroll over the bridge on fine days. I need not state that in a crowded commercial city such a promenade will be of incalculable value." Today the bridge's walkway remains a remarkable city landmark and much-used route—about 4,000 pedestrians cross it daily, along with 3,100 cyclists. Indeed, it's so enduringly popular that widening plans are under way to relieve congestion.

Another contender for great walking-era remnants would be more generic and not city specific: publics stairways linking high and low roads that were built in hilly terrain and often landscaped with platforms for enjoying the views.

A few examples: The city of hills, Cincinnati, had at its peak some four hundred outdoor staircases connecting upper and lower neighborhoods. Many of these have become badly overgrown and are in disrepair today, like neglected Roman ruins in the original city of seven hills, but some—such as the Oregon Street Steps on Mount Adams, which were restored and updated in 1997—are as lovely as when they were built.

Los Angeles is a city often lampooned for its auto idolatry, but it has more than 250 public staircases ascending and descending the hilly parts of town. A guidebook to the stairs was published in 2010, and this lured out a growing cadre of fans, spawning a Hidden Stairs of Los Angeles Meetup group of nearly two thousand. People gather several times a month to explore these artifacts of the walking age.

In Portland, Oregon, you can take guided walking tours of hidden stairways, and in Seattle there's a Stairway Walks Day, with organized hikes based on a new guidebook.

In fact, look in just about any city with hills, and there are good odds you'll find remnants of public stairways—from Portland, Maine, to La Mesa, California. Indeed, there's a Web site (www.publicstairs.com) "devoted to the discovery and documentation of major outdoor public stairways anywhere in the world." And they're worth discovering.

Yet the grandest monument to walking culture may be one that was never built: a fantastical concept city called, curiously enough, Roadtown. In 1910 a man named Edgar Chambless published a book about his big idea. He proposed a series of adjoining concrete town houses ("fire proof and vermin proof") that would go on and on for hundreds or possibly thousands of miles. "The idea occurred to me to lay the modern skyscraper on its side and run the elevators and the pipes and the wires horizontally instead of vertically," he wrote. "You will see the cities spread out in lines amidst the fields and farms, as if by magic." The *New York Times* suggested it could be called an "earthscraper." The houses would feature central vacuum systems, and while the volume of liquid soap needed would be too low to warrant pumping it to individual houses through pipes from a central dispensary, plans called for "a man who will make the rounds and fill the reservoirs at each home" in ten-gallon batches. (Chambless's plan came amid a golden age of utopian ideas, but he wasn't a hapless crank; Thomas Edison made the use of his patents for poured concrete houses available for free to support the Roadtown concept, as did the inventor of the monorail the patents for his trains.)

Transportation was central to Roadtown. Chambless noted that except when asleep, we are invariably in motion. And so he designed his recumbent skyscraper to cater to restlessness and give us room to keep moving. Roadtown would be built on several levels, with two-story homes in the middle and an electric monorail running in a tunnel excavated underneath, its wheels muffled with leather to keep it silent. And above? The contiguous homes would be linked by an unbroken flat roof three lanes wide. The outside lanes would be suitable for biking and skating with "rubber tired roller skates." In the middle, for walking, would be a covered promenade that could in winter be "enclosed with glass panels and steam heated," and dotted with alcoves and benches. Here, one could walk for miles in comfort year-round. The occasional tower would punctuate this linear city, and here one would find shops, recreation centers, and schools. "Certainly no street or boulevard in the history of the world was ever more uniquely located,"

Chambless wrote. Just as Main Street in 1910 marked a transition between the past and the present, the idea of Roadtown sat squarely at the intersection of present and future, where movement on foot and bike and train collided with the desire to improve the grimy, often-dangerous cities and give residents access to nature without sacrificing their big-city access. A magazine article on road towns painted a utopian vision: Not only would city workers live in the country, but also "farmers would live in the houses and commute to their fields . . . avoiding the loneliness of the farm." The author believed that the human love of social life "can be restored . . . to an extent that will surpass the days of Greece and Rome."

Chambless understood that he was up against considerable odds, averring that "the crude horse paths called streets, owned by 'hold-up men' called politicians, do not permit of the general adoption of these great inventions."

He was right. Roadtown was never built.

Howard Frumkin, dean of the University of Washington's School of Public Health and an expert on environmental health, notes with admirable succinctness one of the biggest problems Americans face today: "We have effectively engineered physical activity out of our daily lives." But this wasn't done all at once or by sweeping fiat. It happened through the process of gradual erosion—once public ways were divvied up, one for cars and one for walkers, then came the conquering: making the walker's pathways so uninviting through neglect that almost nobody would choose to use them willingly.

Of course, it didn't have to be this way. Less radical and utopian than Roadtown—and actually built—was the subdivision of Radburn in Fair Lawn, New Jersey, across the Hudson River from Manhattan. Founded as "a town for the motor age" in 1929, Radburn was heavily influenced by the then-popular English garden city, but was adapted for its time and place. It's been credited with popularizing culs-de-sac and residential superblocks not transected by grid roads in America—innovations that have led to heartburn if not heartache for many walkers. Urbanist Jane Jacobs was among those who found fault with the whole concept of the garden city. (She wrote of these "self-sufficient small towns" that they were "really very nice towns if you were docile and had no plans of your own and did not mind spending your life among others with no plans of their own.")

Radburn was built during an early phase of transportation segregation, and so incorporated walking with more than a grudging nod. It actually celebrated walking by creating a lovely, landscaped network of pathways. The developers wove through the community what they called "pedestrian parkways" that passed in front of homes and linked with other pathway networks via attractive rustic wood footbridges and stone overpasses. (Think of New York's Central Park.) As the community grew, so did the network, including a new footbridge over a county highway, making "it possible for children living in the new section to walk in safety to the Radburn school in one of the north parks," as it was reported in the *New York Times*. Radburn's design was influential far beyond New Jersey—newly built communities across America and England implemented the revised concept with varying degrees of success. Even Walt Disney purportedly borrowed some of Radburn's ideas when he designed Disneyland. It likely has been studied by urban planners more than any other development of its size.

Then came the fall in so many communities. As highways expanded, and city streets were widened and converted into one-way sluices to accommodate cars, and subdivisions marched in tidy ranks across the outlying countryside, the walker's geography devolved. Highways cut off neighborhoods that were once connected by sidewalks. Now, when they were connected at all, it was by walking along the unwelcoming edge of a busy multilane roadway, or trekking on dusty and debris-filled sidewalks through underpasses defined by stout columns and steep concrete slopes. Yes, a highway underpass possesses some of the characteristics of the sort of alluring keyhole pathway mentioned earlier: protective cover above; an exit; a beginning, middle, and end. But the particulars are all wrong, starting with the mass of the unyielding concrete, which is both dehumanizing and vaguely threatening in the way a tree canopy is not. There's no refuge in an underpass; it feels like a trap from beginning to end. When you are walking along a car-filled street under a busy highway, it's nearly impossible to not feel small and vulnerable.

Even in some of the more densely settled parts of traditional cities, where the infrastructure favors walking, pedestrians were corralled and redirected—sent underneath roadways and through narrow, tiled tunnels that soon were scarred with graffiti, littered with sandwich wrappers, and redolent of yesterday's urine. In a few short decades, pedestrian underpasses emerged as the natural habitat of droogs, or modern urban highwaymen and perverts. Underpasses are still today's equivalent of a pickpocket-filled lane in Dickens's England, or a dark and thorny wood at the edge of a medieval village. "Pedestrian underpasses generate a lot of fear," notes a report from a Canadian group advocating design for crime prevention. "They limit movement options, reduce visibility and increase isolation. They are often dark and poorly maintained. All of these environmental factors increase feelings of fear." And a scan of newspaper headlines shows no shortage of evidence, ranging from 1953 (Cleveland: "Underpass Victim of Thug Treated") to 2012 (outside London: "Party Woman's Throat Cut in Commuter-Belt Murder: 43-Year-Old Found in Pool of Blood in Underpass Wearing Stiletto Heels.")

Overpasses that deliver walkers over the highways that bisect cities like asphalt rivers may be less odiferous than underpasses. But they're rarely welcoming. Brutally exposed with no prospect of refuge, walkers endure the glare off passing windshields nearby and below, the roar of traffic making it impossible to listen for approaching footsteps, or even to enjoy their thoughts. And increasingly the sidewalks are encased in chain-link cages to ensure errant teens don't toss debris on passing cars.

Pedestrian underpass or overpass—both have one thing in common: None were built for the benefit of pedestrians, no matter what city officials proclaim at their grand unveilings. They're ultimately for the convenience of cars because they take potential obstructions off their roads. "The pedestrian remains the largest single obstacle to free traffic movement," Los Angeles traffic planners wrote some fifty years ago. Keeping pedestrians at a remove from the street was a realization of Bel Geddes's vision.

The other part of Bel Geddes's vision—creating areas where walkers could walk unmolested by cars—did in fact come to fruition, but in a way Bel Geddes probably hadn't imagined: in enclosed shopping malls. These were initially touted as safe, environmentally controlled zones where Main Street businesses could open new outlets and expand their customer bases, but they quickly became outposts for major national chains, which could outbid local shops for occupancy. This subsequently caused many local enterprises to falter in the declining downtowns. Malls offered parking and convenience, and they simply inhaled much of the available economic oxygen from walkable downtowns.

This in turn led indirectly to another sort of blight: the downtown pedestrian mall. Panicked about defections of shoppers to the outskirts, towns with atrophying Main Streets hired consultants, who determined that their downtowns were too 1910. To usher them into the sleek modern age, they recommended imitating the mall by banning automobile traffic and covering the oil-stained asphalt with brick or stone and adding benches and planters to make it more welcoming, pedestrian friendly, and, well, mall-like. Save for a few exceptions (Denver; Burlington, Vermont; Miami Beach, Florida; Charlottesville, Virginia), the concept rarely panned out. "Users only showed up to celebrate a mall's opening," noted one academic paper on pedestrian malls, "they rarely returned to shop."

Pedestrian malls meant well, but they had a central flaw: Like pedestrian overpasses and underpasses, they were never designed for walkers. They were for drivers. So downtowns cannibalized themselves to provide abundant parking for cars. Some leveled the blocks behind their commercial Main Streets to create lifeless oceans of surface parking, flattening the grid and destroying any sort of native downtown charm: Shoppers sometimes must enter by parking behind buildings and their deteriorating brick and rusty fire escapes and ill-tended Dumpsters. Towns that opted to keep their urban fabric more intact often built parking garages instead, which were expensive and created new habitat for droogs. The ornate streetlamps and brick pavers installed along the now-pedestrian-only street often felt inauthentic at best, and, at their worst, unnatural and somehow creepy, like a person with poorly drawn fake eyebrows.

Other big-city downtowns mimicked the malls in another way: by constructing skyways or subterranean passages that linked buildings and parking garages. If they couldn't compete on parking, at least they could offer an environmentally controlled shopping experience. While the idea of downtown sky bridges had been bandied about for decades (not counting early prototypes like the seventeenth-century Bridge of Sighs in Venice), it wasn't until the 1960s and the rising fear of losing business to the suburbs that sky bridges started to actually crop up. Minneapolis opened its first in 1962, and then expanded its hermetically sealed network. Canadians afflicted with long winters also embraced these in major cities like Toronto and Calgary (with more than ten miles under cover), but also in midsize regional cities like Saint John, New Brunswick. In America, skywalk complexes of various sizes cropped up in Rochester, Minnesota; Des Moines, Iowa; Baltimore; and Dallas.

These have met with varying degrees of economic success, but generally have not fared especially well and have been regarded with scorn by urbanists. The zones linked by sky bridges are dismissed as places to transit through, not live in, more like sterilized simulacra of downtown. And by conceding the street level to automobiles, urban life is diminished, and a two-caste system takes shape: the sidewalks are left to the poor and the skywalks are roamed by the more prosperous, many on their lunch breaks from jobs in the adjoining towers. Skywalk networks tend to roll up early in the evening as gates slide across the shop doors and security guards usher out the public. The skywalks are a fantastical *Jetsons*-era concept married to a banal suburban mall. It's likely that these Habitrails for humans would have been applauded by Bel Geddes—and they mark one of those rare moments when the future caught up to the present.

But skywalks, like pedestrian malls, were at heart an alien life-form grafted onto the city. It's no wonder so many cities rejected them as if they were of the wrong blood type.

May 24, 1909. Weston's final leg into Denver—165 miles—should have been a straightforward stroll, an unchallenging three days along railbeds that were flat and smooth and had been recently oiled to keep the dust down. But Weston's abysmal luck with the weather persisted, and he was again buffeted by severe storms that brought rain and hail and cold westerly winds. The rain made the railbed slippery, forcing him to zigzag across the tracks even more often to seek better footing and making it hard to maintain his pace of three and half miles per hour.

And then there was the emptiness of the vast western space. It was all skies and grasslands, with little to break up the monotony. On two days running he didn't see a house for fifteen miles at a stretch. "I sometimes get depressed in my loneliness," he wrote, and he sought to alleviate that by thinking of his friends back in New York and his well-wishers everywhere. For a time, his mind was taken off the loneliness by a herd of antelopes that swooped past and nearly forced him from the tracks.

He caught up to his manager and luggage in Deer Trail, some sixty miles from Denver, and got a long-overdue change of clothes and a filling lunch. The sky cleared, the wind moderated, and he again set off. Four miles later, hail, rain, and a gale swept back in, giving him what he called his "usual daily bath." "I am prepared for ordinary rain," Weston wrote, "but these sudden and fierce storms are new to me. I hardly know how to prepare for the day's walk."

Onward through Limon and Agate ("consisting of a store, warehouse, and eight dwellings"), Weston continued toward Denver. By now he had gathered a bit of company; a reporter from the *Denver Post* named H. A. Anderson joined in and managed to match his pace (although he admitted he was miserably cold). Four others who traveled out from Denver to walk with Weston soon gave up and boarded a passing train. A trestle crossing proved perilous when a terrific wind blew up; after a pause, Weston and Anderson pushed on and made it across. That evening the pair finally arrived in Aurora, a small supply village outside Denver, a day later than Weston had planned. He had hoped to push on to Denver, but city officials, thrilled that he was walking through, had asked that he hold up and instead arrive in the morning. He would be fresh and the day bright, and the city could give him a properly rousing welcome.

That next morning, Weston walked down Aurora's Colfax Avenue when the street was hitting one of its two apogees. A streetcar line had extended from Denver to Aurora in 1900, putting the latter well within the one-hour commuter orbit postulated by Marchetti. A new class of mobile worker had brought prosperity and activity.

Today, Italianate architectural details suggest a former affluence that persists in a feral way near the intersection of Colfax Avenue and Dayton Street, where streetcar suburb buildings once clustered. The understatedly impressive Young Building, a one-story storefront, has an ornate rising-moon parapet presiding over what's now the shop Hair and Nail.

Aurora today is scarcely noticeable as a town—it's largely been absorbed into the Greater Denver metroplex, and Colfax Avenue is essentially a long commercial strip cluttered with hair-braiding shops, payday loan vendors, taco restaurants, and fissured parking lots. Aurora itself has also been atomized and now lacks a single core—a shopping area called Town Center at Aurora is four miles from what was once the actual town center and the site of the original city hall. The old downtown area (dubbed the Aurora Cultural Arts District in 2012) includes the Aurora Fox Arts Center, which was restored and reopened in 1985. Streetlamps nearby play up an art deco

thousands lined his route. He walked briskly and bowed and doffed his hat as usual, then made his way to the downtown offices of the *Denver Post*. The newspaper set off a series of fireworks from its roof, signaling Weston's arrival. He climbed the stairs, stepped out on the balcony overlooking the street, and briefly addressed a jubilant crowd. His message was simple: He was just passing through, and intended to be twenty miles past Denver by nightfall. "I will resume my journey to the coast," he said, and then headed down and resumed his journey.

And that resumption would involve profoundly mountainous country. Weston failed to write about what for the previous week or so must have been the most striking landmarks on his relentlessly flat horizon: the saw-toothed peaks of the Rocky Mountains slowly rising into view, which first ruffled into open foothills before spiking upward into spires that filled the sky. They were like a continent-wide speed bump. And they would require walking of a different order.

CHAPTER 7

WALK,
DON'T WALK

Pedestrian and person with automobile have each the right to use public highway; but right of operator of automobile is not superior to right of pedestrian.

—FROM *O'DOWD V. NEWNHAM*, Court of Appeals of
the State of Georgia, 1913

In first seven months of 1909, 60 people were killed and 1,200 injured on the streets of Chicago alone, mostly because of reckless drivers plowing into pedestrians. This attracted some attention. Police announced they were seeking to improve matters "in the way of closer espionage, more frequent arrests and heavier fines." And if that didn't "check the carnage," they proposed erecting "a bump or ridge extending the full width of the street and high enough to jolt the spine loose in reckless drivers."

The victors in disputes are the ones who control the historic narrative. And so we've been well schooled in the remarkable rise of the amazing automobile and the glorious growth of the seamless American road. (Some examples: *Engines of Change: A History of the American Dream in Fifteen Cars,* and *The Big Roads: The Untold Story of the Engineers, Visionaries, and Trailblazers Who Created the American Superhighways.* And many, many more.) The rise of cars and highways to support them is the twentieth-century version of manifest destiny, the denouement of a fate foretold.

What you don't much hear about are the vanquished, and the scattered battles fought along the way. A rearguard action was, in fact, raised against the aggressors and their "destiny" by a committed cadre of pedestrians hoping to keep the roads open to all and to ensure that the automobile remained one among equals, not the sole and dominant force. Their efforts were both too little and too late, as well as too random and disorganized. Pedestrians lost the battle, and badly, and were exiled to crosswalks and sidewalks.

Yet you may be startled to learn that such a fight actually took place, and that not all Americans greeted cars as saviors, tossing them flowers and confectionaries while waving white handkerchiefs. Look at any newspaper between 1910 and 1930 and you'll see plenty of pushback against the invasive car—from police, from judges, from the everyday urban dweller. It was a battle fought publicly and hard, but as with John Henry's battle against the steam drill, everyone seemed to sense the ultimate outcome. Still, how they fought and how they lost remains instructive.

⸻

When Weston walked to San Francisco, he pretty much had free reign over any street he trod. Not just because he attracted attention and crowds and he and his entourage were often too outsize a presence to be confined to the margins of a narrow sidewalk, but also because anyone on foot could walk just about anywhere they pleased in 1909. That was their right and their habit. Walkers weren't confined to sidewalks; in cities, they wandered streets as if in a public plaza, crossing in midblock or making their way diagonally or rambling in great zigzags if they felt like it. They could stop midstreet and talk to acquaintances, or conduct a bit of business, or simply stroll down the middle if that route struck their fancy. All roads were shared roads—by the end of the nineteenth century, it was common to have streetcars clanging past a rabble of pedestrians, along with jitneys pulled by horses and drays hauling produce to market. No matter how they got around, those doing the getting simply acknowledged and worked around one another. The term "jaywalking" had not yet been coined, because the concept of jaywalking did not yet exist.

When cars initially started puttering down the street, many drivers sought to blend in and moved respectfully and at a speed appropriate to their surroundings—not quite at a walking pace (many early cars would have stalled out at three miles per hour), but at a speed that allowed them to be one of several entities participating in the complicated dance of street life. The government served mostly as a respected chaperone at the dance. According to one study, the median state-designated speed limit in American cities in 1906 was ten miles per hour—faster than a cantering horse, but slow enough for a driver to navigate around others they encountered. The *New-York Daily Tribune* in 1902 ran an editorial cartoon showing a stern woman labeled "Justice" standing next to a sheepish-looking car driver and holding a sign that said, "You must not exceed a speed of ten miles an hour within city limits." (The caption read, "To protect human life.") Even in popular culture, cars were not granted exemptions. In 1910, the first in a series of insanely popular Tom Swift books was published. In this installment, as traffic historian Peter Norton has written, a biking Tom Swift is run off the road and into a ditch by his chief antagonist. "You automobilists take too much for granted," Swift shouts after the car. "I guess I've got some rights on the road."

He did, but they were growing frayed, and a campaign was just getting under way to preserve what was left. "The pedestrian has the undoubted right to cross the street at whatever point he pleases," the *New York Times* insisted in 1913. Motorists "have no superior rights upon our thoroughfares." Two years later, in a letter to the *Times,* a reader echoed this theme and summed up the prevailing belief: "The motorist needs to realize that he is not privileged, that his design to get to a place in a given time should not be satisfied at the expense of others."

On YouTube there's much-viewed and mesmerizing film footage shot in San Francisco in 1906, just a few days before the great earthquake. (Search for "a trip down Market Street before the fire.") An enterprising early filmmaker had rigged up a movie camera on the front of a cable car and filmed the street ahead as the cable car made steady, stately progress down Market Street, the city's chief commercial thoroughfare. The clip runs for more than eleven minutes and nicely captures the amiable mayhem of an urban street in the middle of a day early in the last century. The cable car never fully stops, and open-topped cars, horse-drawn wagons, horse-drawn trolleys (on separate tracks), bicycles, and lots of walkers weave in front of it. Some vehicles travel in a straight line down the street, but not all. Some cars head upstream on what today would be considered the wrong side of the road. It's evident that everyone is aware of the others around them—including some pushy car drivers who in several instances force pedestrians to leap out of the way. For the most part, the chaos just works.

But it wasn't long before car drivers grew weary of the small bedlam and having to share public space. As cars swelled in number and congestion increased, drivers became less complacent about bending their will to convenience other users of the street. They instead turned their focus to reshaping regulations to accommodate their newfound numbers and horsepower. Cars began to challenge the old order. Automobile advocates pulled out all the tools in their toolkits to lay sole claim to the roads: the courts, public opinion, and support for local and national groups intent on altering municipal ordinances in their favor.

Pedestrians started with an upper hand in the courts for one simple reason: ordinances favored them. The laws were based on precedent, and pedestrians had long ago established their rights. Courts understood that cars were the newcomers and were there by the grace of the walkers. So for the first couple of decades following the spread of the automobile, drivers were almost always presumed guilty in any collision with a pedestrian. In 1913, for instance, a judge noted in a Georgia ruling that "automobiles have no priority of right in the use of the public highway" and further averred that "a pedestrian who, in using a public highway, is in the exercise of due care for his own protection and for the safety of others cannot as a matter of law be held to be guilty of contributory negligence merely because he does not run to escape injury by an automobile."

One influential negligence case, *Knapp v. Barrett,* ruled in 1915 that all those sharing the road must demonstrate personal responsibility while doing so, but, notably, must do so equally: "A wayfarer is not at liberty to close his eyes in crossing a city street. His duty is to use his eyes, and thus protect himself from danger," the court wrote. But, the ruling added, "the law does not say how often he must look, or precisely how far, or when or from where. . . . The law does not even say that because he sees a wagon approaching, he must stop till it has passed. He may go forward unless it is close upon him; and whether he is negligent in going forward, will be a question for the jury."

Or as another ruling (*Green v. Ruffin*) put it crisply in 1924: "It is not the duty of pedestrians to make mathematical calculations before crossing streets in front of automobiles, but to exercise ordinary care for their safety."

To prevail in court, auto advocates had to change local laws, and to do that, they needed to get organized. The American Automobile Association (AAA) was founded in 1902, when nine local motoring clubs banded together to form a national umbrella organization. A year later, the Association of Licensed Automobile Manufacturers was formed, although this shut down and was replaced by the more influential Automobile Board of Trade in 1911. (This was renamed the National Automobile Chamber of Commerce in 1913, and then recast again as the Automobile Manufacturers Association in 1934.) Both carmakers and car drivers were intent on reserving streets for cars by more sharply delineating who went where.

If there was one brilliant stroke of lobbying that gave cars expanded rights on the roads, it was the attack mounted on the "greatest good" argument. Municipal ordinances often favored an approach that would bring the broadest benefits to the largest number of its citizens. That makes sense, but this also favored crowded streetcars and teeming walkers over the lesser numbers of cars and drivers. So lobbyists adopted a different tack. "Motorist organizations appealed to minority rights to get favorable rules and legislation through cities and states," writes Peter Norton. Automobilists, in short, trotted out the argument that they were being discriminated against in laws that favored streetcars and pedestrians, and they sought redress. Rule makers listened.

Car advocates were also aided by the ascendency of professional city managers and traffic engineers (mentioned in Chapter 6), who prided themselves on applying scientific rigor to the running of cities. They lobbied their own city councils to establish more laws that codified who belonged where, all in the name of streamlining urban movement. More and more municipal lawmaking bodies began to wonder, as did a New Hampshire editorial writer in 1923, "Why have sidewalks if the pedestrians are to walk all over the street at their pleasure?" The criminalization of traditional uses of the street had begun.

In addition to mounting court challenges and pushing for changes in city ordinances, the champions of cars also launched a series of broad campaigns to sway public opinion. The central argument was invariably built upon their putative concerns about the rising fatality rates among pedestrians: "We're worried about the safety of walkers," their argument went, "and we're lobbying for safer streets." That meant that walkers should stay where it's safe—on the sidewalks—and enter the streets only at places specially designated for them. In short: "We will give you places to be safe, and in return you will agree to remain there; those who disobey should be penalized."

Just as pushing for minority rights in the courtroom was a brilliant gambit, in the court of public opinion car proponents did something equally bold and successful: They invented jaywalking.

In 1916 the *Atlanta Constitution* reported on new "jaywalk" lines being drawn "with brushes and whitewash" near the opera house to show walkers where they could and could not go. A Kansas paper cautioned against walking around motorcars when snow was present, warning: "Don't jaywalk, if you do, it is at your peril." In 1923 the Auto Club in Hamilton, Ohio, made an instructional film "intended to show autoists how to avoid accidents by driving properly"; one man was cast as the villainous "jaywalker."

The term "jaywalk" was defined by the *Oxford English Dictionary* compilers as "one who crosses a street without observing the traffic regulations for pedestrians." The etymology actually doesn't refer to birds—clueless pedestrians hopping around like witless blue jays—but rather comes from slang for a rural rube or country bumpkin: Only someone who didn't know the ways of the city would cross in the middle of a block. This was a nice touch, framing the debate to make urbane city residents fearful of being thought a hick.

And so the AAA clubs and the car manufacturers set about redefining recklessness; what had long been invariably attributed to drivers was now radically shifted to pedestrians. The idea: Make pedestrians equally culpable in accidents in the public mind, taking some pressure off the drivers.

Sometimes, the techniques were subtle. A 1927 article in the automotive pages of one newspaper reported that fully 5 percent of accidents between cars and pedestrians involved someone *walking into the side of a moving car!* The implicit suggestion: Blame must be shared—never mind that cars hitting pedestrians still accounted for 95 percent of accidents.

But more often than not, shifting the blame for accidents was less than subtle. In December 1913, a public safety campaign in Syracuse, New York, featured a man dressed as Santa Claus yelling through a megaphone at midblock crossers, denouncing them as "jaywalkers."

Car manufacturers were eager to tar the jaywalkers as brash and inconsiderate. In 1924 the Studebaker Corporation joined up with "traffic authorities" to launch a campaign in California and elsewhere with the goal of "convincing the man on foot that he, too should do his share to prevent accidents."

"The old common law rule that every person, whether on foot or driving, has equal rights in all parts of the roadway," wrote Miller McClintock, the planner hired to run the Studebaker-funded traffic institute, "must give way before the requirements of modern transportation." He was speaking what many city managers were thinking, and would go on to provide ample justification for those policies in the name of efficiency and expediency.

"The day of the hero with the long, careless stride is over," admitted Elizabeth Onativia in the *New York Times* in 1929. "The more careless it is the quicker it is over. Pedestrianism in city streets today involves executive ability, planning and foresight, specialized knowledge and concentration." The article was titled "Pedestrian Lot Not a Happy One."

Pedestrians did not roll over and immediately cede the streets. Many pushed back. Newspapers are filled with letters to the editor by city walkers in high dudgeon about being displaced from their ancestral turf. Writers commonly referred to automobiles as the "modern Moloch"—referencing a god of the ancients to whom children were sacrificed—and warned of obeying a false and vengeful diety. They objected to the term "jaywalking" to describe pedestrians doing what they'd always done, that is, navigating the best routes for their travels.

"Clearly we pedestrians are getting to be an intolerable nuisance, and something must be done to abate us," wrote someone named Richard Welling in 1916. Referring to the "great battle in the streets," he noted that automobile makers were coming up with new tactics, since "knocking down one of us every twenty-two minutes and killing one every fifteen hours does not perceptibly diminish us."

An article in 1916 noted that the Nomenclature Committee of the Society of Automobile Engineers had just spent six months devising definitions of sixteen different types of cars (including a coupé, a roadster, and a clover leaf, the last of which was a two-door car that seated four). "Not only motorists but the pedestrian public is interested in the different types of cars," someone then wrote in the *New York Times*. "A pedestrian in recounting some thrilling experience in dodging a car in the street can tell his story with much more realism if he knows the kind of car with which he had the encounter, and if he is hit by a car he is surely entitled to know whether it was a lordly 'limousine' or a lowly 'runabout.'"

"Must Jay-Walk or Lose" was the headline of one 1925 letter to the *New*

York Times. The writer pointed out that to reach an Eighth Avenue streetcar, pedestrians had to cross a line of car traffic, and cars rarely stopped to let them across. So the walker stood helplessly on the curb and watched his streetcar continue on its way. "If the pedestrian does not step into the stream of traffic to get a car he may remain on the sidewalk for an unlimited time, and if he does step out he is dubbed a jay-walker by the speed fiends."

The letter writer went on: "A good punishment for inconsiderate drivers would be to make them walk the streets at a good round pace for twelve hours a day for three weeks, giving educational leaflets to motorists." Perhaps best summing up the opposition, one walking adherent wrote in 1922, "the greatest danger of jaywalking is jaydriving." The term "jaydriving" did not catch on.

Ultimately, pedestrians had only sarcasm and facetiousness as weaponry. They lacked any organized opposition to resist the encroachment of cars. (The same applied to streetcar riders, who suffered a similar decline as automobiles gained the advantage.) Walkers didn't coalesce around any shared economic gain or central ideology, and thus spoke with no unified voice to counter the campaign to drive them off the street. Their rearguard battle took the shape of sharp and scattered guerrilla skirmishes, and they were quickly overwhelmed.

As the number of cars increased and more middle-class Americans could afford to buy them, the chore of shifting blame for accidents to pedestrians grew easier—the rock started to roll down the hill on its own. One popular argument: The ubiquity of the car had become such that to discriminate against drivers was now tantamount to discriminating against all Americans. When a New York judge ruled in 1923 that walkers still had a right to the road and motorists were still obliged to avoid them, the resistance was quick. An editorial in a New England newspaper suggested it would now be useful to "break down an artificial distinction" between cars and walkers, because almost every family had a car, and therefore "there are no longer separate classes of pedestrians and automobiles." Car and walker each had their place, and it was sensible to confine them there. "What would they say if automobilists insisted in driving on the sidewalk?" the paper asked. "In principal, surely, the two offenses are alike."

As automobiles dropped in cost, more pedestrians defected and bought cars, which accelerated change in public opinion and allegiances. A Cincinnati paper ran a small joke in 1920 that presaged the shift in attitude:

"'Smith must have bought a car,' remarked Jones. 'What makes you think that?' asked Brown. 'He used to talk about the blank-blank automobiles,' replied Jones, 'but now he is talking about blank-blank jaywalkers.'"

The underlying legal framework that guided street life also gradually changed. Prodded by auto clubs and a shift in the public's allegiance and opinion, municipalities began to formally close off the streets to walkers, imposing fines on those who transgressed. By 1927 Sioux City, Iowa, had implemented a provision stating that "no pedestrian shall cross a public street of this city except at a crossing and at right angles with said street at the end of the block." Violators could be fined a hundred dollars (about $1,300 today) or be jailed for thirty days.

More and more jurisdictions also called for laws prohibiting pedestrians from crossing in the middle of a block. "The individual would suffer no wrong if his freedom to dart about in the midst of moving vehicles were abridged," editorialized the Springfield, Massachusetts, *Republican*. Others embraced this idea, including the Kingston, New York, *Daily Freeman*, which wrote, "How the jaywalkers can be protected 'in spite of themselves' if they persist in 'popping out from behind parked machines in unexpected places' is not readily conceivable."

Much the same was happening abroad. In Germany, jaywalking was referred to as "Dutch crossing"—presumably another "hick" reference—and to control it, the city of Berlin in 1928 printed and distributed two million leaflets outlining the ten commandments for pedestrians. "These edicts can be considered the acme of pessimism," noted one account, "since the walkers are cautioned to look both ways even before crossing a one-way street."

By the late 1920s, the battle for the streets was winding down, with the automobile emerging as the uncontested victor. "Ordinarily, reckless motorists have been the targets of criticism, but pedestrians who persist in taking a chance are now receiving a larger share of the blame than formerly," reported the Springfield, Massachusetts, Safety Council in 1929.

"The pedestrian, says the law, is a free man," wrote Foster Ware in the *New York Times* in 1928, adding that five pedestrians were killed by cars every three days in the city. "But let him try to enjoy this freedom and he will soon enough learn that he has been made the victim of a rather grim joke. . . . Bitter experience has taught the pedestrian to forget most of the 'rights' that technically belong to him."

"This country was founded on the principle of freedom," said Miller

McClintock, then head of the Erskine Bureau for Street Traffic Research, in a 1928 talk to the Society of Automotive Engineers. "Now the automobile has brought something which is an integral part of the American spirit—freedom of movement." (This notion was embraced early on even by the most nimble of minds. Thomas Edison said in 1908 that if New York's horse-drawn carriages and carts "could be transformed into motor cars overnight," this would "so relieve traffic [congestion] as to make Manhattan Island resemble 'The Deserted Village.'")

Freedom of the roads had effectively been redefined. It no longer meant the right to wander at will on foot. Freedom of the road meant driving one's automobile at the top speed it was engineered to drive, the wide-open highway smooth and unobstructed.

Marinetti's *Futurist Manifesto* was, in fact, winning the future.

May 27, 1909. Weston didn't need to ask permission of automobilists to cross streets as he made his way through the west. Cars didn't appear in threatening numbers in these open spaces. But he did need to confront the Rockies. And he opted to do so not by traversing through them directly over passes and through deep valleys between jagged peaks. He chose to first head north, paralleling the mountains, with the idea of angling northwest through Wyoming and then turning southwest toward California. The elevation gains and slopes wouldn't be as severe, and he would face fewer threats of being caught in squally mountain passes. It also would be easier to coordinate baggage transfer, now that he'd been abandoned by car and valet, by sending luggage and supplies ahead by train.

After addressing the crowd in Denver and a short rest, he set off again, "as ambitious and active as a man fifty years his junior," wrote the *Denver Post*. Weston was reverting to form, moving like a metronome, accompanied by a handful of admirers who dropped off first in clumps and then one by one. "He will make no spurts of speed," reported the *Denver Post*, "but will keep up the regular clock-like gait which has worn out the hundreds if not thousands of men who have undertaken to follow him." He was accompanied by one particularly doughty walker, a "young lawyer from New York" named Thomas Hogan, who walked with him as far as Fort Lupton. Hogan "did not show the least sign of fatigue from the twenty-eight mile walk,"

Weston noted admiringly. At Fort Lupton, Weston rested briefly with some distant relatives he'd recently connected with. He was breaking in a new pair of shoes, he noted, and his feet were a touch tender. But he didn't linger for long: After a few hours, he resumed walking north, completing a fifty-seven-mile day upon arrival in the town of Greeley.

The weather continued to plague him. "I thought I had encountered gales before," Weston said of his trek after leaving Greeley, "but yesterday's tornado exceeded the limit." He plunged on into fierce and stormy winds for eleven miles; the last four miles into Nunn took him an hour and forty minutes. The storm continued unabated through the weekend. "The people east of Chicago have no idea of the force and magnitude of these elements of the West," Weston said. "Compared with the showers of the East they are awful and past comprehension."

His health was good and his feet were generally fine, but he was falling behind schedule. He would now need to average forty-seven miles per day to make it to San Francisco within one hundred days.

Weston's western journey was now ironbound—by and large confined to rail tracks, and he no doubt grew weary of the sight of long lines of steel forever converging in the distance, with only the horizontal striping of wooden rail ties beneath his feet providing evidence of speed. But somehow it seems appropriate, given that he was walking at the cusp of the crosswalk era.

———

It's probably just a coincidence that, with its alternating strips of white paint and black asphalt, the common pedestrian crosswalk resembles train tracks, or perhaps more to the point, the bars on a jail cell. But for more than half a century, it's where pedestrians have been confined after their banishment from the broader thoroughfares that were once their natural habitat.

The first iconic so-called zebra crossings—think of the Beatles on the cover of *Abbey Road*—were introduced in England in 1951. These were designed to replace simple metal studs set in the roadway to mark crossings (bricks or stone inlaid in pavement sometimes indicated crossings in an earlier era). These earlier crosswalks were visible to pedestrians but not to cars, rendering them more or less pointless. So bolder colors and patterns were tested out, including blue and yellow, red and white, and black and white. The latter was found to be the most striking and visible for drivers, and by 1951 was made the standard across the British Isles. Pedestrian deaths dropped 11 percent that year.

This made sense: The bold graphics alerted cars that they were approaching a pedestrian zone, and those on foot would have little question of when they had entered a sanctuary. Many jurisdictions around the globe granted pedestrians the full right-of-way within a crosswalk, except when a police officer or a stoplight was directing traffic. A crosswalk is essentially akin to Vatican City within Italy, a sort of subsidiary nation with its own laws existing within a larger republic.

The striping patterns in the United States have changed of late, as municipalities have been testing different patterns and shapes for their effectiveness. The yellow and black "tiger crossings" are now thought to offer higher visibility and to be safer than black and white ones and are seen more often than they once were. Some crosswalks are now diagonally striped, some are painted solid colors, some are demarcated with striped bars in pairs, and many today, in the interest of cost cutting, are "transverse crosswalks," which are a simple pair of thick lines running from curb to curb. (It costs about $4,000 to mark the four blocks of a typical intersection with transverse crosswalks, compared with $10,000 for a full zebra striping.)

All crosswalks share one trait, however: Their effectiveness has diminished. They no longer register as readily with drivers—because of familiarity, contempt, all that—yet pedestrians still perceive crosswalks as offering security. This makes for a bad combination. Some reports suggest that traffic accidents don't decrease at marked crossings that aren't supplemented with other traffic-slowing measures, like flashing lights or speed bumps. In New York City, a study of 1,400 pedestrian-related accidents between 2008 and 2011 found that pedestrians are struck most often when in the crosswalk and when legally walking with the signal. (Those accidents accounted for 44 percent of all incidents, with 23 percent occurring in midblock and 9 percent when pedestrians are crossing against the signal. Six percent of the accidents took place on a sidewalk.)

In part because of their dwindling effectiveness, zebra crossings are disappearing from the very place they were invented—England. They've been removed at many busy intersections in favor of traffic lights that control the crossings. The one place the zebra won't be removed? The Beatles' famous Abbey Road crossing; it's protected as a historic landmark.

Crosswalk technology could be considered a growth field these days, with inventors striving to make the simple act of walking across a street less likely to result in injury or fatality. On the lower-tech end, communities have been trying out new crossing patterns (including honeycombs), textured and reflective crosswalks, and raised platforms for crosswalks that double as speed bumps. Other low-tech approaches border on the farcical, including the caching of orange flags on short sticks at crossings, which pedestrians are to wave to boost their visibility. Astoria, Oregon, set up flag depots at two busy intersections in 2013, but the results were less than stellar. Few walkers used them—perhaps some thought they'd be encouraging cars to charge at them in the manner of a bull charging at a matador—and many flags were tossed in the gutters and became stained and no longer very attention getting. Also, they were evidently popular among souvenir hunters; within the first six weeks, 245 of the 300 flags had been lost or stolen.

High tech gets more media attention, perhaps because as a society we have long believed that technology, smartly applied, will solve any problem, including traversing a street. The use of technology to cross streets—both to give pedestrians control over their destiny and to make them more visible—isn't especially new. In busy cities, walk signals appeared early on (experimentally, as early as the late 1860s in England) to let pedestrians know when it was safe to cross. At first, this consisted of a pennant raised on a mast by a traffic officer. It evolved into a "Walk/Don't Walk" light by the late 1930s, which in turn became the stylized walking figure and raised-hand icons. Pedestrians were granted some control of their environment when button-activated walk signals were installed (again, this was in part for the convenience of cars, since it would allow the skipping of the pedestrian cycle if no one needed to cross). In a wonderfully patronizing story in the *New York Times* in May 1930, a reporter documented the unveiling of an early pedestrian-controlled crossing signal in a suburb north of the city. "The lowly pedestrian has been exalted to master of the broad highway by the Westchester County Park Commission," the reporter wrote, "through the installation today of a device whereby the pedestrian is able to bring all automobile traffic to a halt long enough to cross the street in complete safety."

And what was this magical device? A button on a box. "All he needs to do is to press a button, and the device obligingly flashes a bright red light, in obedience to which all traffic comes to a halt. The light automatically remains at the red 'stop' signal long enough to permit the pedestrian to cross the street. Once the walker reaches his objective the light automatically reverts to green, and traffic proceeds."

These buttons persist, and are what some activists have dubbed "beg buttons" or, at other times, "placebos." Many doubt that they're placed as an actual aid to walkers, believing instead they're installed to create the illusion that one's moment will come only if one presses the button and waits patiently enough. Many are, in fact, inoperative and have the same effect if you press them once or fifteen times—the traffic lights are on their own cycle and will turn when they've been programmed to do so, often in coordination with other lights by computerized systems designed to keep cars moving smoothly. A newspaper in Honolulu reported that more than a third of that city's crossing buttons were nonfunctioning. A 2004 report in New York found that with the implementation of computer-controlled traffic signals, some 2,500 pedestrian crossing buttons (out of 3,250) had been deactivated, but were left on the posts as placebos, along with instructions for use.

Among the more promising emergent crossing technologies these days is HAWK, or high-intensity activated crosswalk. ("HAWK," evidently, sounds more appealing than "HIAC." Also, it carries on the British tradition of goofy, bird-themed crossing patterns—like pelican, puffin, and toucan, the last of which also allows those on bikes to cross—that is, "two can" cross.) These are increasingly installed in areas where pedestrian traffic doesn't merit a full crosswalk or stoplight. HAWK systems, which were inspired by European railroad crossings, consist of a pair of lights that remain unlit until a button is pressed or they are triggered by a motion detector. Flashing yellow lights over the crosswalk then kick on, followed shortly by steady red, then blinking red lights, upon which a driver can proceed if the crosswalk is clear. Then the lights go black again until the next pedestrian comes along. These appear to actually work—in some studies, it's been found that cars are yielding up to 97 percent of the time.

Making crosswalks and those within them more visible has also been a priority of traffic control. One style of crosswalk consists of flashing lights embedded in the pavement aimed toward drivers, which start flashing when someone is about to cross the street. Introduced in Santa Rosa, California, in 1993, the concept was inspired by strobe lights used at airport runways. It's been adopted by others and studied extensively in Kirkland, Washington, which compiled before-and-after data at several crossings. Overall, it did increase compliance—most dramatically after dark, when the percentage of cars yielding jumped from 16 to 100 at one intersection.

Technology for safer crossings is also moving from the streets to the cars themselves. In 2012, the Federal Highway Administration sponsored a study to look at "innovative technologies to detect pedestrians or other vulnerable road users at designed crossing locations and midblock/unexpected areas" using in-vehicle systems. These are essentially dual-lens cameras programed with algorithms to detect pedestrians in the roadway and emit an audible signal within "actionable warning time." A test unit was installed on a Toyota Highlander, and the results were encouraging; although it picked up many false positives, identifying pedestrians where they didn't exist, the developers continue to make improvements. It's still at the experimental stage, and it's uncertain if this will ever become standard equipment.

Failing the ability of technology to detect and deter pedestrian–car collisions, researchers are also looking at the mechanics of what happens when a car hits a pedestrian and trying to improve the outcome. As with just about anything involving cars and walkers, there's long precedent. *Modern Mechanics* magazine in the 1930s reported on a device much like a cowcatcher on trains that was designed to be installed on trucks to remove errant pedestrians. When a driver spotted a pedestrian sprawled on the pavement, perhaps downed by another driver, he would release a steel roller that would clatter down from its former position as the bumper, and in the words of the magazine, "literally sweep a fallen pedestrian before it and thus save him from being crushed to almost certain death beneath the heavy wheels."

More modern versions of the pedestrian cowcatcher have cropped up in recent years. In early 2013 Volvo rolled out the first car with a "pedestrian airbag." It's hidden at the base of the windshield and activated by a collision, when it rapidly inflates (although not so much that it would fully obscure the driver's view). This cushions the impact and reduces the odds of severe head or neck injuries on the part of the pedestrian. And in England, an engineering firm recently paired up with academic researchers and designed a crumpling aluminum hood. Were you to be hit by a car with one of these, you'd evidently sink into the hood as if into a beanbag chair. Early tests suggest that head injuries could be reduced by 50 or 60 percent.

Efforts to make walking safer in an urban environment have required drivers to give up some of the dominance and autonomy they've gained in the past century, including stepped-up enforcement of existing laws and more stops at HAWK beacons. This invariably has led to grumbling and some backlash. In Fort Lee, New Jersey, local police slapped fifty-six drivers with $230 tickets in March 2013 for not yielding to "bait pedestrians"— plainclothes officers using the crosswalk. This did not sit well with drivers. "It's the most bogus thing I've ever seen," one driver groused to a local reporter. Another was more expansive, saying, "Pedestrians are idiots, especially in New Jersey. If someone jumps out into the walkway, what makes you think that that driver can stop in enough time to not strike that pedestrian and not get hit by the cars behind them? Are the pedestrians not endangering the drivers just as much? Where's their ticket?" Which, of course, was the same argument made against pedestrians in 1930. The Fort Lee police took the long view, noting that "people are learning that pedestrians have a right to cross the street and they have to stop."

Blame the pedestrian. It's served as an all-purpose solution for more than a century.

The debate over how to cross the street is just getting started in many parts of the country. In others, the debate has been long over, and it's been settled in favor of the car. No consideration for the walker has been made. Long stretches of roadways lack sidewalks, and pedestrian crossings have been designed by people who, it seems, have never attempted to cross a street.

Ben Ross, a blogger for *Greater Greater Washington,* visited an intersection in a suburb in Maryland not long ago, where a pair of walkers crossing the street at night had been hit by a car and badly injured. They had ignored the legal route for crossing from one side to the other—from a bus stop on one side of the street to a bus stop on the other—and so got little sympathy from the public or press. But what Ross found on his visit was that no crosswalk existed directly linking the bus stops and that to legally cross, a pedestrian would have to walk around the entire intersection, crossing three roads instead of one. He did this, and discovered it required traversing twenty-eight lanes of traffic, some of which were right-turn feeder lanes with no stoplights, making a crossing troublesome at best. It took him eight and a half minutes to get from one side of the street to the other. The couple had made the risky (and illegal) but logical decision to cut straight across.

A not-uncommon story told among walking advocates is of pedestrians being hit while crossing streets illegally (often because, as in that Maryland suburb, no practical alternative existed) and then being fined or arrested afterward. Meanwhile, the driver who did the hitting suffered no legal consequences for failing to stop for pedestrians in the roadway. One of the more egregious cases cropped up in 2010, when a thirty-year-old single mother and three of her children (all under the age of nine) disembarked from a bus along a four-lane road directly across from their apartment. The nearest legal crosswalk was nearly three-tenths of a mile away, meaning that they'd have had to walk about a half-mile to legally travel less than a hundred yards. So they headed directly across when it was clear and made it to the median. While waiting for a gap in traffic in the other direction, the woman's four-year-old son darted ahead and was hit and killed. The car's driver, who had been drinking and consuming painkillers, left the scene of the accident. He was eventually caught and pleaded guilty to a hit-and-run charge, and served six months in jail. And the mother? She was charged with and convicted of second-degree homicide by car, failure to use a crosswalk, plus reckless conduct.

It's a world built for cars, and pedestrians have increasingly been trespassers in a foreign land, subject to arrest and harassment and legal prosecution. Where once common sense prevailed in regulating the streets, it's now seemingly banned.

It's the world we've made.

One consequence of the century-long battle for the streets has been a balkanization of the American landscape. Broadly speaking, we're riven by an unseen border that divides walkable communities, which are largely located in or around downtowns and rail-served suburbs built prior to World War II, and nonwalkable communities, which are generally in outlying postwar suburbs and exurbs built during the scramble to develop cheaper land farther from town and accessible chiefly by car.

This isn't absolute, of course. The rights of pedestrians have eroded and been abridged in many older downtowns as they've been made more car-friendly. And some suburban communities have taken pains to accommodate walkers and build density where none formerly existed. But generally, the broad template relating to walking remains—block sizes, sidewalk placements, and street widths are more or less fixed. As preventive medicine expert Jim Sallis put it, "Every older city is walkable, period. If they were built before cars they had to be."

In contrast, the suburbs took root when cars were running rampant, and thus they were designed on an automobile's template. That's also hard to change—especially shrinking block sizes or placing services closer to one another—although the next chapter will look at some improvements there.

That suburban areas, especially commercial zones, are often hazardous to walkers can be observed by simply driving around. But less obviously, creating an environment that's hostile to foot travel is also more likely to lead to long-term health hazards. In fact, more people may suffer health problems from not walking than from walking, even if it involves playing a real-life version of *Frogger*. By designing communities that make walking difficult or discouraging, we're creating a one-way route to poor health. And again, a negative-feedback loop appears. We walk less because the opportunities diminish, and then we walk less because we're increasingly unfit.

How unfriendly to walking are suburban neighborhoods? Consider one extreme example that was recently featured on *DC.Streetsblog*. It highlighted two houses with adjoining backyards in Orlando, Florida. The yards were separated by a few feet and, apparently, a fence. Yet to travel from the front door of one house to the front door of the other by road—say, to bring a cooler of beer to your neighbor's barbecue—required one to travel a full seven miles, or walk about two hours. Neighbors on foot would need to leave their subdivision and make their way to feeder roads and then to arterials before reversing the process on the other side. Developers of suburban housing have never put connections between adjoining subdivisions very high on their list, because pathways eat up land that could be sold as housing lots, and in some cases, creating those connections is even banned by municipalities out of fear of increased shortcut traffic. And many people choose to live on culs-de-sac for good reasons: It keeps down joyriding and traffic noise, for one. Dead ends also offer the perception of security, since unfamiliar cars or—worse yet—unfamiliar pedestrians creeping through are more readily noticed by neighbors.

But what's the effect of these subdivisions that all but prohibit a natural connectivity? As Winston Churchill once said, "We shape our buildings, and afterwards our buildings shape us." So it is with our cities and towns. And the shape that results is, more often than not, a pear.

One of the seminal works in framing the public debate was "Urban Sprawl and Public Health," a paper published in *Public Health Reports* by Howard Frumkin in 2002. (It became the basis for an influential book published two years later, *Urban Sprawl and Public Health: Designing, Planning, and Building for Healthy Communities,* coauthored with Lawrence Frank and Richard Jackson.) The paper and the book prompted a major shift in the debate over our built environment.

Frumkin in many ways pointed out the obvious: "Land use and travel patterns are closely linked. If distinct land uses are separated, if the distances between them are great, and if roads are more available than sidewalks and paths, then people shift from walking and bicycling to driving."

And the result, he noted, was that those living in areas unfriendly to walking were in worse health. Frumkin notes that many other causes contribute to the nation's rising ill health and obesity, but arrives at an inescapable conclusion: "Sprawl has negative health consequences." In short, the landscape is killing us.

A rather lively debate has flared up about this very assertion, though it seems obvious on its face. The question persists: Do neighborhoods that are better designed for walking—say, with short blocks and sidewalks buffered by street trees and fronting interesting storefronts and architecturally engaging homes—actually encourage more people to walk?

Critics point out that it's not hard to come up with other explanations for the correlations between land-use patterns and health—they note the equally self-evident proposition that people already inclined to walk are likely to be drawn to live in areas where sidewalks and side streets make for better walking, and so land patterns may not actually lead to any change in behavior. If true, it would make it harder to justify investing in improvements in the interest of public health.

Three environmental engineering academics at the University of California in Davis took up this question in a paper published in 2006 in the *Journal of the American Planning Association.* They studied eight neighborhoods, starting with a sample of eight thousand residents in Northern California. They focused on those who'd recently moved from other areas and explored whether an improved walking environment led to more walking. The study was controlled for factors like income (the poor can't afford cars) and age. Among the results: "The residents of traditional neighborhoods walk substantially more than residents of suburban neighborhoods" after they've moved. The authors admit the data aren't definitive and that positive attitudes toward walking still may be more important than an alluring environment. "In the meantime," they write, "the results printed here provide some encouragement that changes to the built environment that increase the opportunities for walking may in fact lead to more walking."

There's a word for factors—like neighborhoods—that discourage walking: "obesogenic." At least that's what social geographers and medical workers have been calling environments that make it hard to bike or walk, and thus contribute to obesity. (The name overlooks the myriad of other diseases also tied to a sedentary lifestyle.) "Safe, walkable neighborhoods are not just an amenity," summarize Michael Mehaffy and Richard Jackson, "they're a matter of life or death."

What makes a neighborhood unattractive for walking isn't particularly elusive—as with US Supreme Court Justice Potter Stewart's description of pornography, you know a pedestrian-unfriendly neighborhood when you see one. Getting around on foot feels unsafe, and it lacks useful services within walking distances from one another. (It may or may not have cold winters: Active transport isn't as dependent on climate as you might guess. More people bike regularly in Minneapolis and Copenhagen than in many more-temperate locales.) Another key element shared by unwalkable areas is a lack of connectivity, of being able to get from where you are to someplace you want to be, like those two Orlando backyards mentioned earlier.

All unwalkable neighborhoods tend to be unwalkable in much the same way. But walkable neighborhoods vary widely—no one would confuse Venice with Manhattan's Lower East Side—each tending to be defined by detail and nuance. But they do share certain broader traits. The urbanist Jane Jacobs identified four qualities in livable cities' neighborhoods: population density, multiple primary functions, short blocks, and buildings of various ages. Jeff Speck, in his highly readable book *Walkable City,* puts forth his "General Theory of Walkability," identifying four main conditions that are broader than Jacobs's, but overlap with them: streets should be useful, safe, comfortable, and interesting.

Various studies have put a finer point on these favorable conditions. A meta-analysis undertaken by two St. Louis University researchers for the Transportation Research Board and the Institute of Medicine reviewed fourteen walkability studies that examined the connection between environment and transport. All concluded that people walk and cycle more when their neighborhoods have higher residential density, a mixture of land uses (shops within walking distance of homes), and connected streets (a gridlike pattern instead of a collection of culs-de-sac). Other studies have pointed to further elements that encourage walking. For example, analysis of diaries compiled by families in Portland, Oregon, found that features that "increase the choice to walk include narrow roads, street connectivity, continuous sidewalks, and zonal household density, as well as proximity to commercial uses and transit." A more highly textured environment filled with intriguing details encourages walking, which engenders better health.

Arguably, modern multistory buildings are like the suburbs: They tend to be designed to encourage laziness. Even in office complexes of just a few floors, the elevator banks are invariably situated by the main entrance. Even if you are inclined to walk two or three floors, you often need to hunt out the stairwells, and more often than not these are unattractive and inhospitable. They seem to be placed grudgingly, required by building codes, hidden away, adorned with warning signs about access ("Emergency Only"). Inside, they feel creepy and are usually constructed with the most rudimentary materials available—concrete and industrial steel plate and rubber tread guards. Just as we've engineered walking out of the suburban environment, so too have we engineered it out of buildings. Only the most brave and indefatigable (or foolishly persistent) get exercise.

"Walking is totally positive and yet we have allowed it to become an extremely negative experience," said Ben Plowden, now director of planning with Transport for London, at a walking conference in 2000.

"Throughout our whole history, people have walked for transportation," said Jim Sallis. "We've deleted that. We've designed that feature out of the world for many, many people and we now have the evidence that our planning and community design decisions and our transportation decisions are reducing activity and contributing to chronic diseases."

We shape the environment. Then the environment shapes us.

———

May 30, 1909. Weston spent his Sunday in Nunn, Colorado, catching up on correspondence and resting. The landscape continued to be open plains in every direction, the chief distraction the shifting clouds billowing high in the sky. The mountains could be seen to the west, but he was continuing his track around them. He left Nunn shortly after midnight. Local residents assured him the weather would improve after the weekend's ferocious storms, and indeed the rain diminished and the savage wind started to abate. He made it eighteen miles to Carr, arriving at 4:45 in the morning. Whereupon he found the wind again rising and the rain starting to fall in great torrents. He sought shelter at a home, took off his shoes, and decided he'd stay put until sunset. Surely by that time, another chorus of locals assured him, the weather would break and conditions would improve.

The weather failed to receive the message. It continued to blow; Weston didn't set off again until midnight, when the wind had finally dropped off, although the rain persisted, and then the temperature fell. Aggravated by the delays, he opted to take a shortcut off the rail line and lopped Cheyenne off his route, shaving off seven miles while disappointing those who had been awaiting him in town. "I arrived at 7XL Ranch at 9:05 A.M.," he wrote, "after passing through Lone Tree Creek, where I got my feet wet." Here he rested up, dried out, and near midnight enjoyed a "substantial meal" before setting off into the dark. He was accompanied by William Acor, a congenial ranch hand who traveled alongside by wagon toward Laramie, shuttling Weston's bags. The long storm had finally passed; a bright moon illuminated the huge sky, and coyotes serenaded Weston as he walked.

When day broke, his adventures resumed. He again intersected the rail line, and soon after he walked through a half-mile tunnel, which gave him "the horrors." He walked on though towering hills capped with snow from the recent storm, reporting that the desolation made "a wild, lonesome picture." His loneliness was compounded when he met up with Japanese rail crews working along the line, with whom he could nod but not converse. (He later reported that he found "the best of treatment and . . . the soul of hospitality" at a section house run by a Japanese man, an encounter that "pleased me beyond expectation.") The hills were full of large rocks and "decomposed granite," which induced in him a sense of melancholy. The good news? The broken granite served as a base for a fine rail bed, which, he reported, was "the best I have walked on."

Finding places to sleep at night was growing more difficult. Towns were fifteen to twenty-five miles apart, presenting his daily schedule with few options for changing up on the fly. Section houses, where men maintaining the rail were bivouacked, were usually filled to capacity (mostly with Greeks, Italians, and Japanese, he said). Still, Weston praised the Union Pacific Railroad for being most accommodating, given the circumstances.

Water was also becoming an issue—not that it proved scarce after a series of heavy storms, but rather its quality. It was extremely alkaline—"heavy with soda," as Weston put it—and made him feel ill when he drank it. He thirsted for fresh cow's milk, which often served as his primary fuel. "Condensed milk is a poor substitute for the real thing, and I feel the loss of it very much," he wrote.

He faced another persistent condition as he pushed westward: hunger. As in Kansas, he was astonished at the distances between homes and settlements and the consequent scarcity of refreshment. He could often count on good samaritans, but here he found few samaritans, good or otherwise. "One day in the week of May 17, I walked thirty-six miles before I could get breakfast or have a rest," he groused, "and for twenty-two miles did not see a house." He arrived in Laramie, Wyoming, "in a very feeble condition because I was unable to get any regular nourishment," he wrote. "The country is full of cows, but no milk can be had; chickens are at a premium, consequently no eggs. I depend mostly upon eggs and milk, and without them I feel lost."

"The country itself," he noted later, "affords no encouragement for one engaged in a task of this kind."

He wasn't utterly alone walking through basins and canyons. From time to time, he crossed paths with people who weren't employed by the railroad. In Castle Rock, Wyoming, a man named John Moore came out from town to meet him, bringing him a welcome supply of milk and a dozen eggs. Moore seemed to be the sort who thirsted for company as well. He confided to Weston's manager that he'd captured two young eagles and had been training them so he could attach a wicker basket between them. He was planning to sit in the basket and fly to New York, and then continue on across the Atlantic Ocean. He hoped Weston wouldn't be too cross with him when newsmen abandoned the walker to cover his flight.

Weston also had encounters with train-hopping vagrants, who stared sullenly at him. The hoboes made Weston uncomfortable. "Some of them don't look good to me," he reported. He bought a revolver and now carried it with him. "But for what purpose I hardly know," he admitted, because "if I were attacked they would also take my gun." After he told local law enforcement his worries, they sent instructions down the line to deputy sheriffs, asking them to clear the tracks of vagrants. "I feel safer since this is done," Weston wrote.

Weston rarely had anything but good to say about the railroad workers; they returned the affection and seemed to enjoy being a small part of a long walk. On one gusty day, Weston's hat blew off and down a ravine. He deemed it foolhardy and time-wasting to attempt to retrieve it, and he pushed on. A short while later, a railman, having heard of the loss, went back and scrambled down to fetch it. He sent it ahead to Weston on a passing freight train. "All the working class wish me the best of luck," Weston said.

The weather, as usual, did not proffer good wishes. "There is hardly a day in which I don't encounter some extreme elements of weather, such as a wind storm and sudden rains, snow, hail or sleet," he wrote from Wyoming. "However encouraging the indication may be on starting out, invariably I am caught when miles away from any town or haven of safety. I am never sure of reaching the destination for the day."

Another big storm blew through, flooding creeks and rivers and sweeping away rail bridges, when he neared Rawlins, Wyoming. Men were dispatched to repair the washouts, and trains were delayed up and down the line. "The prospects for today's walk are not very encouraging," he wrote. "The sudden changes and the daily drenching I get are becoming monotonous."

He eventually made it to Rawlins. It was his seventy-third day since leaving New York, and he'd walked some 2,783 miles, averaging slightly more than 38 miles a day. Impressive, perhaps, but not quite impressive enough to ensure he'd arrive San Francisco on time. His margin of error had evaporated. He cut back his sleep, often finding time for just a quick evening nap, then setting off again late at night. "I won the Astley Belt on two hours' sleep, and probably will win this effort in the same way, weather permitting," he said.

And on he went.

———

In Weston's era, talking about a town's walkability or neighborhood was might have seemed nonsensical. All were walkable, more or less, although some had muddier streets and others were more clotted with horses and their waste. But in the following century, with communities starting to sprawl along the margins as the car secured its domain, divisions arose, with older neighborhoods being more foot-friendly than the new ones developed to accommodate the car.

So, as will often happen, people devised systems of measurement. Among the first and most prominent is the Walk Score, which began as a side project by a trio of software engineers. They'd heard a report about "food miles"—the labeling of food with the number of miles it had traveled from its source—and thought to create a sort of mirror image by figuring out how far a consumer had to travel to buy basic products or find entertainment. If it was within walking distance, the score was higher. This became a marker of how walkable a neighborhood was.

A rudimentary site went live in 2007, and the founders sent an e-mail to a few dozen people letting them know about it. By the end of that day, some 150,000 people had clicked through to check out the site. Evidently, it was information people wanted.

Walkscore.com was, and remains, a remarkably simple site to use. You type in an address, and a proprietary algorithm gives you a score between 0 and 100. Anything below 50 is "car dependent," and anything above 90 is a "walker's paradise." This is determined largely by proximity to places you might visit on a regular basis, like a grocery store, a bookstore, a movie theater, a city park. Older, livelier downtowns tend to have higher scores; locales far out in the suburbs rate lower.

It's far from perfect—the algorithm is pegged to the proximity to restaurants, banks, retail, and the like, so if your home is surrounded by malls, you'll likely have a high Walk Score, even though every errand will involve trekking across parking lots and no sidewalk may exist within a mile of you. The creators have been working to patch these shortcomings and in the meantime have been developing another scoring system called the Street Smart Walk Score that takes into account other factors, like the size of blocks (smaller block sizes are more conducive to walking), the number of intersections per square mile (more is better), and the speed of traffic on adjacent roads (slower is better). It has some nice extras, like a shaded zone showing everything within a fifteen-minute walking radius, but is still in beta testing as of this writing.

Other competitors have joined the action. There's a smartphone app called Walkonomics, created by an Englishman named Adam Davies, which strives to gauge the walking environment using more nuanced criteria. (A recent blog post was titled "Why Walkability Isn't Just about Proximity to Shops.") Among the variables it considers are the ease of crossing the street, sidewalk quality, hilliness, crime, and the attractiveness of the street and its buildings. (It's currently available for use in San Francisco, New York, and a few cities in England.) Overall, it's a bit quirky and arbitrary—for instance, 555 Hudson Street in Manhattan's West Village, where Jane Jacobs once lived, earns only two stars out of five; her old neighborhood is penalized for road safety, fear of crime, and not being "fun and relaxing," although it gains points for being "smart and beautiful."

Architect Steve Mouzon, who has been advocating for a new urbanism that adopts a more human scale, has been shopping another idea—a measure for "Walk Appeal." It's built around what might be called Mouzon's law, which notes that the average person might walk two miles in Rome but maybe only a quarter-mile in a squalid, surnburnt area of suburban strip malls. "Europeans are reputed to walk much further than Americans," Mouzon notes on his blog, "and for this reason: their streets have much better Walk Appeal." Among other things, they've got shorter blocks and more to look at. "Narrow storefronts change the walkers' view frequently, which is more entertaining than long blank walls or long stretches of the same building," Mouzon writes.

Proof of his point: Just look at all the drivers circling and waiting for parking at a supermarket or mall to avoid having to convey themselves an additional seventy-five feet or so from the nearest available slot. Part of it is laziness, to be sure, but also at work is that, as Mouzon notes, "the walking experience is too dreadful." Yet, crossing a parking lot doesn't earn the lowest Walk Appeal score: "The worst sidewalk you could possibly choose to walk on is one with an arterial thoroughfare on one side and a parking lot on the other." Here, he estimates, people are willing to walk a grand total of twenty-five feet, although no one actually does this unless their car quits on them. Among the "measurables" he lists are "goals in the middle distance," "view changes," and "street enclosure"—the sorts of things that could be worked into an algorithm. But he also suggests that reducing a complex environment to a single number may be a fool's errand, just as afflicted with tunnel vision as measuring a city street solely by the number of cars that can traverse it in an hour.

Walk Score and its competitors may be imperfect and misleading. But the fact that they exist and are gaining traction—especially in real estate listings, where walkable neighborhoods tend to have higher land values—is significant, and suggests that we may be returning to something many assumed has long since been abandoned: a renewed appreciation for walking as a way of getting around.

June 16, 1909. Weston crossed the state line and entered Utah. He was relieved to be out of Wyoming, with its barren rock and constant wind and perpetual storms and frightening hoboes and long stretches devoid of lodging and food. "I'm glad to have reached Ogden," he said. "It's the end of one of the hardest parts of my journey." ("I pray to be protected from Wyoming," he said later and more dyspeptically. "It is the worst state in the United States.")

But he'd managed to survive so far and he was still headed west—and this singular fact was deemed worthy of comment. The *Washington Post* rejoiced that at a time when residents of Indiana and Tennessee fired on hot-air balloons overhead ("folks who suspect spies in the very birds of the air"), Weston had not once been held up or attacked or otherwise molested. He was vulnerable, aged, and often alone, yet no one had caused him harm. "Bad roads, bad weather, and a wind that blew him bodily against a fence, are the worst accidents that have happened," the paper noted. "Many things that are remarkable pass without remark. This phase of Weston's long journey should be taken as a remarkable proof of the good sense and honesty that prevails throughout the country."

Utah continued to please Weston immensely. "By gum, this is God's country isn't it?" he gushed to a local reporter, ingratiatingly adding that he was content to arrive in the land of Mormons. "As I crossed the line from Wyoming the grass began to grow on this side within two inches of the post, by thunder. And it's been getting greener and thicker ever since."

But time was not on his side; he couldn't dawdle and enjoy the state as much as he may have liked to. He eliminated some planned detours, like a tailor taking in a suit. He trimmed off a long-planned side trip into Salt Lake City. The disappointment there was palpable. The city had been bristling with excitement about the great walker's impending arrival; a Weston

Walking Club had formed and was marshaling to greet him, and several long-distance walkers from the local YMCA had announced plans to walk toward Ogden, meet him en route, then escort him into town. All plans were scuttled as Weston veered west.

Yet the biggest revision was to come: He abandoned his original (and ill-considered) plan to first walk to Los Angeles, then head north to San Francisco. The Los Angeles route had the merit of allowing him to stay on Union Pacific rails, but Weston had been apprised of the disadvantages: the distances between work stations would be longer than what he'd endured even in Wyoming, meaning there would be more vexing gaps between the barrels of drinking water set out for station men.

The most compelling reason for the change, though, may have been an unexpected offer that came in from the competing Southern Pacific Company. It had a line that ran from Utah through Reno and Sacramento, and then onward to the San Francisco Bay Area. Southern Pacific officials informed Weston by telegram in Ogden that, if he'd like, they could arrange for a railroad velocipede and a driver to accompany him along their rail lines westward as far as Sparks, Nevada.

This was very good news. Weston had earlier asked for a cart and driver from Union Pacific to help get him through Colorado and Wyoming. They hadn't responded during two months of requests. So he was delighted when Southern Pacific made its offer, and he merrily abandoned his plans to walk via Los Angeles.

Velocipedes—low vehicles that scuttled crablike along the tracks, ridden by rail inspectors checking for washouts and rotted ties—were once common. Many velocipedes were powered by arms and legs, and a sitting driver would push and pull a handle with his arms, and do the same with a bar and his legs. But Weston was lent a new gasoline-powered velocipede sort of like a railroad go-cart, complete with a platform to store lunch tins, coolers, and baggage. The velocipede driver assigned to him was a Southern Pacific employee named Joseph N. Murray—a fortuitous choice, as Weston would later write that Murray was "the very best helper I have had."

He'd now no longer have to worry about finding water or milk or eggs on the more desolate stretches of track. It also brought the immense luxury of ice: the conductors of passing trains had been instructed to give him a fresh supply, which could be kept in a cooler. The vast Nevada desert still awaited him, but it now didn't look quite as bleak. He later reported that he was so pleased about resuming a regular eating and drinking schedule that he scarcely slept the night before he left.

He departed Ogden shortly after midnight, setting off just above the surface of the Great Salt Lake on a long and low train trestle. He walked seventy-two miles within that twenty-four hours, one of the best days of his entire journey. His spirits were buoyed. San Francisco was now just 768 miles away.

But the lush landscape he enjoyed in northeastern Utah proved fleeting. Moving west toward the Sierras, he was soon deep in the desert again, and walking was taxing and unpleasant. The heat steadily rose as he continued west of the Great Salt Lake and into Nevada. "The heat is so intense that the natives complain," he wrote on June 29. "It was 90 degrees in the shade this morning and about 5 degrees warmer in the hotels."

Even with the velocipede and driver, he continued to fall behind schedule. He spent two long days crossing the windblown desert. "When the wind blows I am in a sand storm," he wrote, "the particles filling my eyes, nose and mouth, and almost choking me." He said he often couldn't see a hundred feet at time. For such occasions, he donned sand glasses, and doubtless cut quite the figure for those who saw him: long coat, wide-brimmed hat, thick sand glasses. But those who saw him weren't many, because he was usually walking in the dead of night. He now regularly favored night over day for trekking, often leaving at one in the morning and walking by lantern light. This wasn't without cost—the darkness forced him to slow his pace to about three miles per hour. And when he rested during the day, sleep came uneasily, as he was tormented by the stifling heat. "The nights are passable," he wrote, "and I could do the walking then were it not for the want of sleep which is impossible to get during the day, when the heat of the sun is doing its worst."

By the time he hit Lovelock—about 315 miles from the Utah state line, and with more than 100 to reach the California border—it was growing clear to anyone with a calendar and a map that any chance Weston had of making San Francisco by his self-imposed deadline of July 9 was slipping away. He'd now have to average a Herculean sixty miles each day. A few cracks started to emerge in Weston's stubborn confidence. At one point, he sheepishly expressed regret for taking his northerly detour up to Albany and across New York State rather than trekking straight through Pennsylvania.

By his calculations, that had added 323 miles to his route. "Under ordinary circumstances this would have made little difference," he wrote, "but the extraordinary circumstances, combined with the elements, has made the difference very material."

At last, entering the Sierras, he acknowledged that his hundred-day goal had slipped out of reach. "There have been many examples of overestimation of durability in this heat, and it serves as a warning to me not to attempt to injure myself in my anxiety to accomplish what I have set out to do." He noted the death of another septuagenarian, a fellow Rhode Islander who had recently expired while walking across the same desert. This may have prodded him to rethink increasing his already heedless pace.

Referring to the man's death, he said, "This has been the only proposition which has completely taken my nerve, and, conscious of this fact, am considerably depressed. I will, however, continue to walk to San Francisco, and will make as good time as conditions will permit."

CHAPTER 8

LEARNING TO WALK AGAIN

He has nothing to invest in a walk; it is too slow, too cheap.
We crave the astonishing, the exciting, the far away, and do
not know the highways of the gods when we see them.

—JOHN BURROUGHS, 1873

Pedestrian islands—those raised concrete slabs situated midway across busy streets, sometimes adjoined to median strips—first started to appear in cities around the time of Weston's great walk. They were originally called "safety islands" or "isles of safety," and were described in 1909 as "squares of concrete built up high enough to discourage automobilists," thereby creating "refuge spots" where "women and children flee when they see machines approaching." A 1915 account noted another use for them: They allowed a pedestrian to "confine his attention to one direction the first half of his cross, and the opposite direction the second half."

One might guess this term was devised by the pro-automobile faction, just as "jaywalking" was invented to achieve a strategic goal. The term "island" suggests idyllic splendor, but these plainly were not that sort of island. They might be viewed more like Napoleon's St. Helena, a knobby, uninviting rock to which one is exiled to live out one's days, endowed with abundant time to nurse ancient grudges. They might also be likened to the Galápagos Islands, territories so isolated that new species could evolve to adapt to local conditions. In fact, in 1909, the *New York Times* speculated about evolutionary changes in the new ecosystem of the car-clogged byway:

"Will the pedestrian of the future be armed with a shell like a turtle which shall ward off and render harmless the blows of passing cabs, cars, vehicles, buggies, hansoms, limousines, fire engines, vans, gigs, steeds, and other means of locomotion that are destined to inherit the earth?" the editors pondered. "Will the pedestrian come to be limber and semi-vertebrate like the reptile and arise from the shock of collision with an unnoticed vehicle to crawl away unbroken and unhurt? Will his legs and arms, which are the most easily breakable parts of him, shrivel up and disappear, and will he be able to roll across the street as a sort of rubber sphere that may be dented and run over and driven across without mutilation or injury? What is the future of the pedestrian, anyway? Darwin might tell us if he were here, but he is not here and we must look elsewhere for enlightenment."

The vista from a pedestrian island, it turns out, can be instructive. The waters around it, freely flowing with cars a century ago, are often now fouled and congealed with slow-moving, honking vehicles piloted by cursing, peevish drivers. The ecological niche the automobile once invaded with such predatory charm, dominating and displacing the pedestrian with only token resistance, has changed strikingly in the past century. As sometimes happens with other invasive species that succeed in establishing themselves amid bountiful resources, the car experienced a population explosion, and promptly overextended itself. The car has been rapacious in consuming land resources, and due to its overpopulation has been forced in the past half century to spar over territory with other cars. Cars still clearly dominate the roadscape, but are lapsing into a somewhat weakened state. They may now be on the cusp of colony collapse.

Under these new circumstances, some walkers have sensed a chance to reassert themselves and strive to retake their former niche. They're making a push to claim their space about a century after they conceded defeat by moving to the sidewalks or defected by getting their own cars. And many walking advocates—call them "predatory walkers"—have sensibly concluded that now is a propitious time to launch a campaign to retake the former habitat, starting in the places originally built for them: the cities.

===

July 4, 1909. Weston generally seemed more content in cities, where roads were firm and enthusiastic crowds came out to applaud and lend him the encouragement to continue. But that was rare in the West, and in early July conditions had taken a turn for the worse—yet again. Not so much because of inclement weather this time, but because of the general bleak and trying conditions: heat, dust, poor water quality, sandy soils, and voracious, swarming mosquitoes.

"Is it any wonder I long for something else than sand, alkali, tremendous heat, mosquitoes and sage brush?" Weston wrote on July 4, still in Nevada. "There is nothing here that tends to encouragement or induce pleasant walking." He noted that many people complained about crossing this part of the country by rail. "What would they say if they walked?" he asked.

He finally strolled into the town of Reno and thence to the Golden Hotel just after midnight on the evening of July 6. He walked, his lantern in hand—this image was becoming iconic in the press—with some two hundred supporters and the merely curious bobbing along in his wake. The crowd included the mayor and police chief on horses as the guard of honor, then the Reno City Band, with the city council walking just behind them. He marched into town, proffering waves to bystanders, then bid the crowd good night, took an elevator to his hotel room, and went directly to sleep.

After a day spent resting up, filing dispatches, and meeting with reporters, he left Reno at 6:00 p.m., walking through the Truckee Valley, which he found "exceptionally fine." Also, the "fresh air from the field and river" was particularly appealing, invigorating and refreshing him. His companion on the velocipede, J. N. Murray, concluded his duties in Reno and began his return trip; Weston was entrusted to the care of a new velocipede driver and guide, also provided by the Southern Pacific. He, a young man from San Francisco named C. E. Brown, was charged with guiding Weston through the peaks of the High Sierra. Brown's first task? Convince Weston to detour around the forty-two miles of snowsheds that were protecting the train tracks from heavy snows and avalanches, since Brown feared that Weston would find the going in the dark both slow and dangerous. This turned out not to be a hard sell—Weston had no love of long, dark passages (he worried about "suffocating" in them). Brown convinced Weston that he'd make better time by walking along the rough roads down the Yuba River canyon to the Sacramento Valley rather than doggedly sticking to the tracks.

Weston made it to Truckee, thirty-five miles to the west, shortly after noon, traveling again at a good clip. After resting two hours, he set off on the Donner Road down the canyon, then pushed on toward Colfax. He was stepping up his schedule, even though he knew he couldn't arrive in San Francisco in time. He did walk through a few snowsheds, but found the experience unnerving—he could make only two miles per hour through the darkness, the locomotives came every half hour and were "deafening," and he had to stand with his back to the wall, the train passing a mere foot away. Out of the sheds and up over Clipper Gap, the rising heat got the better of him, and at one point he was found stretched out under a tree in the middle of a planned sixty-mile day. He said he felt "somewhat tuckered out." The railroad dispatched the velocipede with ice and beverages. To relieve the heat, he took leaves of cabbage—"the kind used by Chinese vegetable peddlers"—and wrapped them around chunks of ice, placing the cooling packages in his hat.

═══════════

Were Weston alive today, it seems likely that he would be appalled by the dominance of the automobile in so much of the landscape and by the narrow, restricted lanes of travel left for travel by foot. But perhaps he'd be pleased to see that, block by block, pedestrians are beginning to reclaim their dominion. This isn't happening in every city or neighborhood, but it's a noticeable trend. Officials in many jurisdictions and some developers are starting to understand the links between opportunities for walking and long-term sustainability. Secure beachheads are surfacing in many places where walking has made small but welcome inroads. These include a prime stretch of Broadway in New York City that has been given over to walkers and sitters; New York has also revised municipal ordinances to allow some neighborhoods to apply to become Neighborhood Slow Zones, adding traffic calming treatments, such as speed bumps and special signs, and implementing twenty-mile-per-hour speed limits to return more space to the public realm. A bill making its way through the New Jersey legislature would give community associations in many towns the right to petition to reduce speed limits to fifteen or twenty miles per hour on low-volume streets lacking sidewalks, effectively telling cars they must share space with pedestrians. Raleigh, North Carolina, also recently adopted a progressive city plan that encourages planners to design more space for walking. Throughout the United Kingdom, the "20's Plenty for Us" movement now has launched more than two hundred campaigns that encourage municipalities to make twenty miles per hour the default speed limit.

If there's a saint of the modern pedestrian revival it's the late Hans Monderman, a Dutch traffic engineer who was faced with a small budget and a big problem. The Dutch village of Oudehaske was having issues with cars striking pedestrians (two children had recently died) when he was given an underfunded mandate to make streets safer. So Monderman did the unthinkable: He removed curbs, put sidewalks and streets at the same level, and let cars, bikes, and pedestrians come together and sort it all out on their own.

To the surprise of many, it worked. The more nuanced environment slowed down drivers, and the intermingling required communication using body language and eye contact. Every interchange between car and pedestrian was a small negotiation rather than action by rulebook. Accidents decreased, yet traffic continued to flow smoothly. The concept—called "naked streets" or "shared space" (or *woonerf* in Dutch)—has been expanding across Europe, and is slowly, tentatively, making its way to American shores. It's been implemented at a small-scale, generally experimental level in Cambridge, Massachusetts; Portland, Oregon; Seattle; and even in new developments in places such as St. Charles, Missouri.

There's also Complete Streets, a term increasingly heard in town council chambers around the country. It's an effort to end the partitioning of streets into isolated ecosystems (highways, bike lanes, etc.) and instead to redefine what a street is supposed to do. Opening the streets to multiple users is not only more equitable and democratic, but also often safer: In highly segregated environments (cars here, pedestrians there, bikers over there), drivers tend not to see the others and focus more narrowly on the rules that apply solely to them. When uses are mixed, drivers broaden their horizons and pay attention to what's going on.

The idea of Complete Streets has even been getting a nod at the federal level: "When it comes to transportation, we need to have people with a vision," said former US transportation secretary Ray LaHood. "People that understand that DOT is not just about roads and bridges anymore." The Complete Streets movement is bringing walkers and bikers to the table with traffic engineers and car advocates and finding ways to design streets that benefit all. It's certainly a step up from pedestrians being referred to as VRUs (vulnerable road users), as they often are in highway safety research papers.

This whole approach has been deemed radical by some, a complete reversal of How Things Are Done. But it's not. It's simply a return to the way things once were after a century-long detour, when streets were taken from people and handed over to cars and converted into sluices. It took about three generations to eradicate pedestrians from the road, and it might take three generations to make it safe for them to come back. But the pivot is well under way.

What's behind the return to walking? Some clues might be found in looking at baby boomers, a cohort that loves to set the social agenda and can get a little pouty when it doesn't. Boomers browbeat the public into jogging and running marathons in previous decades, but they are now getting on in years—the peak of the bell curve is headed toward sixty—and they're feeling it in their knees, ankles, feet, and backs. Walking gives them a chance to move and burn calories and be active and be outdoors, and to feel like they're living an active life, but without the jackhammer wear and tear of running on pavement. They're also now becoming empty nesters and retiring (however they decide to define that) and are weary of lawns and the upkeep required by showcase homes. A compact condo or apartment in a walkable downtown is an environment where they can get around on foot and leave the car behind and, they hope, age gracefully. Also, if they give up the car keys voluntarily, then they needn't suffer the indignity and trauma of having their kids take them away when they become incapable of driving safely. If nothing else, boomers are adept at avoiding indignity and trauma.

Yet, it turns out that boomers may not be setting the walking agenda after all. This time, they may be tracing the steps of their kids and grandkids, who are leading a larger and more formidable change. The embrace of walking—and biking—by the generation that was brought up in the backseat of a car is a more relevant shift culturally. The millennials, many of them fresh out of college and grad school, are figuring out what to do with their lives. And one of the things they've figured out is that they don't really need a car, nor do they want one. They're giving up driving in large numbers, and choosing to live in communities that are more compact, offer more services nearby, and, in short, are more walkable.

Statistics show that millennials are abandoning driving more rapidly than their boomer elders. Research by the Federal Highway Administration found that drivers between the ages of twenty-one and thirty accounted for just 14 percent of the total vehicle miles driven in 2009—down from 21 percent in 1995. That's a drop of a third, and evidence of a respectable realignment that's under way.

To be sure, a number of outside factors are making driving less attractive to a younger generation: the price of fuel, along with the rising expense of buying, insuring, and maintaining a car. Then there's the growing inconvenience and cost of parking in cities. And all this is set against a backdrop of economic expectations tempered by a persistently dismal economic reality—the jobs they were told to expect just aren't materializing.

But signs abound that millennials are not only being pushed out of the nest of the driving world but are also finding the world of walking freeing and inviting. It could be that it's simply Marchetti's Constant exerting itself in a recalibrated world. The parents of millennials moved to the suburbs, occupying the outer range of the one-hour round-trip commute. More people followed, traffic ossified, and the one-hour commute gradually grew to ninety minutes. Their kids may have simply rebelled against this and are moving back into the cities, abandoning cars, and finding work within a half-hour's walk, bike, or bus ride.

Or it could be that they're just rediscovering their genetic predilections and finding that walking is what they were meant to do.

Even if free fuel were discovered tomorrow and some emerging market figured out how to produce and export half-priced automobiles, it seems unlikely that millennials would clamor to get back behind a wheel and move to the suburbs. Many were brought up in suburbia and have discovered that there's a more pleasant alternative to spending a measurable fraction of their lives waiting for the cars ahead of them to make the left-hand turn so they can move up in the line waiting to do the same. They want to live in places where land uses are mixed and diverse (perhaps reflecting the fractured attention span of a digital generation), where entertainment and recreation are within walking or biking range, where there's easy access to transit and close-by shopping opportunities. (They also want affordable housing and good jobs, but appear ready to compromise on both in order to live in desirable places.) As land-use expert Chris Leinberger has noted, the parents of millennials were raised on the idealized suburban life depicted in *The Partridge Family* and *The Brady Bunch*. Millennials were raised on the urban alternatives *Friends, Seinfeld,* and *Sex and the City.* The very notion of what constitutes a desirable environment has shifted. One hears occasionally that we have passed "peak driving," suggesting that from here on out vehicle miles traveled per capita will slowly if steadily decline. In surveys, more than three-quarters of millennials now say they want to live in one of America's urban cores, where they can fare just fine without a car. (Whether they remain in cities or decamp to the suburbs as they start having children, like their parents and grandparents once did, remains to be seen.) Writing in Toronto's *Globe and Mail,* reporter Anita Flash noted that more and more people are leaving their cars behind: "Finding themselves caught in an uncomfortable tangle of urban sprawl, population growth and plain individual inconvenience, people, one by one, are just quietly opting out." They're returning to their feet.

———————

"Walkability" is an unfortunate, ungainly word—it has the sound of a term invented by a bureaucrat embittered from being confined too long in too small a cubicle. But it's serviceable, and it's also less likely to provoke head-scratching today than it would have five or ten years ago. It's become part of general urban conversations among a certain class, thanks in part to Walk Score and its derivatives (mentioned in Chapter 8). It's a term that's especially common in conversations about real estate.

New planned communities are increasingly establishing useful, attractive walkways from the outset, not tacking them on merely to meet local codes. In part they're drawing on the elements people like about prewar villages, such as the streetcar suburbs and garden cities like the subdivision of Radburn in Fair Lawn, New. Jersey. And it's influenced by New Urbanism, a school of thought in urban planning that advocates for reviving some elements once common in older towns and villages, such as walkways, pocket parks, short blocks, and abundant visual variety that's appealing to those on foot. Builders realize that useful pathways are valuable amenities, like community pools and open space, and can boost the value of homes nearby. According to one study, a one-point increase in the Walk Score translated into an increase of between $700 and $3,000 in home value; another study found that a ten-point increase in the Walk Score boosted commercial property values by 1 to 9 percent. In 2009, the economist Joe

Cortright looked at data from more than ninety thousand home sales in fifteen major markets. In thirteen of those markets, he found that better walkability (that is, higher Walk Scores) translated to higher home values.

"Until the 1990s, exclusive suburban homes that were accessible only by car cost more, per square foot, than other kinds of American housing," reported land-use expert Leinberger in 2012. "Now, however, these suburbs have become overbuilt, and housing values have fallen. Today, the most valuable real estate lies in walkable urban locations." Leinberger and his colleague Mariela Alfonzo studied the value of real estate in and around Washington, DC, and classified neighborhoods on a five-step ladder of walkability, from least walkable to most. Each step up the ladder increased prices for homes by $82 a square foot, and added $9 per square foot to annual office rents. Walkability was once a throwaway quality associated with poor neighborhoods where residents couldn't afford cars; now, if you want walkability, expect to pay a premium. "People are clearly willing to pay more for homes that allow them to walk rather than drive," Leinberger wrote.

Not surprisingly, Leinberger found that household incomes were also higher in walkable neighborhoods—people who could afford to pay more to walk were happy to do so. Which raises the question of whether walkable neighborhoods are simply boutique neighborhoods, limited in scope and number and available only to the more affluent.

While that may be the case at present, it could well be that we're in a transitional period—like when drinking good coffee or craft beer was being adopted by the better-off before becoming accessible to a broader market. In time, walkable neighborhoods will be more in demand by those farther down the economic food chain. And that will likely happen even if they don't move to a more walkable community, because walkable amenities will come to them.

As architect and *Washington Post* contributor Roger Lewis noted, the "suburban planning and zoning templates" that have guided land development since at least World War II have been predicated on four assumptions. These include an unlimited supply of land on which to build and an unlimited supply of oil to meet transportation needs. The other two assumptions decreed that segregating land uses—retail here, residential there—was the best way to preserve property values, and that the surest route to the American dream was to own rather than rent.

All four assumptions are now being sharply tested, if not teetering on the verge of collapse, Lewis noted. While many Americans still yearn for a freestanding house on a secluded piece of land—an ideal fueled by Thoreau's *Walden* and Thomas Kinkade's paintings and much else—and there's some debate on whether the trend toward urban areas is a trend at all, the economics of living in the scattered suburbs has become less defensible. Density is already moving to the inner suburbs in the form of zoning that allows mother-in-law apartments above garages and along alleys, and infill development, in which mall parking lots are being colonized by new shops (often restaurants) along the outer margins, where parking lot meets arterial. In more ambitious conversions, housing is taking over parking lots, such as at Seattle's Thornton Place, where 387 apartments, a medical center, and additional retail outlets were built atop a parking lot adjacent to an older regional mall. ("What exactly is 'plaza living' at Thornton Place?" reads the marketing material. "Well, it's walking to everything—the movies, a world of great restaurants, transit, [and] shopping.") Indeed, shopping mall parking lots may prove to be one of history's great investments, offering space for the building of future village centers, which is likely to attract denser housing nearby, and homes and apartments within walking distance. (More on retrofitting suburban areas in a moment.)

In short, a century after we forgot how to walk, we're starting to remember what we liked about moving around on foot, as we were programed to do some six million years ago. According to a recent report by the Centers for Disease Control and Prevention, 62 percent of Americans were walking at least ten minutes a day in 2010. That may not be a figure worth lighting fireworks over, but it's better than the 55 percent who reported a ten-minute walk just five years earlier. The fading allure of the American road also shows up in other statistics. The total distance Americans drive each year ceased rising around 2007 and has been gradually edging downward. On a per capita basis, by 2013, Americans were driving roughly the same amount each year as they were around 1990, a downward trend at least in part driven by those nondriving millennials. That's still far more than our counterparts in Europe or Japan, but nevertheless a reversal of a long-standing trend.

The number of miles driven tends to narrowly ebb and flow based on general economic conditions and gas prices, but this time the shift away from cars and toward more active transport appears to be more structural, and less a passing fad. That's not to say that it doesn't have elements of the faddish—the walking desks that are appearing in corner suites and bedroom offices may be just the latest alternative to sitting on a large rubber ball at one's desk in a relentless search for distraction from actual work. (Walking and standing desks are "the new ergonomic office craze," as described in one article, which gives one pause.) But desks attached to treadmills aren't driving trends; they're indicators of a broader, more systemic pull toward walking, of sitting less and moving more.

July 9, 1909. The morning of July 9 was surely a sour one for Edward Payson Weston: it marked the one hundredth day (less Sundays) since he'd left New York City. It was the day he had told the world, frequently and confidently, that he would arrive full of pep and vigor in San Francisco. Yet when the day broke, he found himself in Cisco, California, still about 170 miles from his goal.

Weston didn't try to gloss over his defeat by the calendar. He called his inability to make it in a hundred days a "wretched failure" and "the most crushing failure I have encountered in my career. . . . This has been an effort which should be called one chapter of mistakes from beginning to end," he said. He told people he wasn't offering any excuses. Whereupon he offered excuses. Among them: a "miserable and worthless automobile" that accompanied him to Chicago and slowed him down with its troubles; the unrelentingly horrid weather, including drenching rains that kept him off the road for, by his calculation, fifteen days; the lack of decent roads, forcing him to walk on railroad tracks, which reduced his pace by a half mile to one mile per hour; and the strategic error of walking into the prevailing winds instead of putting them at his back and starting his walk in San Francisco, then heading east.

But mostly he reserved his antipathy for Wyoming. "I would have made this walk on scheduled time," he said, "but for the fact I had to go through the state of Wyoming." He couldn't get either water or milk enough to rinse his mouth, he said. "I never saw even one cow in Wyoming." When he did finally see one in Utah, he added, "I took off my hat to her, and I said 'Pardon me, madame, if I intrude.'"

This certainly wasn't the first failure in his career as a walker—he'd missed self-set goals often enough early on—but this may have been his most crushing defeat.

Weston's manager, John Schenkel, arrived in San Francisco on July 9. He began to arrange for events to celebrate Weston's arrival. Schenkel also took a moment to offer further excuses for Weston—slow going in Wyoming, hailstorms in Kansas and Colorado. He admitted that Weston was "slightly downcast" about failing to make it on time. Still, the pedestrian was "vigorous and energetic as a boy," and he urged others to regard his trek as an accomplishment.

Meanwhile, Weston pushed on, getting back up to four miles an hour on a country road that paralleled the rails outside Sacramento, where a contingent of Southern Pacific employees applauded him as he arrived. And then through Davis and Dixon and Elmira and Suisun City, where he rested for several hours before returning to the rails after nightfall. The wind blew out his lantern—"a Kansas gale took possession of the track and hurled me around merrily," as Weston put it—and he injured his foot after stepping in a hole. He spent the night at a station house in Goodyear, then continued on at eight the following morning, now accompanied by a pack of San Francisco newspapermen eager to document his finish. Before arriving at the ferry at Benicia, on which he would cross the Carquinez Strait, he reversed course for a mile and a half to compensate for the three-mile crossing by boat.

———

The phrase "rise of pedestrianism" may carry an excess of optimism. It might be more realistic to talk of the "unprivileging of the automobile." After decades in which transportation planning revolved largely around the car, the discussion has taken a different turn of late, and other forms of transit—bus, train, bike, foot—are being invited to sit at the adult table and participate in the conversation. And that creates an opening for a more pedestrian-friendly environment.

Pockets of walkability are like seed corn. When successful, they spur the revival of other areas, especially those already blessed with good bones for walking. Cities both large and small with short block lengths and visual variety will benefit first, as the heavy lifting has already been done. When cars rose in prominence and walking faded, many of these areas were simply neglected—street trees were cut down or died, their sad and empty circular gratings filled with fast-food wrappers; storefronts were boarded up or overlaid with fluorescent-backed plastic signs and tattered awnings; buildings were demolished to make way for barren parking lots; sidewalks were narrowed as streets were widened to squeeze more traffic through. But today these areas are attracting people drawn by their human scale, and making them eminently walkable again is mostly a matter of cosmetics.

Not that this will be easy; even modest improvements to urban walkability require diverting money away from widening roads and toward Complete Street improvements or better transit, and this can result in hostility from drivers stuck in traffic who still believe that simply adding another lane would resolve their life's woes. If you listen carefully, you can hear faint echoes from 1909, with walkers and automobiles again facing off for control of public spaces, although now under vastly altered circumstances. When Weston was walking west, cars were ascendant, edging pedestrians off the streets. With those on foot (and bike) now more assertive and politically savvy, they're slowly taking back space. Drivers increasingly feel bullied after their decades-long run of the roads and are now pushing back. Like walkers a century ago, car drivers are sending sarcastic screeds and letters to the editor about how they're being villainized and forced to give up what's rightly theirs. As Justin Davidson groused in *New York* magazine in 2012 (opening sentence: "Bless me, Father, for I have driven"), drivers are the victims of crusading walking advocates: "Urban transportation is no longer purely a matter of efficiency and comfort; it's acquired a moral charge," he wrote. "Every time you caress the gas pedal, you threaten lives, inch the planet closer to calamity, give some sheikh more control over our foreign policy, and tighten the knot of urban dysfunction. The only remedy is abstinence. Park. Walk. Repent."

While Davidson has no use for holier-than-thou walkers, to his credit he prescribes strong if bitter medicine: Make driving cost much more. "If New York is to become a better habitat for automobiles, it should never be cheaper to drive than to take a less convenient form of transportation. To put it another way: Saving time should cost money, and vice versa. That way, car-haters can stop spluttering about the ills of driving and let the rest of us whip around the city in motorized tranquility."

Efforts to make driving more expensive in cities, such as boosting bridge tolls or imposing a stiff fee on those wishing to travel during peak hours (as was done in London), have had their own blowback problem. It's spun as being antidemocratic, allowing only the wealthy to drive in the cities. (The spin in this case is, of course, accurate.) Other efforts to make driving reflect its true economic cost to society—insurance pegged tightly to the number of miles one drives, far steeper rates for parking on public streets—are also roundly attacked as being unfair and favoring the wealthy.

But all this points up a widespread perception problem: that keeping driving cheap is fair and just, while funding pedestrian facilities or transit is catering to special interests. "There are many situations where private transport interests are claimed as public and public, democratic interests such as walking and use of public space as private ones," noted Daniel Sauter, a transportation researcher in Zurich, in 2005. A decade later, that's shifting as influential boomers and car-weary millennials move to reclaim walking in our cities.

"Increasing densities to levels near or exceeding those typical of cities in 1910 by concentrating housing, jobs, schools, stores, parks, and populations is the best way to shrink commute zones from 80 or 20 square miles to ones as small as two and a half square miles," writes urban designer Julie Campoli in her 2012 book, *Made for Walking*. For that to happen, she adds, we need to create fewer Houstons "and a lot more Jamaica Plains."

Urban planner Jeff Speck writes in *Walkable City* that if you live in New York, Boston, Chicago, Portland, San Francisco, or a handful of similar cities, your sense may be that things are moving in the right direction, walking-wise. But outside those cities—on the endless asphalted plains of America built in the post–World War II era—not so much. As Fleming El Amin, a transportation planner in Raleigh, North Carolina, put it, "Some folks would walk if they had the opportunity, but there's no opportunity." Most of this space—strip malls, cul-de-sac developments, big-box stores surrounded by vast parking lagoons—was designed around the car, with little or no accommodation made for walkers. Large block sizes, a profusion of parking lots, wide and fast roads, narrow or nonexistent sidewalks, and long distances between destinations: How to make this more friendly to walkers? And how to do this if local planners and transit engineers retain the belief that moving more cars more quickly is their sole job?

Creating the opportunity for walking will require time and a change in mind-set. Low density isn't a genie you can put back in the bottle. The six-lane arterials flanked with strip malls and fast-food restaurants won't be walkable until their parking lots are built up with commercial or residential or mixed-used buildings and then the roads themselves are narrowed and rebuilt on a scale more suitable for walking.

The grid upon which a neighborhood is built is among the most predictable determinants of whether people will walk or drive. One highly useful measure is "intersection density," and one analysis has shown that a greater number of intersections in an area strongly increases the amount of walking. Suburban developments, built on long and sinuous lanes that double back on themselves or dead end, don't lend themselves to retrofitting to increase the number of intersections. Few homeowners would be pleased to see a new road or even a new pedestrian walkway put through their backyard.

But some big-box and mall developments are learning that smaller block sizes and better connectivity, as opposed to the imperial fortresses of slabby, massive mall buildings surrounded by asphalt moats, have a salubrious effect on the bottom line. Fewer enclosed malls surrounded by lots are being built today, and it appears that they've had their moment (roughly from 1970 to 2000) and are now being supplanted by retail centers that mimic Main Streets, such as Belmar in Denver, which consists of twenty-two urbanlike blocks (and even a farmers' market) on the former site of an enclosed mall. The more progressive developers, like those behind City Creek Center, which replaced the 1970s-era Crossroads Plaza Mall in downtown Salt Lake City, are even incorporating residential units.

"Sprawl recovery is an act of enticement, not one of contrition," writes New Urbanist Steve Mouzon. He's compiled of a set of twelve steps essential for making sprawl more sustainable and walkable—something he notes won't be a nicety when gasoline hits $20 a gallon. (And he's sure it will: The price of gas has gone up twentyfold since he was child, he says, and it doesn't take much of a leap to believe it will increase fivefold in another half lifetime.) Among the steps he calls for: adding more civic space (like plazas), adding density through zoning that permits accessory apartments (like mother-in-law units over garages), and subdividing large lots in the suburbs to allow small cottages to be added. Efforts to carry out such measures will be certain to hit resistance (has already in some places, including Missoula, Montana, where a group called Save Our Neighborhoods has fought new, more permissive ordinances), largely from those who moved to the suburbs to flee density and enjoy more privacy and less traffic. But this is unlikely to hold over time: Housing prices in far-flung developments aren't keeping pace with those in more central, accessible communities, and a later generation of homeowners may find themselves more willing to compromise to protect their investments. If the market wants density, density will thrive. Add to this the fact that many millennials who want to live in walkable downtowns won't necessarily be able to afford it. They'll compromise and settle in the nearby suburbs, and once there, they are likely to support zoning changes and civic endeavors that create urbanlike amenities, such as improved pathways and grocery stores within walking distance of their homes (which are other steps from Mouzon's dozen).

The Danish architect and urban planner Jan Gehl offered what might be the single best suggestion for changing society's approach to getting about on foot: "If you want to promote walking," he said, "don't talk about walking."

He's right. In fact, perhaps "walkable cities" is the wrong term. It has the sound of slightly bitter medicine. Maybe it should be simply "livable cities." Instead of talking about walking, talk about building community, about reducing the stress of everyday life, and about freedom of movement. Walking advocates would do well to take a page from modern automobile ads, which still capture the allure of the open road, even as that open road becomes extinct in many areas (think: suburban Washington, DC). In ads, drivers shrug off the burdens of life as they speed along unencumbered, as if they're hawks soaring on their own private thermals. If one judges by car ads alone, one might reasonably conclude that all roads are empty of all cars except one's own, and that these roads always meander along open ridges and through meadows that offer breathtaking vistas of more ridges and meadows, except when these are interrupted by views of the ocean. (If your television diet is restricted to car ads during National Football League games, however, you have a different view of freedom. There, freedom means driving a large pickup truck carrying outsize cargo through a landscape consisting chiefly of shallow rivers to be forded and rugged buttes to be ascended.) Car ads promote unfettered mobility; car manufacturers never extol their ability to help you maintain your equanimity while you wait through two stoplight cycles to make a turn into a chain restaurant parking lot. (As urban planner and author Jeff Speck puts it, cars are "an instrument of freedom that has enslaved us.") That's the reality for many drivers, yet the idea of the open road often remains foremost in our minds, thanks to the ubiquity of car ads.

Walking has the benefit of providing us with actual freedom: freedom of movement in any direction, freedom from sluggishness and torpor, freedom to walk where we want to without having to always watch for lights and signals and lanes. About the only people seen walking in television ads today are those promoting dietary supplements for the aged, or those who slow their pace to admire a sleek new car driving past.

It may be more effective to craft another message—that of community. This is an equally powerful message, and one that's the yin to the yang of the open road. Rather than being about escaping and freedom of movement, it's a message about being connected and rooted. Automobile makers, no matter how impressive their advertising budgets, can't win the argument that cars build community. Cars atomize community and fragment it into competitive, hard-shelled nuggets.

Community building starts with the simple matter of speed. You can't build a community at fifty miles per hour, or even at twenty-five miles per hour. To begin with, speed consumes space; a road engineered for forty miles per hour needs far more space than one engineered for twenty miles per hour. And as roads widen, they become less human scaled and more scaled for automobiles. Human connections fray. We lose eye contact with one another at about twenty miles per hour (humans' maximum running speed), and that's the point when human links are further eroded—studies show that lower speeds in urban areas correlate with lower crime rates. What's more, as transportation philosopher John Whitelegg has noted, the speed of auto travel tends to make the concepts of "near" and "far" less distinct, which contributes to what he calls "loss of place particularity." One of the foundations of community is having a place that's distinctive: This is here, and this is not there. Walking speed allows one to notice the layers of a fine-grained environment, whether natural or built; a sense of place is contained in the details. In a 2010 survey, a majority of people agreed that walking and a sense of community were linked. The respondents cited "seeing neighbors when walking and the presence of interesting sites." The study also found that a mix of residential and commercial uses strengthened a sense of community.

Building community is a draw. A study on how best to market using local walking trails in Pennsylvania found that urging people to walk for their health did little to increase trail traffic. More successful were messages about enjoying fresh air and spending time with friends and family—again, the social side of walking. A walkable community is a true community.

Community is a good launching point for changing the discussion about walking. But it's also essential to begin a discussion about time. Walking clearly isn't the fastest way to get around. Walking is too slow to be used as transportation, and also too slow for exercise—running burns more calories per minute, and so is more efficient than walking.

But that doesn't make walking inferior. Consider a notion called "effective speed" that's gotten a bit of traction in some transportation and public health circles. This was spelled out in a 2010 paper in the *Journal of Urban Health* titled "Speed Kills: The Complex Links Between Transport, Lack of Time and Urban Health." The author, Paul Joseph Tranter, outlines "a paradox whereby 'faster' modes of transport lead to a loss of time." He reaches this conclusion by not just looking at the time it takes to travel a set distance by a certain mode, but also calculating "all of the time costs associated with a particular mode of transport." For those who drive cars, for example, foremost among these hidden costs is time spent at work just to pay for an automobile, insurance, maintenance, parking, and fuel. (Not to mention the time standing on line at government motor-vehicles departments to deal with paperwork.) When this is all factored in, walking has one of the best "effective speeds" because it has "virtually nil time costs apart from the time spent walking."

Encouraging more people to give up their cars for trips of under a mile or two will still require significant prodding. One surefire way to guarantee that the prodding will fail is to attack drivers at every opportunity— lambaste them as selfish, wasteful, and lazy. People love their cars, and two hundred years from now, people will still love their cars, even if it's only a handful of people and they keep them in car museums and take them out once a year on National Car Day, when local nonprofits hold fund-raisers to buy a gallon of gasoline to entertain the kids.

Most everybody travels at least sometimes by car, and they'll get their hackles up when attacked. The positive message gets lost. Whenever someone tries to legislate or decree where or when someone can or can't drive, it offers a point of resistance to rally around. A more effective tactic for getting people to rethink their relationship with their car may be to let them stew alone in a forty-minute traffic jam. Or simply to encourage a reduction in driving.

A good model is the flexitarian diet, in which you don't give up meat entirely, you just cut back a lot. It makes sense to follow this approach for transportation diets: Walk when you can. Bike if it's a bit farther. Drive if you must.

One of the brilliant moves a century ago among those advocating for cars was to claim more of the road by loudly complaining that they were being discriminated against. It was a clever way to neuter the commonsense notion that public transit and walking were more populist and democratic. Interestingly, we're starting to hear a return to that argument, with drivers saying they feel persecuted and beleaguered by sanctimonious walkers (and bikers) as they see their freedom to speed and occupy public real estate at the expense of others beginning to erode. Claiming discrimination worked for drivers a century ago; it may well work for walkers today.

———

July 14, 1909. The beginning of the end of Weston's great walk occurred on the night of July 14, when Weston, wearing a white cap and an olive army shirt, walked into the dispatcher's office at Oakland's Sixteenth Street Station, where the rail lines ended and the San Francisco ferry carried passengers onward to the west side of the bay. He walked in at 9:41 and inquired about the next ferry. He had walked thirty-nine miles that day, plus an additional six miles when he doubled back to compensate for the distance he planned to travel via ferry. The end of his trip was in some ways like the beginning: Crowds flocked to see the curious walking man. Here, though, he lacked the police guard he'd had in New York, so when thousands gathered to cheer him, he was reduced to shouting at people to *please, please stand back* while "swinging about him vigorously with his stick."

Although Weston often seemed an uncomplicated man—and certainly his writings in newspapers and quotes given to newspapermen don't reveal a complicated inner life—one might guess his mood was conflicted, happy to be finishing his long journey but plagued by what-ifs. What if he had not taken that 323-mile northerly detour through upstate New York? What if his car and chauffeur had worked out and hadn't had to be dismissed in Chicago? What if his replacement car had stuck with him and made his walk through Kansas, Colorado, and Wyoming less of an ordeal? What if the spring and summer weather had been more cooperative, ushering blizzards and torrential rains and blinding sandstorms around him rather than putting him in their crosshairs, one storm after another? He told a reporter that if he did it again, he'd "dodge cyclones and blizzards, . . . leave automobiles strictly alone as a means of carrying his baggage, [and] court the west winds at his back instead of forever pushing against them."

"It was a great walk," he told some of those around him, "and but for unforeseen difficulties and hardships in the last three weeks of my journey, I would have been here on the hundredth day. Still I am feeling fine and could do it over again."

In the end, the numbers he amassed were impressive. He walked 105 days, five hours, and 41 minutes and averaged a little more than thirty-eight miles per day. (These were "secular days"; he also rested on seventeen Sundays.) He walked a total of 3,925 miles, roughly 2,500 of which were on railroad tracks, owing to the lack of decent roads across the West. (Weston actually claimed, although without much ardor, that he'd walked 4,200 miles if one counted all the veering from one side of the road to another in search of a better route, and from one side of the train tracks to the other.) For 1,800 miles, he was alone and without a support vehicle. He wore out three pairs of shoes. Expenses for the walk, Weston reported, totaled $2,500—about $63,000 today.

The call for the ferry to San Francisco came, and Weston boarded, opting to stand during the crossing. He'd walked too far to sit. He chatted with those who had followed him on board to witness his finale, along with passengers simply drawn to the hubbub around this slight but picturesque man. "He is bronzed so deeply that his flowing mustache, time-bleached to snowy whiteness, shows with startling distinctness against his ruddy cheeks," the Associated Press reported.

He disembarked in San Francisco at 10:50 p.m., then walked another twenty minutes through a city still rebuilding from the great earthquake and fires of three years prior. Small knots of people stood along the streets and applauded and cheered him as he arrived at the St. Francis Hotel on Union Square. Here, well-wishers clotted the lobby, and "hundreds" of letters and telegrams awaited to congratulate him on his feat. But it was late, he was tired, and he quickly slipped upstairs to his room.

And yet, his trip wasn't completely over. There was still the matter of delivering the letter to Postmaster Fisk the following day. "I dare say it can wait a few hours," he told reporters.

―――――

When Weston strolled from the ferry terminal through downtown San Francisco to his hotel, he walked amid what, a little over a century later, would be considered the nation's second-most-walkable city, having departed 105 days earlier from the most walkable one. At least that's according to the latest ratings from Walk Score, although these appear to be somewhat arbitrary; prior to 2011 San Francisco was ranked the most walkable, and New York was the runner-up. (Walk Score's other highly walkable cities include Boston, Chicago, and Philadelphia.)

Whether first or second, San Francisco has long been a pedestrian-friendly city, provided you don't mind mounting a hill or two. The urban blueprint was solidified in the mid-nineteenth century, so it was built around a walker's template. Its location on a constricted peninsula meant the growth couldn't migrate to the margins in every direction when the car become dominant (although it did spill southward), and so it had to build higher and denser near the economic engine of the port. And an early and excellent transit system offered an alternative to owning and garaging a car, which was already difficult in a city built on steep hills. San Francisco's boom times arrived during an era when small shops below and residential dwellings above were the norm, and the big money from gold and shipping fortunes encouraged architectural flamboyance. After the 1906 earthquake, the city's rebuilding was in large part based on plans by Daniel Burnham, one of the leaders of the City Beautiful movement in the late nineteenth and early twentieth centuries. The result? A finely textured urban environment with narrow lots, manageably sized blocks, and copious architectural detail to catch the eye. The hills can be challenging, but along the way there is much to captivate and entertain. In many ways, San Francisco is nearly at the eye of a perfect storm of walkability. It's no surprise that it's also been called the one of the "best walking cities in the country" by the American Podiatric Medical Association and *Prevention* magazine.

San Francisco's pedestrian-friendly history and enviable Walk Score hide one disconcerting fact: A lot of pedestrians die there. Statistically, it's a dangerous city to get around in by foot. In 2012, 16 pedestrians were killed and

948 injured by cars—almost three accidents a day. In the broader Bay Area, 434 pedestrians were killed between 2007 and 2011. A third of those fatalities occurred in crosswalks, about triple the national rate.

San Francisco is working to reduce injuries in a variety of ways. Mayor Ed Lee in the spring of 2013 announced a goal of cutting pedestrian deaths in half by 2021. Measures include streamlining the approval process for pedestrian-friendly improvements to roadways; stepping up enforcement of cars not yielding to pedestrians at crosswalks; and launching the nation's first Walk to Work Day (held in April 2013), with giveaways like free coffee and bus passes (to get home) to encourage greater awareness of walking.

And the city has an effective advocacy group riding herd on these changes. Walk San Francisco was founded in 1998 with the goal of making walking in the city safer and more enjoyable. It's pushed to increase funding for street improvements for walkers, to make areas around schools safe from speeders to encourage walking to school, and for stronger enforcement against antipedestrian behavior, such as blocking sidewalks with parked cars. Its success could make it a model for pedestrian activism in many other cities.

That level of success has required reversing decades of movement in a car-centric direction. As Andres Power, then an urban designer in San Francisco's planning department, told *Metropolis* magazine in 2010: "What's happening here is a response to the depopulation of San Francisco in the fifties, when people fled to the suburbs. All the people that you would want to be on the street left, and so all that remained was vagrancy and publicly detrimental behavior. And so basically everything that made the street comfortable was taken away. They removed virtually every bench. It was a scorched earth policy. What we're trying to do now is break that cycle."

Homelessness remains a highly visible issue in the city, and many residents and shopkeepers remain wary of bringing back benches that offer places for the homeless to congregate. (As many have pointed out, the homeless and park benches are not necessarily related. The homeless still congregate in large numbers at United Nations Plaza, even though its benches were removed more than a decade ago. Figuring out how to reduce homelessness is an issue separate from creating walking-friendly streets.)

The San Francisco idea attracting the most attention—and a fair dose of ridicule—has been the Parklet Program, which was inspired by PARK(ing) Day. The original idea, launched in 2005 by Rebar, a local design and art studio, was to encourage citizens to take over parking spots by feeding the meters as if they were parking. But instead of using them to store large and cooling pieces of steel, they'd roll out old carpets, add some furniture and a few potted plants, and *voilà!*—they'd create mini parks measuring about thirty-four feet long by six feet wide, where passersby could sit and enjoy the street. What started as a guerrilla effort went official in 2010, when the city instituted a program allowing community organizations and shop owners to petition to create their own parklets (and also pay the city up front to compensate for the lost parking revenue), and the movement boomed. As of this writing, nearly forty parklets have been installed.

Parklets have been hailed as a new way to claim public space, but of course, it's anything but new. It's really a recapturing of the verge, that zone that had long been a scene of urban social life before the days of cars. It was a spot for socializing, maybe enjoying a snack from a local vendor, and letting city life unfold between the sidewalk and the streets. While criticism has been mounting—"It's real hard to find a place [to park]" was one (typical) complaint from a suburban visitor to a local television reporter—parklets are generally popular among city residents, and help offset the city's relative dearth of public space.

San Francisco has led the way in another innovative program involving parking meters, one that effectively ends one of the subsidies for driving. The idea is simple: Instead of having officials or administrators set low rates for metered parking, let the market—that is, drivers—determine how much an hour is worth block by block. The city's goal is to price parking so that, at any given moment, one space is open and available per block, which makes it convenient for drivers coming in from a distance and looking for a space. The catch, of course, is cost. The hour at the meter needs to be priced to cause some pain, making drivers think twice about that second hour. Rates are revised quarterly and analyzed on a block-by-block basis. Around popular destinations, it might be significantly more expensive to park, with rates dropping the farther away one parks. The ultimate goal, of course, is to tilt the balance toward those for whom public transit is an option. Buses and trains might not be the most convenient ways to get around, but if they're significantly less expensive than street parking, more people will use them. The emphasis on letting the market determine behavior seems to be one that could be embraced (in theory) by everyone from Tea Party advocates to urban activists and environmentalists, although enthusiasm for the idea will no doubt be offset by ingrained resistance to making it more difficult to get around by car.

Mayor Lee seems to understand that making the city safe and more appealing for walkers is an essential part of an overall strategy for the city. "A great walking environment is essential to our city's prosperity" is how a 2013 report by his Pedestrian Safety Task Force puts it. More walkers makes for healthier residents, and more opportunities for walking attracts businesses and workers. The official "Pedestrian Strategy" (which has benchmarks and suggestions but is largely toothless compared with a official plan) puts forth suggestions on how to "make walking more attractive [to] lead people to choose to walk for most short trips." The city estimates that 40 percent of all trips taken by car within San Francisco are under a mile, leaving much room for improvement.

"Cars already have more space on the roadway than they should, and we need to reclaim that space for the public," says Nicole Schneider, current executive director of Walk San Francisco.

San Francisco—like New York—is a serving as a crucible for trying approaches and strategies that will make cities more walkable and friendly to pedestrians. In its hills and intricate architectural details and progressive policies, there's a blueprint forming for healthier and more sustainable cities nationwide. The past is informing the future.

July 15, 1909. Weston enjoyed a late and leisurely breakfast and then walked his final half-mile from the hotel to the post office. He arrived precisely at noon. People spilled out of buildings and hurried down side streets to watch him complete the last leg of his trip. In the postmaster's office, a small posse of postal officials waited to greet him and shake his hand. Weston arrived and, with his customary formality, handed Postmaster Fisk the letter addressed to him.

"My Dear Mr. Fisk," the letter read. "This letter will be presented to you by Mr. Edward Payson Weston, a pedestrian who at 4:15 P.M. on the seventieth anniversary of his birth, will leave this office on a 100-day walk to San Francisco. It is a big undertaking for a man of Mr. Weston's years, or for any man, but he is not made of the stuff that fails, and from what I know of his past performances I am sure that he will make good." It was signed "E.M. Morgan, postmaster of New York." Weston apologized for delivering the message five days late, then used the opportunity to make a few more unkind remarks about Wyoming. It is not known whether he collected the eighty-five cents in postage due.

Throughout the day, the accolades flowed in. The *San Francisco Chronicle* framed his walk as an act of heroic athleticism, noting that Weston wasn't paid to do it, nor were wagers involved. His goal instead was "Ulysses-like, to make one final hike." The writer went on: "This journey set an athletic mark that may not be equaled for years to come." Other laudatory editorials hailing his spunk and determination filled newspapers across the nation in the following days. (Not all were smitten with the long-walking codger; a columnist at the *Chicago Tribune* wrote, "Edward Payson Weston has fetched up at San Francisco after hoofing it across the continent, thereby proving what we have always maintained, that two times two are four.")

Dr. Osler's jocular if misinterpreted comment that aging people should get "chloroform at sixty" resurfaced at Weston's finale, in large part because the whole idea still got people sputtering and newspaper editors knew that sputtering was good for readership. Weston also seemed pleased to sustain the debate. "Well, can Osler do what I did?" he asked. "Can some of these youngsters do it?" (The *Oregonian* ran a one-line report the day after Weston's arrival in San Francisco: "We haven't noticed that Edward Payson Weston has received a congratulatory telegram from Dr. Osler.")

Weston didn't announce any firm plans for the coming months, but mused that he might now turn north and walk to Seattle to attend the Alaska–Yukon–Pacific Exposition. He told others he was thinking of starting a walk back to New York, and that he was sure, having learned from his mistakes, he could do it in ninety days. He wouldn't even need to rest before he set off. He could leave tomorrow, he said.

"I have been walking all my life and expect to continue walking until I drop," he told a reporter. To another, he asked rhetorically, "Is this to be my last long walk?" Then he answered himself: "No. But I cannot tell when the next will be, or where.

"I must keep on the move."

EPILOGUE

A month after Weston completed his walk, the new Indianapolis Motor Speedway held its first major "speed race" on a brand-new two-and-a-half-mile circular course initially constructed of crushed stone bound together with a mix of tar and oil. (The surfacing was less than ideal. A driver was temporarily blinded when a stone kicked up and shattered his goggles, and it was soon repaved in brick, giving the speedway the lasting nickname of the Brickyard.) The first races involved three days of competition with autos racing at distances of 250 and 300 miles. The series attracted widespread attention, fueled in part by accidents and small mayhem. During the first day's final race, a driver and his mechanic were killed when the driver lost control and the car flipped over in a ditch in a crash so violent both axles flew off the track. On the third day, two spectators and a mechanic were killed when a racecar plowed through a fence and into a knot of cheering fans. About fifteen thousand spectators showed up the first day; attendance had doubled by the third day.

Two days prior to the race, a *Chicago Daily Tribune* sports column reported that a convoy of some fifty cars carrying two hundred people was making the twelve-hour drive south to Indianapolis ("maintaining an average of seventeen miles per hour"). A minor notice was appended to the bottom of that report: "Edward Payson Weston, 70 years old, who recently walked from New York to San Francisco . . . has just returned to New York and announces that next spring, when he will be 71 years old, he will start again to walk to the Pacific Coast."

"I do not feel inclined to close my public career with a failure," Weston announced.

Newspaper readers at the time may have been skeptical about Weston's pronouncement, and not without reason. Weston's puffed-up talk after finishing up in San Francisco—about walking to Seattle, about walking back to New York—came to naught. He quietly returned home by taking the train east, albeit making stops along the way to deliver lectures and earn some cash in the doing. This offset some of the expenses he incurred, and, in his words, helped "elevate in popular esteem the exercise of walking."

As it turned out, he *was* serious about a reprise walk; he really didn't want to conclude his walking career with what he deemed a failure. So on February 1, 1910, after traveling by train westward from New York to Los Angeles to put the prevailing winds at his back, Weston again set off on foot from one ocean to another. He would turn seventy-one years old six weeks into his trek.

Weston also altered the route for his second transcontinental crossing, opting for a more southerly course that would take him through Arizona, New Mexico, Colorado, Kansas, Missouri, and Illinois, mostly following the rail lines into Chicago. He walked the tracks of his latest sponsor, the Atchison, Topeka and Santa Fe Railroad, which also provided him with a motorized velocipede and two assistants to accompany him. (This included "a gentleman instead of a laborer," Weston noted with some satisfaction. Weston also had the backing of a wealthy New Yorker, who insisted on remaining anonymous.)

From the outset, Weston made good time, averaging an impressive 45.5 miles per day over his first forty-two days. (Some questioned his figures, including the normally supportive *New York Times,* noting that the mileage in the timetable he'd printed up and distributed was at variance with that found in the railroad's booklets.) But no one questioned his vigor and determination. And unlike the year before, he was blessed with better luck and consistently cooperative weather that allowed him to maintain a good pace. He was even feeling confident enough to make a detour to the Grand Canyon, and another to see the fossilized wood at the Petrified Forest. (He had but one serious mishap: He injured his left leg in a slip on a train trestle in Arizona, but managed a quick recovery and lost little time.)

In Albuquerque, a reporter wrote that between three thousand and five thousand people came out to greet Weston as he walked through. But for the most part, his 1910 walk didn't attract the same sort of clamor as that of the previous year. The *New York Times* declined to publish his regular dispatches, likely because his cross-country walk was seen as old news. As the *San Jose Evening News* put it, "There is always a demand for novelties and Weston and his walking have become an old story."

From Chicago he took a fairly familiar route, although this time did deign to walk through Cleveland once he learned the former police chief was no longer in office and that the current mayor had promised to protect him from crowds. Then back up into New York State for his fourth walk across it, passing through Erie and Buffalo before heading eastward through Syracuse, Utica, and Albany. Then southward along the Hudson River, where his final days were marred by a minor automobile accident: a car clipped a young walking companion, throwing him four feet into Weston and knocking both down. Weston was dazed and his right ankle bruised, and he was taken to a farmhouse where he rested up overnight. He resumed walking the next day, but cars continued to plague him. "Mr. Weston has been particularly irritated over automobiles to-day," a reporter summed up, "and he said that if he had had a revolver he certainly would have taken a shot at a touring car party which passed him near a bridge" and forced him to jump out of the way.

This time, Weston was utterly triumphant. He arrived in New York seventy-eight days after leaving Los Angeles—thirteen days ahead of the ninety he'd planned. By one account, nearly five hundred thousand people turned out throughout New York City to watch Weston as he made his way south through Manhattan toward City Hall—"a speck in a human whirlpool," wrote a reporter. At the finish, he handed a letter to New York mayor William Jay Gaynor, sent from Los Angeles mayor George Alexander. "Weston, my old friend," Mayor Gaynor said, "I am mighty proud of you. The whole world is proud of you."

Soon after, Weston admitted something that few thought they'd hear escape his lips: He allowed that his walking days were behind him. He proffered none of the bluff or bluster about doing another ocean-to-ocean walk in better time. He'd done what he set out to do. "I guess I've taken my last walk," he said. "The public doesn't care anything about me, except as a sort of curiosity, a young old man."

Following his 1910 transcontinental walk, Weston slipped from the public eye back into obscurity. When he did resurface from time to time, he appeared somewhat unmoored and adrift. Separated from his wife, Maria, since 1893 (she refused to grant him a divorce), he spent many of his later years with Annie O'Hagan, a young woman variously referred to in newspaper accounts as his adopted daughter, his secretary, or his housekeeper. They claimed to have adopted a boy, but speculation was rife that it was their own child. They moved here and there.

Weston and Annie made do, living a life that appeared to be as confused and mysterious as it was short of glamour, wealth, and fame. Weston licensed his name to a manufacturer who sold "Edward Payson Weston Long Wear Hose" ("100 percent more durable than the great majority of guaranteed hose"). Also on the market was Weston Heel and Toe Walking Sox ("no seam of any kind"). He roused himself for an ambitious long walk or two—including a walk from New York to Minneapolis in 1913, at age seventy-four—and these brought him a small measure of renewed attention and presumably a bit of cash on the lecture circuit. He sought the quiet life in the country, moving outside Kingston in the Hudson Valley in 1914.

When he was eighty-three, he laced up his leather boots again and walked from Buffalo to New York City, taking a fairly leisurely thirty days. This time, he complained more loudly about the cars all along the road. He even made a stop in Albany to lobby the governor for a law that would require drivers to beep their horns when passing pedestrians.

His upstate retirement was interrupted by one mysterious episode when he was eighty-six. In 1924, a gang of men attacked his home with sticks, rocks, "and at least one gun," smashing out all the windows and pummeling the aged walker, who was in an upstairs bedroom. In the course of the mayhem, Weston was shot in the leg. "The motive of the attack is unknown," the *New York Times* reported. There was speculation that it was country people fed up with city people invading their domain, as the new arrivals were preventing them from cutting firewood wherever they desired. (Other theories: He was attacked for living with an unmarried woman with whom he had possibly fathered a child, or that the whole attack was fabricated for publicity.)

Whatever the true story, Weston left upstate New York and relocated for a time to Pennsylvania. His financial situation, never strong, deteriorated. After the *Times* reported on his unfortunate situation, donations came in ("thirty-one dollars, the promise of further funds, a bottle of soup, [and] some sandwiches"). He was also offered a job by a publisher to haul proofs around town on foot, but Annie "was afraid Mr. Weston might not be able to remember directions and might get lost while doing messenger work."

At age eighty-seven, he was discovered one day wandering around New York City, unable to identify who he was. Police figured it out from a pocketful of newspaper clippings about his glory days that he carried with him. Afterward, he moved back to Manhattan and lived in what the press referred to as a "tiny, dingy flat" on the Lower East Side. He continued to struggle to make ends meet—although scattered help arrived. A Civil War veteran who'd seen Weston walking on his way to Washington, DC, and Lincoln's inaugural and gave him $35 to cover a month's rent, "for old time's sake."

Just before Weston turned eighty-eight in 1927, the playwright Anne Nichols, who had amassed a modest fortune from her play *Abie's Irish Rose*, set Weston up with a pension of $30,000 that provided him a small but helpful income for the rest of his days.

It was a welcome bit of good fortune, but good luck was not to last. Less than two weeks later, he walking to church in Manhattan when he absent-mindedly stepped off a curb at Seventh Avenue and Eleventh Street. A bystander hollered for him to look out.

The call came too late; the sound of locked wheels skidding on the wet pavement filled the city street. A taxi hit Weston full-on, and he was thrown to the asphalt, his head bleeding. The cab driver lifted Weston into the backseat, then took him to the hospital. Doctors announced that his prospects of surviving were slim. Yet he survived the night, and the following day he rallied, although talking confusedly about his long walks. He fully regained his senses after a few days and was sent home. But from here on out, he was confined to a wheelchair, and by the time he turned ninety, he was largely confined to bed. The walker would walk no more.

The automobile had won.

On Sunday, May 13, 1929, Weston died of natural causes, two months after his ninetieth birthday. He was buried at St. John Cemetery in Queens, in a plot reportedly bought for him by Anne Nichols.

"Weston's life may well be dubbed 'The Story of a Man Who Learned to Do One Thing Well," a reporter had written before his death. And it could make a fitting epitaph—by one account, he'd walked ninety thousand miles in his lifetime.

But he did so much more—he reminded a nation that we could walk, and at a time when we were all abandoning our feet in favor of the car.

―――――――――――

On a recent December morning, with the temperature just above freezing, I took the Bay Area Rapid Transit train from downtown San Francisco across the bay to the end of the Richmond line. My plan was to retrace part of Weston's final day, when he walked to Oakland on July 14, 1909, then took the ferry across to San Francisco. The stretch I picked wasn't that daunting—about a dozen miles, mostly down the long commercial stretches of Carlson Boulevard and San Pablo Avenue through Richmond, Albany, Berkeley, and Oakland.

At Richmond, I disembarked from the train and followed a pedestrian walkway under a trestle painted salmon with "Richmond" on it in large, art deco–ish lettering. Richmond was incorporated in 1905, just a few years before Weston's walk, after being carved out of the adjacent town of Rancho San Pablo and named after the city in Virginia by an early businessman. It was an active port with rail lines terminating and passing through. Yet it rose and fell in large part with the automobile. Standard Oil had bought up land along the deepest water for a port, where it situated a refinery to provide oil for the growing number of cars; black tendrils of smoke were no doubt rising from it when Weston walked by. And from the 1930s until the 1950s, Ford maintained a large assembly plant here, churning out cars that were then shipped out by rail.

All this industry provided Richmond with its own economic center of gravity. (It's now a city of some one hundred thousand.) It had a low-slung downtown, with stores that included J. C. Penney, Thrifty, Macy's, and Woolworth. But then came the 1970s, and as with so many other vibrant downtowns, much of the economic dynamism migrated to a newly opened mall outside town. Downtown became the slightly sad place it is today, a little threadbare and home to chain pizza restaurants, auto parts stores, wig shops, and furniture clearance outlets.

The first three miles or so of my walk were down Carlson Boulevard, which is scaled for cars rather than humans. The road is simple and utilitarian—four lanes broad and unshaded. Train tracks run along the far side of the road, and on the sidewalk side I passed housing complexes distanced from the road by tall fences, a sort of modern moat. (A sign posted on one fence had an arrow indicating "This way to nearest pedestrian gate with telephone entry system.") Although the landscape wasn't inviting, walking felt good in the sun as the day warmed, and after a couple of miles I felt limber and had settled into a loose, natural gait.

I had an edge on prehistoric man in navigating and tabulating: My smartphone tracked my route, and the Fitbit on my wrist counted my steps. Over the course of working on this book, a day's walk of about twelve miles had ceased to be an event for me. It was more or less just a comfortable and normal day, when I could find the time to do it. At some point, I'd tasted the ten-thousand-steps-per-day Kool-Aid (about five miles) and found it to my liking. Ten thousand steps makes a good base, and walking two or three times that no longer seems the challenge it once was. Nor does it take a day or two afterward to work out the stiffness. (I did learn, however, that forty miles is out of reach. I attempted several times to walk what I'd come to think of as a "Weston," but would fade quickly after about twenty miles and find an excuse to stop. I continue to marvel at Weston's stamina.)

Toward the end of Carlson Boulevard, I passed a house with a small fiberglass waterfall on a postage-stamp-size lawn. It was a gateway of sorts—from here on out, the homes were unbordered by iron fences and had a cozier relationship with the street. The roadway didn't seem to be a separate sluice, but was now on a first-name basis with homes. Then I passed beneath an echoey highway overpass, and I soon was walking on San Pablo Avenue, another long commercial corridor, although one with multiple personalities. It follows one of the older routes through the Bay Area and was originally called Camino de la Contra Costa ("Road of the Opposite Shore") when the Spanish still maintained a network of missions. Later, a streetcar ran between Richmond and Oakland. Walking through the town of Albany, I noticed the streetscape reflected more of the automobile era, with four lanes and a median strip and low-slung chain stores and parking lots lining the street itself. But as I neared the city limits of Berkeley, the shop fronts somewhat conspiratorially edged closer to the street, and trees offered shade. The bones of a former streetcar suburb started to emerge. I also passed the California Typewriter Company and the D. C. Piano Company, which offered a passing glimpse of what once was.

It turned out that I couldn't follow Weston's exact route to its conclusion. The ferry and rail terminal where he'd boarded the boat going across the bay was now landlocked. The bay is now nearly a mile from the old Southern Pacific station, thanks to a long-term project to fill in the tidelands and increase industrial and docking space, launched in 1912 and continued until after World War II. The old railroad terminal building still stands, although it's been shuttered since the 1989 Loma Prieta earthquake. So I veered east, continuing down San Pablo into downtown Oakland, intersecting Broadway at Frank H. Ogawa Plaza. I continued on toward the water at Jack London Square, where the ferry to San Francisco now lands. This required walking under a broad overpass carrying a dozen or so lanes of traffic on I-880. It was made slightly less foreboding thanks to a sculpture by local artists consisting of bands of shiny highway guardrails abstractly flowing between the red-painted concrete columns supporting the freeway. I guess this was more pleasing than raw underpass space, but it seemed a vaguely territorial gesture, as if highway engineers were making sure walkers knew they were in an area through which they could pass, but could not claim as their own. It was designed to be viewed from a car.

Jack London Square is billed as a "popular entertainment and business destination on the waterfront" and has all the festival marketplace trimmings—open greensward, benches facing the water, restaurants with outdoor cafés, a big neon-lit archway sign to let you know you've arrived at a place of manufactured festivity. It boasts a badge of authenticity in Heinold's First and Last Chance Saloon, a battered tavern that's been serving up beer and liquor since 1883. The floor tilted when the 1906 earthquake caused pilings to sink slightly, and no one has leveled it since. It was the inspiration for scenes in some of novelist Jack London's fiction.

I sat on a bench and awaited the ferry. Then I boarded with about a dozen others, and we puttered past massive container ships freshly arrived from Asia before crossing preternaturally scenic San Francisco Bay. Views opened up of the Bay Bridge and hills ringing the water, with San Francisco looking like a snow-globe city across the way. A half hour later, I disembarked at the grandiose ferry terminal, the prominent tower marking a lapsed era. It was completed in 1898 and once had ferries running to points all around the bay, but it is now largely a mall for foodies. I walked up Market Street, which is flanked by wide sidewalks. (I wanted to walk down the middle of the street, as I'd seen in the 1906 film mentioned earlier, but this seemed foolhardy.)

My stroll into San Francisco was essentially a mirror image of my walk out of New York City, when I tracked Weston's first day. I had then started deep within a city built for people on foot and ended up in a less dense neighborhood designed largely for cars. In California, I began walking the far margins of a road built to ensure automotive speed and efficiency, and I ended up in a city with narrow streets and sidewalks and storefronts meant to be experienced on foot. The cars here were aggravated by traffic lights and pedestrians. I was a half-continent away from where I lived, but somehow I felt as if I were returning home.

At Post Street I angled uphill for a few blocks, edging by Union Square, and then walked through the front door of the St. Francis Hotel, where Weston had concluded his walk. It had opened in 1904 and survived the 1906 earthquake, although the fires afterward damaged it badly. I looked at pictures in the lobby that showed it standing proudly if a bit uncertainly amid the city's rubble. The hotel was quickly rebuilt after the devastation, and another wing was added in 1908.

I stood in the hotel's lobby more than a century after Weston. What hadn't changed—the century-old hotel, the venerable city built on a pedestrian scale, the crowds of people on foot on sidewalks just outside the doors—captivated me more than what had changed in the broader world beyond. After five million years, it struck me, we can still get around the way evolution meant us to, and in cities designed for feet.

"Anyone can walk," Weston said in 1910, at age seventy-one. "It's free, like the sun by day and the stars by night. All we have to do is get on our legs, and the roads will take us everywhere."

A NOTE ON SOURCES

Edward Payson Weston left only footprints, for the most part. He never wrote an autobiography, nor kept a journal . . . at least not one that I or anyone else has found. He penned a couple of pamphlets earlier in his walking career, but little else. Much of what I've gleaned about Weston has come from articles he wrote for various newspapers (mostly the *New York Times*) and through articles written about him while he was alive, which often involved interviews in which he revealed a little of his thinking.

Two self-published books by Paul S. Marshall have been incalculably helpful in filling in considerable gaps about Weston's life. Between them, these total nearly 1,500 pages, harvest many of the newspaper accounts about Weston, and offer some insight into the man.

Marshall's *King of the Peds* (Milton Keynes, UK: AuthorHouse, 2008) covers the rise of pedestrian competitions from 1860 to about 1890, with much solid information about Weston's early career. Marshall's other book, *Weston, Weston, Rah-Rah-Rah: The Original Sporting Superstar* (Bloomington, IN: AuthorHouse, 2012) covers Weston's career until nearly the end of his life, including such detailed information as his times and placements in various races and an impressive compilation of newspaper accounts covering his long-distance walks.

Marshall was also coauthor, with Nick Harris and Helen Harris, of *A Man in a Hurry: The Extraordinary Life and Times of Edward Payson Weston, The World's Greatest Walker* (London: deCoubertin Books, 2012), which provided abundant detail and historic context. I especially recommend this to those who'd like to learn more about Weston's early career.

Further information about Weston and his walks was gleaned from hundreds of newspaper and magazine articles appearing throughout the late nineteenth and early twentieth century. The *New York Times* had the most consistent coverage, but other papers featuring stories about Weston (chiefly accessed through GenealogyBank.com and Newspapers.com) include:

Anaconda Standard (Montana)
Baltimore American
Biloxi Herald (Mississippi)
Chicago Tribune
Cleveland Plain Dealer
Colorado Springs Gazette
Dallas Morning News
Duluth News-Tribune
(Minnesota)
Idaho Daily Statesman (Boise)
Lock Haven Express (Pennsylvania)
Marion Daily Star (Ohio)
New York Sun

New York Tribune
Piqua Leader-Dispatch (Ohio)
Pittsfield Sun (Massachusetts)
Riverside Daily Press (California)
Salt Lake Telegram
San Francisco Chronicle
San Jose Evening News (California)
Syracuse Post-Standard
Oregonian
Wilkes-Barre Times Leader
(Pennsylvania)
Los Angeles Times
Washington Post

Key books and articles helpful in understanding the evolution of biped-alism, cognitive mapping, the rise of the automobile, and other aspects of walking history, culture, and physiology are listed below. For more detailed sources listed by chapter, please visit www.lastgreatwalk.com for a down-loadable file.

Allen, Frederick Lewis. *The Big Change: American Transforms Itself, 1900-1950.* New York: Harper and Brothers, 1952.

Allen, Gary L. *Human Spatial Memory.* Mahwah, NJ: Lawrence Erlbaum, 2004.

Booth, Frank W., Manu V. Chakravarthy, Scott E. Gordon, and Espen E. Spangenburg. "Waging War on Physical Inactivity: Using Modern Molecular Ammunition against an Ancient Enemy." *Journal of Applied Physiology* 93(1):3–30, 2002.

Campoli, Julie. *Made for Walking: Density and Neighborhood Form.* Cambridge, MA: Lincoln Institute of Land Policy, 2012.

Chatwin, Bruce. *The Songlines.* New York: Penguin, 1988.

Coverley, Merlin. *Psychogeography: The Pocket Essential Guide.* Harpenden, UK: Pocket Essentials, 2010.

Cumming, John. *Runners and Walkers: A Nineteenth Century Sports Chronicle.* Chicago: Regnery Gateway, 1981.

Downs, Roger M., and David Stea, eds. *Image and Environment: Cognitive Mapping and Spatial Behavior.* Chicago: Aldine, 1973.

Goffman, Erving. *Relations in Public: Microstudies of the Public Order.* New York: Basic Books, 1971.

Groeger, John. A. *Understanding Driving: Applying Cognitive Psychology to a Complex Everyday Task.* Philadelphia: Taylor and Francis, 2000.

Halprin, Lawrence. *Freeways.* New York: Reinhold, 1966.

Hill, Michael R. *Walking, Crossing Streets, and Choosing Pedestrian Routes.* Lincoln: University of Nebraska, 1984.

Hillman, Mayer, and Anne Whalley. *Walking Is Transport*. London: Policy Studies Institute, 1979.

Hoffecker, John F. *Landscape of the Mind: Human Evolution and the Archaeology of Thought*. New York: Columbia University Press, 2011.

Hole, Graham. *The Psychology of Driving*, Mahwah, NJ: Lawrence Erlbaum, 2007.

How to Walk: Describing the Whole Art of Training without a Trainer. Full instructions and hints for those who intend entering walking contests either for short or long distances; special chapter on Walking for Women. London: Evening News, 1903.

Ingold, Tim, and Jo Lee Vergunst, eds. *Ways of Walking: Ethnography and Practice on Foot*. Aldershot, UK: Ashgate, 2008.

Jackson, Kenneth T. *Crabgrass Frontier: The Suburbanization of the United States*. New York: Oxford University Press, 1985.

Lummis, Charles F. *A Tramp across the Continent*. New York: Charles Scribner's Sons, 1892.

Marchetti, C. "Anthropological Invariants in Travel Behavior." *Technological Forecasting and Social Change* 47:75–88, 1994.

Marples, Morris. *Shanks's Pony: A Study of Walking*. London: J. M. Dent and Sons, 1959.

Mauch, Christof, and Thomas Zeller, eds. *The World Beyond the Windshield: Roads and Landscapes in the United States and Europe*. Athens: University of Ohio Press, 2008.

Nicholson, Geoff. *The Lost Art of Walking: The History, Science, Philosophy, and Literature of Pedestrianism*. New York: Riverhead Books, 2008.

Norton, Peter. *Fighting Traffic: The Dawn of the Motor Age in the American City*. Cambridge, MA: MIT Press, 2008.

O'Sullivan, Timothy, M. *Walking in Roman Culture*. Cambridge, UK: Cambridge University Press, 2011.

Ratey, John J., with Eric Hagerman. *Spark: The Revolutionary New Science of Exercise and the Brain*. New York: Little, Brown, 2008.

Rodaway, Paul. *Sensuous Geographies: Body, Sense, and Place*. London: Routledge, 1994.

Rose, Jessica, and James G. Gamble, eds. *Human Walking*. Baltimore: Williams and Wilkins, 1994.

Rudofsky, Bernard. *Streets for People: A Primer for Americans*. Garden City, NY: Doubleday, 1969.

Self, Will. *Psychogeography: Disentangling the Modern Conundrum of Psyche and Place*. New York: Bloomsbury, 2007.

Solnit, Rebecca. *Wanderlust: A History of Walking*. New York: Viking, 2000.

Speck, Jeff. *Walkable City: How Downtown Can Save America, One Step at a Time*. New York: Farrar, Straus and Giroux, 2012.

Stanford, Craig. *Upright: The Evolutionary Key to Becoming Human*. Boston: Houghton Mifflin, 2003.

Tenner, Edward. *Our Own Devices: The Past and Future of Body Technology*. New York: Alfred A. Knopf, 2003.

Tolman, Edward C. "Cognitive Maps in Rats and Men." *Psychological Review* 55(4):189–208, 1948.

Vanderbilt, Tom. *Traffic: Why We Drive the Way We Do (and What It Says About Us)*. New York: Alfred A. Knopf, 2008.

Welsh, Charles, ed. *Chauffeur Chaff or Automobilia*. Boston: H. M. Caldwell, 1905.

ACKNOWLEDGMENTS

Every journey beings with a single step, and for me that first step is often toward someone who can give me better directions to where I'm headed. My thanks to all those I've encountered along the way who've done just that.

My friend and former *Atlantic* editor Amy Meeker patiently listened to me explain why I wanted to write about this over the course of a couple of summer evenings and then helped me think about how to do it better.

In Ann Arbor, Dr. Caroline R. Richardson and Dr. Michelle L. Segar were kind enough to fill me in on their walking and exercise research as we took a long stroll around their city. And I appreciate Courtenay Coughenour taking the time to meet with me in Las Vegas and tell me about her research on what makes neighborhoods walkable (or not).

Sandy James in Vancouver helped me make connections at the Walk 21 conference and later gave me a great tour of a city that understands mixed use. Patrice L. Smith of Kaiser-Permanente helped open doors at the 2013 Walk Summit in Washington, DC.

Also thanks to Jim Sallis for sharing his work on walking and mental and physical health; Chris Bradshaw, founder of Ottawalk, for his insights on walking activism in Canada; Nicole Schneider of Walk San Francisco for helping me understand that city's efforts to become more walkable; L. J. Dean, a volunteer at the National Railroad History Society who didn't find my questions on walking on nineteenth century rail lines all that strange; and Michael Hauser for showing me around the La-Z-Boy Museum. Joyce Litz was helpful in suggesting some avenues of research on her great grandfather Edward Payson Weston.

Dozens of bloggers have taken it upon themselves to document and advocate for better walking conditions around the country. Every day seems to bring news of a couple steps forward, and often a step back. Thanks to all of them. I've especially appreciated the coverage at the blog Atlantic

Cities (now CityLab), particularly that by Sarah Goodyear, Emily Badger, and Kaid Benfield. And thanks to Katie Matchett for her outstanding coverage of pedestrian issues on her blog, "Where the Sidewalk Starts."

Additionally, my thanks to everyone at Rodale for helping to keep this book on track, especially project editor Nancy Bailey, copy editor Nancy Elgin, and fact checker Sonya Maynard, all of whom were dogged and persistent, in a good way.

And special thanks to my editor, Alex Postman, who was always kind, encouraging, and wise.

Any missteps are, of course, my own.

Finally, thanks to Jennifer Gates of Zachary Shuster Harmsworth for finding this book a home.

And to my wife, Louise, for listening to me talk about Edward Payson Weston for a long time. I mean, a really long time.

INDEX

Traffic engineers/engineering (*cont.*)
data lending power to, 145
divide-and-conquer strategy of, 142–43
expanding influence of, 144, 145
New York World's Fair exhibit, 1939, 141–42
pedestrian deaths and, 144
pedestrian islands, 190–91
police regulation prior to, 143, 144–45, 160
pushback against, 166–67
rise of, 136, 142
sidewalks slighted by, 146
trees removed by, 145
Traffic rulings
associations for drivers' rights, 163–65
blaming the pedestrian, 175–76
on influential negligence, 163
jaywalking, 161, 165–66, 167, 168
pedestrian pushback against, 166–67
pedestrians favored early on, 144, 160, 163
shift to favoring cars, 167–69
Tranter, Paul Joseph, 207
Turkle, Sherry, 125

U

Underpasses, pedestrian, 152–53
University of California Transportation Center, 109
University of Southampton, England, 24
Urban planning, 197–99. *See also* Traffic engineers/engineering

V

Vanderbilt, Tom, 115
Verge, the, 137
Video games, 100–102
Virtual reality navigation, 101–2

W

Wagner, Jon, 84
Walkability
of Brooklyn Bridge, 148–49
community building and, 206–7
crosswalks and, 175–76
factors increasing, 179–80
factors reducing, 179, 203, 204
intersection density and, 204
lacking in suburbs, 176–79
as liveability, 205
malls and, 153–54
of older cities, 176–77
public health and, 178
of Radburn subdivision, 152
real estate prices and, 197–98
reclaiming, 201–7
of San Francisco, 210–11, 213
scores and measures of, 184–86
skywalks, 154–55
spread of pockets of, 201
underpasses or overpasses and, 152–53
in Weston's era, 183–84
Walking (in general). *See also* Exercise
amount before modern era, 56–57
average steps per day in US, 5
brain benefits from, 96–97
brain function aided by, 89–90
brain not required for, 103
cognitive development aided by, 104–5
complexity of, 80
dérive, 117–18
effective speed of, 207
efficiency of, 60
electronic device use during, 124–27
evolution and, 36–43
extra dimensions known by, 124
by *flâneurs,* 116–17, 119
freedom as benefit of, 206
French army method, 22
gaits, 22–30
health benefits of, xv, 68–71, 88–89